INTIMACY:
The Need to Be Close

INTIMACY

THE NEED TO BE CLOSE

DAN P. McADAMS, PH.D.

DOUBLEDAY

Excerpt from "The Road to Self-reliance," by Michael Norman, from *New York Times Magazine*—"About Men," December 13, 1988. Copyright © 1988 by the New York Times Company. Reprinted by permission.

Excerpt from *The McGill Report on Male Intimacy* by Michael E. McGill. Copyright © 1985 by Michael E. McGill. Reprinted by permission of Henry Holt and Company, Inc.

Lines from "With the Door Open" and "Two Friends" by David Ignatow. Copyright © 1963, 1961. Reprinted from *Poems 1934–1969* by David Ignatow, by permission of Wesleyan University Press. "Two Friends" first appeared in *The Nation*.

PUBLISHED BY DOUBLEDAY
A division of
Bantam Doubleday Dell Publishing Group, Inc.
666 Fifth Avenue, New York, New York 10103

DOUBLEDAY and the portrayal of
an anchor with a dolphin
are trademarks of Doubleday, a division of
Bantam Doubleday Dell Publishing Group, Inc.

LIBRARY OF CONGRESS CATALOGING-IN-PUBLICATION DATA

McAdams, Dan P.
   Intimacy: the need to be close / by Dan P. McAdams. —1st ed.
     p. cm.
   ISBN 0-385-24266-2
   1. Intimacy (Psychology) I. Title.
BF575.I5M32   1989
155.9'2—dc19   88-30761
                                                     CIP

Book design by Patrice Fodero

June 1989

FIRST EDITION

for Rebecca

Contents

Preface

We have many desires in life, but none may be more compelling than the desire for intimacy. Each of us wants to be close to somebody else: to feel and to believe that—in some place, at some time, and in our own idiosyncratic way—we can connect with another person; we can come to know the other and reveal what can be known about ourselves. The desire for intimacy is the desire to share one's innermost self with another. In the sharing, we come to know better the other and ourselves, and we come to care for the other, and perhaps even to care for ourselves as well. This book is about the different ways in which this universal desire for intimacy—what I call the "intimacy motive"—reveals itself in the lives of relatively normal people, from birth to old age.

Intimacy is one of a handful of basic psychological needs that give form and substance to our lives. Each human life is a unique story with a content and structure that are significantly influenced by both the strength of a person's intimacy motivation and the characteristic way in which intimacy motivation plays itself out. Over the past twelve years, I have explored the workings of intimacy motivation in human lives from a scientific perspective, seeking to bring some rigorous discipline to the study of a rich and mysterious phenomenon, without stripping it of its richness or reducing it to trite formulas or simplistic, common-sense solutions. Most of the research I have conducted has taken place in university settings, where I have worked predominantly as a teacher, scientist, and writer. Therefore, the focus of my investigations into intimacy has been on "normal," as opposed to pathological, people—relatively normal students in college, children in elementary schools, adults in typical American communities. In their imperialistic zeal to discern the various ways in which we are "crazy," "abnormal," and "maladjusted," psychologists often lose sight of the tremendous variability in personality among people in the "normal majority." I have tried not to fall into this trap. Normal people experience the full gamut of the human condition, the peaks and canyons of emotional and interpersonal experience that make the normal man and woman the most fascinating subjects one can study.

This book celebrates the wonderful diversity of human lives, emphasizing variations among people with respect to their desires to be close to others and the ways in which these desires are expressed. We shall see in Chapter 1 that people vary considerably in the strength and the meaning of their desires for intimacy and that these desires interact in complex ways with competing needs for power and autonomy. In Chapter 2, I describe how the private fantasies of normal people are the windows through which we gain the most direct view of intimacy motivation. The strength of a person's desire for intimacy is reliably measured by analyzing the imaginative fantasies that he or she creates. Chapter 3 explores a number of different ways that intimacy motivation translates itself into human behavior and experience, from the subtle nonverbal expressions of a person's face to the international efforts of peacemakers to stop wars among nations.

Intimacy motivation and intimate relationships contribute in a wide variety of ways to human health and happiness, as we shall see in Chapter 4. Over the past twenty years, scientists have examined carefully the healing power of human love and intimacy, revealing intriguing relations between mind and body that we are just now beginning to understand. Chapter 5 examines the development of intimacy and intimacy motivation over the human life-span, focusing on such formative experiences as the bond of love between caregiver and infant, the love triangles of early childhood, and the intensive "chumships" of preadolescence. Finally, Chapter 6 considers the pervasive influence of gender on intimacy. Are women more intimate than men? Do men fear intimacy? Do men and women typically "fail" in their search for intimacy in characteristically masculine and feminine ways?

This book draws on a wide range of scientific research into intimacy and love, much of which has appeared at one time or another in professional journals and books that are read exclusively by psychologists and other social scientists. The general public rarely catches a glimpse of this rather arcane literature on personality and human relationships. I have taken what I consider to be the most instructive and interesting studies from these professional forums and blended them with a wide range of other sources, such as poetry, myth, biography, and personal experience. The result is both a *theory* of intimacy and intimacy motivation, stemming primarily from my own empirical research, and (more importantly) a *story* about the meaning of intimacy in human lives. It is the story that excites me more, a story that—I hope—entertains, illuminates, and provokes. The hero of my story is the intimacy motive itself, the desire to share one's innermost self with another. He is a capricious and enigmatic hero, of uncertain birth and destiny, mischievously difficult to pin down, likely to disappoint, to break your heart and mess with your mind, but oh-so riveting, so compelling, so deliciously enrapturing when he takes center stage and dominates the plot.

This book is for anybody who has encountered the hero of my story and found him more than a little puzzling to figure out. It is for people who have wondered about and struggled with their own desires to share that which is innermost with another. And it is for those who know intimately the villains in my story—loneliness, alienation, narcissism. No story is complete without its villains, and few villains are as menacing as these.

This book is not a formal scientific report. Do not worry about getting bogged down in the methodological and statistical details of research. No statistics and only one or two numbers appear in the entire text. I have saved some of the technical details about the studies I discuss for the Notes, which are grouped at the end of the book. The rest of the details are in the original sources themselves, the references for which also appear in the Notes. And I have outlawed most forms of psychological jargon.

I wish to thank some of the many people who have, in one way or another, contributed to this book and to the research that I have done on intimacy motivation over the past twelve years. I am most grateful to two professors from graduate school who guided and inspired my earliest explorations. George Goethals taught me about intimacy, and David McClelland taught me about motives. The concept of an intimacy motive, therefore, is the offspring of their most generative efforts, and I am something of a midwife.

Since graduate school, I have collaborated and conversed with a number of colleagues, students, and friends who have promoted and enriched my understanding of intimacy and intimacy motivation. Some of the most helpful and most gracious include Skip Alexander, Don Allen, Jackie Allen, Eileen Bernat, David Berndt, Laura Booth, Rick Boyatzis, Fred Bryant, Michael Carney, Dave Cella, Alice Chatillon, Dante Cicchetti, Carol Constantian, Roberta Drews, Bob Emmons, Jeanne Foley, Sheila Healy, Jeffrey Jackson, John Kihlstrom, Carol Kirshnit, Steven Krause, Denise Lensky, Renee Lester, Michael Losoff, Alan Lundy, Dick Maier, Jim McKay, Rick Ochberg, Dan Perlman, Joe Powers, Stan Rothman, Rick Selvik, Abigail Stewart, Donna Van De Water, Joseph Veroff, Jeff Wilbert, David Winter, and Peter Zeldow. I wish to thank Katinka Matson for her guidance in preparing the original proposal for this book and Loyola University of Chicago for providing me with the time off to complete the writing. Finally, I wish to thank Rebecca Pallmeyer, my wife, for her unflagging encouragement and support and for her discerning editorial contribution.

Dan P. McAdams

CHAPTER 1

Connection and Separation

Only connect! That was the whole of her sermon. Only connect the prose and the passion, and both will be exalted, and human love will be seen at its height. Live in fragments no longer. Only connect, and the beast and the monk, robbed of the isolation that is life to either, will die.

—E. M. Forster, *Howard's End*

I want you to listen to me. I want you to hear of the wonderful things I have seen and of the great things I have done. I want you to know how I once made love to Pat Simpson—not on the night of the prom (no way!), but many years later in a special place that I will describe to you. I want you to know how I once wished to kill the boy who embarrassed me in class—wished so hard and so long that I could not bear to be with him unless I pretended the opposite—pretended that I thought he was the smartest kid I'd ever met, admiring him, fawning all over him every time I saw him for two years thereafter. I want you to know of the joy I felt when my father came home—finally came home after so many times when he didn't—to take me to that ballgame. I want you to feel that joy for me, and to care that I felt it.

And more important, I want you to know of the dumb things I've done; the terrible things; even the evil things: how I pretended that I didn't hear the phone ring when that old but now unfashionable friend called me in college. How I was too busy to visit him in his sickroom. How my cousin saw me naked

1

when I was twelve. I want you to know that I love to watch very sad movies, that I hate shopping malls, that I greatly fear that my children will grow up to be mediocre, that I'll grow up and quit caring—it seems to have started already—about the misery that is all around me, on the TV, in the newspapers, next door. I want you to know why I don't like coconut and why I sometimes think that there is a God and sometimes don't. And why I am afraid to tell you all of this.

And most important, I want *you* to tell *me* things like these, as they are for you. Note how I will discern the true meaning in what you say and return your small gift—the secret you have offered—with empathy and with a response of my own that I desperately hope will not seem to be a cliché. I want to listen, too.

In all of this, what do I *really* want? What I am really asking is to be close to you. I am asking that we find connections between our lives, that we bind ourselves to each other by communicating what is "innermost." Like every human being who has known what it means to be alone, I am asking for *intimacy*.

The desire for intimacy is the desire to share that which is innermost with another person. In intimacy we share parts of ourselves with others, who share parts of themselves with us, and in the highly enjoyable sharing we come to *care* for those with whom we share. The desire for intimacy is a fundamental psychological need in human lives, one of a few basic needs that organize our behavior and experience and provide our lives with meaning.

As we shall see, all human beings are endowed with intimacy motivation; all people desire intimacy in one form or another. But there are important individual differences among persons with respect to the intimacy motive. Some people consistently desire intimacy to a greater degree than others. They seem to be more ready or open for opportunities to share that which is innermost in everyday life. These people have relatively high intimacy motivation. People who are high in intimacy motivation are very different from others who are lower on the motive in a number of important ways having to do with

2

their behavior in groups, their relations with others, and even their health, happiness, and adaptation to life. Further, while there appears to be some consistency in intimacy motivation over time, changes can occur in a person's life. Therefore, your intimacy motivation is *not* a fixed personality trait, set in concrete at a very early age. Intimacy motivation may change somewhat with life experience and development.

The Experience of Intimacy

What does it mean to say, as I did above, that intimacy motivation may "organize" our behavior and experience and provide our lives with "meaning"? Let me offer as a first answer a particular life. Conducting a psychological study a few years ago, my students and I interviewed a number of men and women between the ages of thirty-five and fifty years. One of them was Sara N., a forty-three-year-old high school counselor who was formerly a Catholic nun.[1] On the one hand, Sara is hardly typical: her strong intimacy motivation is characteristically expressed in a wide range of activities and in ways that are probably relatively rare. On the other hand, Sara is hardly unique: there are many people whose intimacy motivation is just as strong and encompassing. There is no "perfect example" of intimacy motivation—no single life that tells all that can be told about the wonders of intimacy. People express the motive in a great variety of ways, and there are many different kinds of intimate lives. Sara's life is but one testament to the possibilities of intimacy motivation.

Sara tells the story of her life in soft but confident tones. She was four years old when the Japanese bombed Pearl Harbor and the United States entered World War II. Her father joined the Air Force, and her mother followed him on duty, leaving Sara and her brother in the care of grandparents till she was nine. This first "chapter" in Sara's life story is an extremely happy one. She loved her grandparents dearly and felt especially close to her grandmother, whom she describes as her "first heroine," "the perfect human being," always "loving, independent, feisty, committed to God and to others." Now, thirty-four years later, she is still extremely close to her grandmother, who is well into her eighties.

When her father and mother returned from the war, Sara was forced to leave her grandparents' paradise and begin life anew with her parents and other "strangers." Although Sara did well in school and made some friends, she was very unhappy at home. She reports that her parents often left her alone when they went out on weekends. Another problem was religion. Her parents were "Yankee Baptists." But Sara had made some Catholic friends when she lived with her grandparents, and a Catholic priest had once been very nice to her. At the age of nine, she had what she describes as a "religious experience":

> It was quiet and dark and I was aware of the silence. I was alone there and remember thinking back on myself and saying, "Oh! Who is this person here?" And I was also aware of another presence. I don't know if I even thought God, but there was something there. And I made up my mind then that I had found something, like, that was home. And knew then that I would like to be Catholic.

Notice that whereas Sara seems alone in this key event from her childhood, the experience itself is profoundly interpersonal. There are two intimate connections being made. First, Sara experiences a reflexive splitting of the self. She senses that she is watching herself, that she has temporarily become both the observer and observed. She expresses a longing to be intimate in this regard: a desire for "Sara the observer" to know what is innermost in "Sara the observed." Next, Sara senses another presence in the room. Implied is a communication between Sara and the presence that, as she tells it to us years later, changed her life for good. She was to defy her parents and become a Catholic. She was to find a new and more loving "home."

After the religious experience, Sara began sneaking out of

her parents' home to attend Catholic Mass with her friends. As her ventures became bolder, her faith grew stronger. At the age of eighteen, Sara graduated from high school, started college, and began formal instruction in Catholicism. Learning of her daughter's decision to become a Catholic, Sara's mother "got hysterical," but her father expressed only mild disappointment and affirmed that "you have to do what you feel is right." Her father's acceptance of Sara's choice mirrored a growing closeness between him and his daughter and a contrasting coldness between Sara and her mother. The bond between father and daughter grew and deepened but ended tragically when Sara was twenty-one, as she experienced the lowest point in her life:

> When I was twenty-one and a senior in college, my father was killed in a mid-air collision. He flew jet refuelers. He was forty-two at the time. He'd flown all my life and I had never even thought about this happening. He and I were very close, not overtly, but a deep, knowing bond. I just went numb when I heard, and couldn't even cry for a couple of months after. Dad and I had spent some time together the summer before and were beginning to share lots together in terms of our beliefs, dreams, values, and loves in life. I felt as though, again, I had lost someone I loved and cared about, like losing a chunk of myself, a part of my own being. I still miss him and ache to see and talk to him about important things. Again my faith has sustained me so I did reconcile the loss and learn to integrate it into my life with understanding, rather than anger. I still feel his presence in my life. The things I loved in him have helped me get through lots of things. I have a more realistic picture of him with faults and greatness, which has helped me accept both in myself.

Sara's account of her reaction to her father's death highlights a few classic themes of intimate experience. First, when Sara remembers her father, what she points to first is the growing closeness of her bond with him and their increasing ability to share what is innermost. More than twenty years later, she still "aches" to be with him so that she can "talk to him about important things." Second, the relationship has continued *even after the father's death*. Although when he died Sara felt that she had lost a chunk of herself, her father has now become part of her, helping her to grow and adapt to the world. With her father's death, part of Sara died but part of her father was also born anew within Sara, and that part continues to live and grow. Finally, as the relationship has grown, even after her father's death, Sara has come to see him in less idealized and more realistic terms, which has in turn helped her understand herself. Here Sara suggests a cardinal attribute of intimate experience that can be contrasted to what sometimes happens in romantic or erotic love. As we shall see in Chapter 2, romantic lovers often *idealize* each other, even believing that their love partners are perfect in every way—the paragon of feminine beauty or manly strength. With growing intimacy, by contrast, we come to see each other in more and more realistic terms, as complex human beings with whom we desire to forge lasting connections, rather than as one-dimensional perfections to gaze upon from afar.

Returning to Sara's Catholicism, we next hear of a tremendously symbolic event that occurred during her first year of college. She was finally baptized as a Catholic *on Valentine's Day*. As Sigmund Freud and other highly intuitive psychologists realized years ago, there are a surprising number of instances in which events take on symbolic psychological significance.[2] In Sara's case, the symbolism is pretty obvious. Sara became a Catholic on the day that traditionally celebrates love, especially erotic love. We might say that she achieved a symbolic intimacy with the "presence" who first appeared in her childhood religious experience by uniting herself as a young, passionate woman with the Catholic church—the church of her friends, the church that, for her, was "home"—on *the* day of lovemaking.

The Valentine's Day event foreshadows, as well, the integration of spirituality and passion in Sara's future years as a nun. About six years after her father's death and shortly after her

6

best friend developed breast cancer, Sara entered the religious life to become a nun. After joining the religious order, Sara worked to integrate faith in God and love for people and developed the reputation among her Catholic sisters as "the earthy one"—the nun steeped in the world and people instead of abstractions and the dogma of the church.

Throughout her life story, Sara describes a large number of long-term friendships in unabashedly passionate terms. She relates that her friendships have always been the greatest source of satisfaction in her life. Virtually all of the major changes in her life involve some major influence from friends, from her early rendezvous with Catholicism to her decision to leave the religious order in her thirties and become a school counselor. She also found herself involved in romantic relationships in her early adult years, falling in love with at least two men. In one instance laced with irony and missed opportunity, she fell in love with a priest as he was deciding to leave the religious life. She, by contrast, had decided to enter the religious life largely because of the example he set for her as a servant of God. Thus, she declined his proposal of marriage and became a nun.

In her current work as a school counselor and in her free time, Sara continues to live out her life role as "the earthy one." While her relations with God and the church have become enriched even as she has withdrawn from the religious life, her relations with other people continue to define her life and provide it with ultimate meaning. When she is not counseling students, she may be organizing workshops and retreats or working with the elderly in a retirement home. Of course, she does other things too, things that do not involve intimacy. For instance, she is now taking a course in investing money. Still, her life is organized around people and relationships, especially relationships through which she can be of service. She believes that she is especially effective in helping other people because she is able to listen more keenly and sympathetically than anybody she knows. This quality makes her a good friend, too. Yet not all of her relationships are rosy. Her mother and she are still not on good terms, which causes Sara considerable distress. And a few of her closest friends have died.

7

Sara's dream for the future is to set up a religious community in a rural area where people can live in peace with one another and with God. Again, we see the emphasis on love, faith, and "home." She speaks of continuing to minister to others both in her work and in her play. Summing up, she states, "I see my life as becoming more and more integrated—to be able to be a space for ministry in my work and with friends, and to enable people to grow and be who they are." When I asked her to tell me the overall "theme" of her life story, she replied simply, "a lot of living, dying, and loving."

Loneliness

In the Garden of Eden, Adam's first problem was not disobedience, pride, or even the serpent. Rather, his first problem was *loneliness*. As the book of Genesis tells it, God created the Earth and the animals and then created Adam, the first man. But Adam was not immediately happy. Perhaps it was difficult to share one's innermost self with the animals:

> The man gave names to all the cattle, all the birds of heaven, and all the wild beasts. But no helpmate suitable for man was found for him. So God made the man fall into a deep sleep. And while he slept, he took one of his ribs and enclosed it in flesh. God built the rib he had taken from the man into a woman, and brought her to the man. The man exclaimed: "This at last is bone from my bones, and flesh from my flesh!" (Gen. 2:20–23)[3]

Now, some people take offense at this passage because it suggests that woman was made from man. I myself find that notion more than vaguely offensive. But I still like the passage because of what it says about intimacy and loneliness. It suggests to me that the need to be close to another may be the most basic of all psychological needs. And it suggests that the experience of loneliness may be one of the most devastating of all human experiences, and one of man's and woman's eternal and most ubiquitous problems.

A number of prominent psychologists have asserted the same, though they do not necessarily go to Genesis for their inspiration. The great psychoanalyst and social philosopher Erich Fromm claimed that humankind's most basic fear is a dread of being separated from other humans. Fromm believed that the experience of separateness, first encountered in infancy, is the source of all anxiety in human life.[4] Child psychologist John Bowlby agrees, citing a good deal of scientific research and many clinical case studies to support the idea that separation from one's caregiver—usually mother or father—in the second half of the first year of life inevitably produces fear and eventual sadness in babies. According to Bowlby, interpersonal separations are unavoidable in life, and we all experience them as babies and young children. Beginning about eight months of age or so, we begin to show signs of fear when separated from those caregivers with whom we have formed loving attachment bonds. Prolonged separation produces an experience of grieving and bereavement in babies, akin to the painful melancholy that we experience as adults when we lose somebody we love. Thus, separation and interpersonal loss are at the roots of the human experiences of fear, sadness, and sorrow.[5]

The renowned psychiatrist Harry Stack Sullivan took a slightly different tack on loneliness. As we will see in Chapter 5, Sullivan distinguished between the infant's experience of anxiety in the face of separation and other tensions on the one hand and the older child's experience of loneliness on the other. According to Sullivan, early experiences of anxiety result from failures in meeting basic *security* needs. In later childhood, however, a new kind of need—the need for *interpersonal intimacy*—arises in the life cycle, and it brings with it the new and extraordinarily painful possibility of loneliness. According to Sullivan, we do not feel loneliness until we experience the longing for intimacy. And we do not feel the longing for intimacy until about the age of eight or nine years, at which time we desperately seek to find a close friend, or what Sullivan called a "chum."[6]

What is important in Sullivan's ideas for us at this point is his suggestion that intimacy and loneliness are closely linked in development. Indeed, the two experiences develop in tandem. We do not feel loneliness until we know, at some level, intimacy. And we cannot be intimate until we are capable of being lonely. Indeed, intimacy with another person is the only human means for staving off the horrors of loneliness. In an essay entitled "The Intimate You," the popular psychologist and lay preacher of love Leo Buscaglia writes:

> I truly feel that if there is, in this world, *one* person whom we can touch totally, unabashedly and unashamedly, we will never die of loneliness. One person! I don't say fifty, a hundred, a thousand. It really doesn't matter who that person is, woman to woman, man to man, someone you can go to and lay it on the line with, who will listen. Someone you don't have to hide from. Someone to whom you can say "These are my feelings," and they say, "Good. It's all right." "This is me." "That's O.K."[7]

But Buscaglia sounds awfully optimistic. It is hard to take him seriously when he first intimates that we can die of loneliness and then claims that the cure is relatively easy.

Others who write of intimacy and loneliness are less sanguine. The novelist Joseph Conrad laments "the tremendous fact of our isolation, of the loneliness impenetrable and transparent, elusive and everlasting; of the indestructible loneliness that surrounds, envelops, clothes every human soul from the cradle to the grave, and perhaps, beyond."[8] In his celebrated novel, *Look Homeward, Angel,* Thomas Wolfe wonders if any of us can escape the relentless devil of loneliness:

> Naked and alone we came into exile. In her dark womb we did not know our mother's face; from the prison of her flesh have we come into the unspeakable and incommunicable prison of this earth.
> Which of us has known his brother? Which of us has

looked into his father's heart? Which of us has not remained forever prison-pent? Which of us is not forever a stranger and alone?[9]

As overwhelming as human loneliness may be, we cannot help but find even more discouraging the possibility, expressed by many, that as intimacy increases so does the potential for loneliness. Leo Buscaglia to the contrary, when we develop and sustain ever more intimate relations with our friends, lovers, children, and families, we may unwittingly be raising the stakes of loneliness. While intimacy may be the only solution to dreaded loneliness, experiencing greater and greater levels of intimacy increases the likelihood that we will ultimately experience greater and greater levels of loneliness when confronted with separation or loss. Intimacy is tremendously risky, and it will ultimately bring suffering. There seems to be no way around it, for all intimate experiences are short-lived and all intimate relationships, sooner or later, must end. The termination of an intimate relationship—through death or separation—is doubtless one of the most traumatic of all human experiences. In short, intimacy and loneliness are forever wrapped together. When we feel no intimacy, we are lonely. But when we experience intimacy with someone else, we risk even greater loneliness should that someone and we part.

In the past twenty years, psychologists have begun to study loneliness in a scientific manner. Armed with new questionnaires designed to assess just how lonely we are, empirical psychologists have examined the experience of loneliness in otherwise "healthy" and "normal" people of all ages. One of the most striking findings of these studies is that virtually all people report that they do experience loneliness in their current lives or have experienced it in the past. In a large survey, over one-fourth of American adults reported that they had felt extremely lonely at least once within the previous two weeks.[10] Although we often think of loneliness as more common among the elderly, research suggests that teenagers and young adults are just as likely to report that they are lonely as are members of the older generations.

New scientific research on loneliness has led to a number of other conclusions.[11] First, whereas almost everybody experiences loneliness at one time or another, some people appear to be lonely almost all of the time. Chronically lonely people report that they are also depressed, anxious, and bored in their lives and that they have lower self-esteem. They tend to criticize themselves to a greater degree than do people who are not chronically lonely, and they tend to hold rather cynical and rejecting attitudes about specific other people and about humankind overall. They do *not* report fewer friendships. But their satisfaction with their friendships is especially low, partly because they rarely share themselves with their friends. Indeed, in one study of nearly four hundred accounts of loneliness, 75 percent of the lonely people explained their loneliness as resulting from the inability to discuss personally important and private matters with someone else.

A central problem in loneliness is what psychologists call "self-disclosure." Lonely people report major problems in disclosing or relating personally meaningful information about themselves to other people. Indeed, not only do lonely people perceive that self-disclosure is a problem in their lives, but laboratory studies of lonely people engaged in conversations show clearly that chronically lonely people are less effective than nonlonely people in making themselves known to other persons. They seem to miss opportunities for disclosing important information about themselves by failing to pick up on subtle cues from the other person that signal a readiness to listen and share. Chronically lonely people seem less responsive when talking with other people. They ask fewer questions during a friendly conversation and seem to be less interested in what the other person has to say. They often interrupt the flow of conversation by jumping arbitrarily from one topic to the next. Even when lonely people do talk extensively about themselves, they still appear to be "hard to get to know."

The implication of much recent research on loneliness is that chronically lonely people lack certain social skills that would enable them to engage in intimate, sharing behavior with other people. They are not good listeners. They are not tuned

12

in to the subtle nuances of conversations. They make other people feel that they do not care to get to know them. Many psychologists believe that these deficits in social skills can be remedied through systematic behavioral training and therapy. Workshops and special therapy regimens for "the lonely" have sprung up in clinics, colleges, and many other settings across the country, as professionals have sought to address the needs of this special group of Americans. And a spate of self-help books designed to cure loneliness has also appeared in recent years.[12]

While there is much to praise here, I must admit that it all makes me a bit nervous. It hints of "quick fixes" and blaming the victim. While I am certain that chronically lonely people do sometimes lack key social skills, I find it troubling to suggest that the complex experience of loneliness can be reduced to a matter of skills, as if one were talking about riding a bicycle. To say that the chronically lonely are just not very good at "doing intimacy" is to imply that their "failure" is their fault and that it can be turned into instant success with a little "skills training."

Certainly there is truth in the view that loneliness stems from social incompetence. Such a view also, however, seems to undermine the integrity and complexity of the human experience of loneliness. Further, it tends to obscure other scientific findings on loneliness that set the experience into the biographical context of the lonely person. For instance, research suggests that living through the divorce of one's parents, especially in early childhood, seems to predispose a person to later experiences of both loneliness and low self-esteem.

I believe that it is worth thinking hard about the complicated associations between loneliness and human intimacy. Even in our most intimate moments, when we are as close to another as we can be, we are haunted by the specter of loneliness and loss. And experiencing deep and pervasive loneliness in one's life can sometimes enhance our intimacy, making it more precious, more delicious and well-savored. Social scientists William Sadler Jr. and Thomas Johnson Jr. observe that intimacy can be the bearer of loneliness. They speculate that "those with the greatest capacity to love and for whom love has been a primary value are those who experience the greatest depths of loneliness on an interpersonal dimension." They add, "the most loving people can also be those who are most aware of loneliness in themselves and in others."[13]

Narcissism

In the ancient legend, the beautiful boy Narcissus falls so completely in love with the reflection of himself seen in a pool of water that he plunges into the pool and drowns. If we are to believe a number of contemporary journalists, psychologists, and social critics, something very much like the fate of Narcissus is happening to people all around us today. The contemporary narcissist has fallen in love with the self and thus finds it virtually impossible to be intimate with others.

Contemporary American society is a "culture of narcissism," wrote Christopher Lasch in 1979.[14] The ethic of the "me generation" encourages us all to love ourselves first, to seek, develop, perfect, and master the self. As a result, many of us are incapable of mature love for and commitment to others and are unwilling to devote ourselves to pursuits that go beyond our own selfish concerns. In the eyes of the popular press, the modern-day "Yuppie"—the young, upwardly mobile, urban professional—stands as the perfect example of the contemporary narcissist, obsessed with perfecting his body at the health club, desperately trying to "be all that she can be," "born to shop" and to accumulate high-priced possessions and exotic personal experiences. Popular novels such as Jay McInerney's *Bright Lights, Big City* (1984) and Louis Auchincloss's *Diary of a Yuppie* (1986) dramatize what many observers believe to be a serious social problem among those between the ages of approximately twenty-five and forty who are well educated and relatively well-off.

A number of prominent psychoanalysts consider narcissism to be the representative psychopathology of our time, rendering the "narcissistic personality disorder" one of the most talked-about clinical syndromes of the 1980s. Psychoanalysts tend to regard serious narcissism as a product of very early deficits in the child's relations with parents. According to Otto Kernberg, narcissism develops from parental abandonment and rejection. Because of cold and rejecting parents, the child defensively withdraws from others and comes to believe that it is only him- or herself that can be trusted and relied on and therefore loved. The narcissist's haughty attitude to others is in fact a defense against a burning rage within and an extraordinarily fragile sense of self. Because love was spurned in childhood, the narcissist holds back love for others as an adult.[15] The high-tech, consumer society in which we live reinforces narcissistic tendencies, providing us with a thousand and one narcissistic delights —spectacular sound and video systems, recreational drugs—all at our fingertips, provided we have the money to pay for the delights.

The extreme narcissist considers him- or herself to be the center of the universe, the most important man or woman on earth. Internally, he or she is preoccupied with fantasies of unlimited success, power, beauty, even ideal love. Interpersonally, narcissists crave constant attention and admiration and seem to expect that they are entitled to all that they desire, without having to pay people back for what they give. Other people may initially find that the narcissist can be charming and fun, but they usually change their minds later, as they come to see that they are being exploited as objects for the narcissist's private delight.

While the narcissistic personality disorder exists as a significant clinical diagnosis, strains of narcissism can be seen in varying degrees among relatively "normal" persons as well. Psychologists Robert Raskin and Robert Emmons consider narcissism to be a personality trait that can be measured in normal people with standard questionnaires.[16] Raskin has developed the Narcissistic Personality Inventory, or NPI, to measure this trait. People who score high on Raskin's measure of "mild narcissism" tend to endorse items like the following:

I really like to be the center of attention.

I have a natural talent for influencing people.

I like to look at my body.

I think I am a special person.

Everybody likes to hear my stories.

I insist on the respect that is due to me.

I will never be satisfied until I get all that I deserve.

Psychologists employing the NPI have found that people scoring high on narcissism tend to carry on conversations with others in ways noticeably different from those used by people who do not score high on the measure. People with high scores on narcissism tend to use the words "I," "me," and "my" frequently, reflecting their preoccupation with the self. Other studies have shown that people high in narcissism show less empathy and understanding for others, tend to be highly dominant and exhibitionistic in their relationships, to report lower self-esteem, and to say that they have greater mood swings in everyday life. With respect to the last two findings, it is believed that the narcissist's superficial smugness masks a deeper insecurity and vulnerability. Narcissists may be more sensitive to both success and failure in experiences than most other people, experiencing intense joy when the self is uplifted but devastating depression in the wake of even minor setbacks.

At the center of the narcissist's experience in life is a sense of being completely alone in the world. The narcissist cannot engage in the reciprocal sharing of the innermost self that is at the heart of intimate behavior with others. Fantasies of omnipotence and immortality substitute for real intimacy in everyday behavior. If intimacy is seen as a risk, we can say that the narcissist shudders in the face of such risk today, perhaps because yesterday, in early childhood, he took the risk and was repeatedly rebuffed. Fantasy is safer than intimacy, but desperate and eternal aloneness is, of course, the result. If we examine further the fantasies of people who are clinically diagnosed as suffering from extreme narcissism, we find that their internal images of other people are often stark, cold, and unfeeling. It is as if the narcissist views other people as akin to inanimate machines. Like Adam without Eve, like the Old Testament God without his creation, the narcissist exists in a world in which no help-mate can possibly exist. The failure in intimacy resides in the psychological fact that, for the narcissist, there truly is nobody in the universe with whom one can share one's innermost self.

Intimacy Today and Yesterday

If narcissism is a greater problem today than it was years ago, as many psychologists seem to suggest, is intimacy currently under siege? Does psychology's upsurge of interest in the phenomenon of loneliness signal that intimacy is a greater problem for us today than it may have been two or three decades ago? Are contemporary adults, in fact, lonelier, more self-centered, and less intimate than they were in earlier times?

One of the few observers to answer "no" is literary scholar Phyllis Rose. In her analysis of the marriages of such Victorian authors as Charles Dickens and George Eliot, Rose finds no evidence to support the idea that people of the nineteenth century were less preoccupied with intimacy and loneliness than we are today.[17] Social historians have suggested that intimate relationships as we understand them today emerged as a special problem in the lives of middle-class Europeans and Americans in the early years of the nineteenth century, with the rapid urbanization of Western life. It is at this time in history, the argument goes, that the world of work was separated from the world of home, and men in large numbers began to abandon farming and other home-based occupations to find work in other places, leaving women behind to tend to family and friends. Intimacy became a "feminine" issue confined to the domestic front. "Masculine" business and industry became divorced from all that was domestic. Men experienced alienation at work, but they were rewarded with intimacy at home. Life became compartmentalized.[18]

17

Our current problems in intimacy, therefore, may stem partly from social changes that occurred almost two centuries ago. Nonetheless, many things seem to have become a lot more complicated in the past thirty years or so. Pointing to such recent social changes as the rise of the women's movement and the skyrocketing divorce rate, psychologists, journalists, and novelists have asserted that Americans are increasingly troubled by problems in intimacy. Psychotherapists like Lillian Rubin observe that, with rapidly changing expectations about what it means to be a male and a female, men and women no longer know how to relate to each other. As she sees it, couples are left blindly groping for a common ground as "intimate strangers."[19] Sociologist Ann Swidler observes that American adults are likely to view intimate relationships as either something to be "worked on," like improving your golf stroke, or virtual impossibilities, never to be attained. Finding proof for her second assertion in recently popular works of fiction, Swidler writes:

> [Fictional] heroes refuse to join society, but they cannot quite escape it either. Indeed, even the hero of Vonnegut's *Slaughterhouse Five* escapes his sordid earth life only to find himself a caged pet of beings from another planet. In *One Flew Over the Cuckoo's Nest,* while the hero creates a band of buddies who defy the head nurse (now the paradigm of the overwhelming, repressive, female social force), their triumph is ambiguous. The men recover their masculinity and their will to resist, but the hero is destroyed as a person, though his spirit lives on. And in high culture—the novels of Saul Bellow or Thomas Pynchon, for example—unstrung heroes, with no social attachment anywhere, twist and turn through a world which has disintegrated around them. Madness makes the world incomprehensible and real contact with anyone in it impossible. Society, and the world of love and of women, has become positively sinister—a senseless, overpowering juggernaut. The individual must defy society, but he can never hope to overcome it.[20]

In their penetrating analysis of contemporary American society, Robert Bellah and his coauthors of *Habits of the Heart* examine Americans' traditional preoccupation with *individualism*. Since at least the time of Thomas Jefferson, Americans have tended to see themselves as self-sufficient individuals. We cherish freedom and independence, and we view society as comprising autonomous individuals who freely choose to engage in intimate relationships and make commitments to the social good.

For all its blessings, however, American individualism exacts a tremendous price, and the price may have risen dramatically in the past two to three decades. Bellah's interviews and observations suggest that we are increasingly unable to make meaningful commitments to community groups, churches, and other institutions that traditionally affirm the common good. Moreover, we appear increasingly unable to discover and create intimacy in our personal lives. Bellah believes that we are more socially and emotionally isolated than we have ever been. Yet the yearnings for commitment and for intimacy are still strong. Most people, however, find it very difficult to put these yearnings into words. Even more difficult is translating the yearnings into behavior.[21]

Although I strongly affirm Bellah's analysis, I am aware of no large-scale scientific studies that provide clear evidence that people are generally lonelier today—more socially and emotionally isolated—than, say, fifty years ago. And I do not know of studies to support directly the claim that people are more frustrated or perplexed by intimate relationships than they were years ago. This should not be surprising in that social scientists have only begun to study these sorts of questions in recent years.

One important study, however, does suggest that American adults have become increasingly concerned with the general issue of intimacy during the past thirty years.[22] In 1957 and again in 1976, the Survey Research Center at the University of Michigan interviewed a large cross-section of American adults living in the forty-eight contiguous states. The adults represented virtually all walks of American life. The men and women were interviewed in their homes. They were asked a variety of questions, covering topics such as life satisfaction, marital and job relationships, use of leisure time, attitudes, and values. They were also administered a number of standard psychological tests.

In their important book *The Inner American*, Joseph Veroff, Elizabeth Douvan, and Richard Kulka report some of the results from the 1976 survey and compare them to what was found in 1957. Two of the most interesting findings concern social relationships. First, Americans in 1976 were less interested in committing themselves to community and civic organizations than in 1957. In keeping with Robert Bellah's analysis, contemporary Americans seem reluctant to put their time and energy into large group endeavors, focusing more attention, it seems, on work and family. A second, related finding is a shift over the twenty-year span in the importance Americans place on intimacy in their daily lives. The authors write that warm and intimate relations with other people constituted a major life concern for many middle-class, well-educated Americans in 1957. But in 1976, this concern was stronger and broader, spreading to Americans in all class categories:

> Related to this thinning of the social commitment and social investment, we note an increased sensitivity to interpersonal relations—a desire for friendship, warm relationships at work and in the family, a desire for personal impact in everyday encounters. In all of the major life roles we looked at—work, marriage, and parenthood— respondents in 1976 stress interpersonal aspects in their definitions and in describing their satisfactions, problems, and inadequacies. The search for satisfying warm relationships which was primarily a feature of middle-class, educated life in 1957 has spread more broadly in 1976.[23]

We are not sure whether people are lonelier today than they were years ago; and we cannot say for certain that narcissism is on the rise, though clinicians seem to think it is. But the Michigan study does reinforce our sense that people today are more concerned about intimacy in their daily lives than they were thirty years ago. People appear to be seeking intimacy in a greater number of their daily activities—at work, at home, in their play. The desire to be close to another and to share that which is innermost with another is more than a transient need that is fulfilled in, say, a single relationship with a person's spouse or lover. Rather, the need for intimacy manifests itself in many different life domains, guiding our behavior in the office, at church, at the supermarket, in both our public and our private spaces. Indeed, we may even define who we are in terms of our intimate relationships.

Intimacy, therefore, is a surprisingly broad and influential force in our lives—a central motive that organizes our behavior and experience. It is not, however, the only motive. Intimacy often runs up against an equally influential force—the desire for *power*—the need to have an impact on the world, to feel strong and effective. While intimacy brings connection, power brings separation and mastery. A major life task for many of us is balancing, integrating, or finding a common ground for our contrasting needs for intimacy and power.

Intimacy Versus Power

Living on the southern coast of Sicily about 440 B.C., the ancient philosopher Empedocles asserted that two grand forces rule the universe. One is love, the other strife. All that exists in the world and in the heavens is guided and organized by these twin forces. Love unites all things; strife separates. The clouds in the sky, the animals in the forest, the people in the city come together through love and separate violently through strife. History, too, is ruled by the two masters, as periods of unity are followed by epochs of discord. After love brings things together, strife gradually sorts things out again until all is divided. Then love again begins to reunite. A person's life is the same.

Empedocles' vision has found its way into many modern theories of human behavior and experience. In 1920, Sigmund

21

Freud presented his final theory of human motivation, in which he speculated that two fundamental forces exist within the human being to organize and direct behavior and experience. Freud termed these the *erotic* "life instincts" and the *aggressive* "death instincts." Freud believed that at the basic instinctual core each of us desires to unite ourselves in loving and pleasurable oneness with other people (life instincts) and to assert ourselves in ever more aggressive and deadly ways against others and even, sometimes, against ourselves (death instincts). These desires remain unknown to us, Freud maintained, operating as unconscious forces that ultimately shape all of our behavior and experience.[24]

A number of other twentieth-century psychologists have offered similar theories.[25] One of the most appealing variations on this idea is offered by psychologist David Bakan.[26] Bakan distinguishes between two "fundamental modalities" in all living forms. He calls them *communion* and *agency*. Communion is the tendency of living forms to come together in unions, to surrender the self and become one with a larger whole. Agency, by contrast, is the tendency to assert and expand oneself as an autonomous "agent," to master and control others and the environment. Intimacy motivation can be seen as an expression of communion. An expression of agency is the "power motive."

Let us consider the life of Roberta K. from the standpoint of power motivation.[27] Roberta is a thirty-eight-year-old divorced social worker who has traveled the world over. Her life reads like an adventure story. She sees herself as a restless heroine encountering one dramatic challenge after another. In describing her philosophy of life, Roberta states, "Life is a journey. It is the journey that matters, not the arrival. I will not stop running; I refuse until I'm in a wheelchair." The key events in her life—those moments in her story which stand out in bold print —are virtually always set in exotic, faraway places, like Mexico and the Orient. There are illicit love affairs, experiments with drugs, tempestuous relations with lovers and friends, strange foods and customs, captivating conversations. Her life is populated with forceful people who have an impact on one another and on their worlds. The most important people in her life tend to reflect the character traits that she most values in herself: they are ambitious, adventurous, restless, cosmopolitan, dramatic, and sophisticated.

Roberta is a forceful "agent" who makes big things happen. This image of herself goes back at least to her elementary school years. Attending a Catholic school, Roberta found herself repeatedly "moving against" the nuns who were her teachers. Although she was not generally considered a troublemaker, she drove the nuns daffy with her incessant questions. Although her teachers complained to her parents that Roberta was a bit of a pain, Roberta's mother encouraged her further, taking secret delight in her daughter's ability to ruffle the feathers of the status quo. One of Roberta's aunts, too, consistently supported her adventures. This aunt is one of Roberta's greatest heroines in life because "she always believed in trying new things."

Roberta left for Mexico shortly after high school graduation. In retrospect, she sees this move as an example of "running away." It is by no means the last example. Even though she has held the same job for the past eight years, Roberta continues to travel, regularly visiting Latin America where she has some dear friends. In Roberta's life story, physical travel mirrors the psychological and spiritual journey she perceives. In her eyes, she is ever expanding, ever growing, and ever changing. If you stay in one place, she maintains, you get bored. Movement, both physical and psychological, brings with it excitement and a worldly wisdom that cannot be found in books. It is important to Roberta that she see herself as a worldly and sophisticated woman who, in many senses of the term, has "been around the world." She scoffs at those who never move, who "stay home" in a physical and a psychological sense. In Roberta's view, these people are stagnant and naïve.

Yet Roberta has been naïve herself, and she tends to "stay home" more than one might think. She tells of her early years, before the nuns, in which she was always "the good little girl," and of a later period as a young adult when she naïvely "wanted to save the world." She sees these chapters in her life story as necessary stages in her own growth, through which she needed to develop in order to attain the maturity that she now feels she has found. Another necessary "stage" was her marriage. In her late twenties she married a man she met in Latin America, but the marriage seems to have been a failure from the start. As Roberta tells it, she was still too unsophisticated to know what she wanted in an intimate and sexual relationship. Although she and her husband were compatible in bed, they fought most of the rest of the time, and neither ever fully understood the other. Shortly after they divorced, Roberta's mother died, and her younger brother developed a serious kidney ailment that required hospitalization. This was the low point in her life.

Roberta rebounded with gusto. She began to date older men whom she felt she could respect. She resumed her travels to distant lands. She found a job as a social worker that provided her with not only a good deal of authority in her work but also the fulfillment that comes with "doing my bit for mankind." She began caring for her ailing father. Roberta's rebound has enabled her to strengthen her agency in the world, and she has begun to have a major impact on events and people around her. She is no power-hungry tyrant who exploits other people in a narcissistic way. Far from it. Like Sara N., whose life reflects strong intimacy motivation, Roberta surely cares for many people in her work and in her personal life. But her life is not organized by intimacy in the same way that Sara's is. Rather, the organizing principle is power. Whereas Sara lives for love and service, Roberta lives for change and adventure. While Sara values equality and peace, Roberta values freedom and strength. Roberta's life story celebrates Bakan's concept of agency: she is motivated to assert and expand the self, to keep moving and growing with each new adventure.

Intimacy and power. Like Empedocles, Freud, and Bakan, I believe these to be two of the great organizing principles in human lives. I have spent a lot of time over the past ten years listening to people tell the stories of their lives. Again and again, these narratives seem to revolve around issues of intimacy and power, feeling close and feeling strong. The two themes are dramatically apparent when people tell of the most wonderful moments in their lives, what some psychologists term "peak experiences." In my research, I routinely ask people to describe their peak experiences. Invariably, these involve some aspects of either intimacy or power, or sometimes both.[28]

Peak experiences laced with intimacy often highlight communication and sharing between people, friendship and love, sympathy and compassion for others, and tender interpersonal contact. As one of many examples, a sophomore woman in college described this experience, the most wonderful moment in her life:

> In the last month I had the opportunity to experience a true peak experience—an actual "rebirth" of sorts. I have become very close to an individual who has a very high moral system—one which I myself used to have and an innocent beauty I want to recapture. Together we have discussed all the events that have occurred between us and the guilt that hovered over some of our actions. And we decided to start over in purity. We went walking down the beach after going to Mass one night and it was beautiful! It was a warm night—stars were everywhere. Never before had I felt so close to God and so close to another human being. We waded into the water—next thing I knew we were up to our waists in water. We laughed and cried and hugged while the water swirled around us and we promised to each other a new start—a new fidelity to God and to our faith, and a promise not to tempt but rather to help each other. When we left the lake that night and walked back squishing and dripping we were happy—totally one with each other and with the heavens above. It was absolutely the most wonderful happiness possible.

Like Sara's approach to intimacy, this young woman sees close relationships with other people as reflections of a closeness to God and to the natural world around her. Peak experiences of intimacy, however, need not be so mystical and religious. A male student from the same college describes a peak experience that may be a bit more common:

25

My experience involved a relationship with one of my friends. We had known each other for a short while but there was a certain feeling of being closer, of feeling like you have known this person longer. One day, we were both talking and suddenly we both began telling things each of us had never told anyone before. We were having a completely honest and open conversation with each of us exposing some of ourselves that had never been shown to anyone else. It was just the two of us talking and pouring out our hearts. We both cried. Some of the things I spoke about were painful, but an immediate sense of relief came over me after I had opened up. I was thinking of how good it felt to be so open with this friend. Our friendship was strengthened as a result of this. We have a strong bond between us, and our friendship is something I cherish. The experience changed my concept of myself. I learned to be more tolerant of my faults. It helped me to feel more alive, more loved than ever before.

Peak experiences of power emphasize a physical or mental "strengthening," having an impact or influence on others, movement and action, and heightened prestige or status. A forty-three-year-old man tells of a great moment in his life that occurred in the Army:

During a particularly exhausting physical training session in military service, I experienced an immensely high sense of unity with a group. While being observed by training officers, several groups were being put through intense exercise routines for the better part of an hour. A strong sense of competitive attitude became apparent between the groups which one by one began to falter and break pattern very obviously due to the pressure and discomfort. My own feelings were mixed ones of resentment against the training officers and a responsibility to the unit coupled with a sense of pride in still being able to keep the pace. All of this was consistently overridden by physical pain. In the final minutes we seemed to become aware that the other units were faltering and without outside direction we began to function as one large being, rather than sixty men. I felt, as did the others, a tremendous surge of energy and our precision of movements was faultless. The bond we had been seeking for so many weeks suddenly was there and petty differences and jealousies no longer existed.

While this experience begins and ends with a mention of the "union" experienced by members of the group, it is essentially a power experience, emphasizing physical strength and action, competitive advantage, and heightened prestige. The union described is less an intimate exchange among partners than a solidarity of powerful agents. The experience was especially meaningful for this man because of the incredible power that he and his group experienced during very trying circumstances.

A less physical experience that, nonetheless, highlights the person's ability to have a powerful impact on another, is described by a twenty-four-year-old woman:

Oddly enough, a confrontation with a man I highly respect and admire resulted in what you might call a "peak experience." I am normally intimidated by those whom I greatly admire. The incident occurred at a school board meeting. Present were members of the board, a few parents in the audience, the principal, and our pastor, the man with whom I debated. I had been working on a parent survey from March through November. The pastor wanted to dismiss the value of the survey findings purely on the basis of a few points with which he disagreed. We were sitting face to face across a table. As I listened to him tear down months of work, I thought, "I can't let him do this." Then the confrontation began. For approximately twenty minutes we debated and compromised. All the while, I was sure that he would dislike and resent me from that time on, but I had to risk it. I was wrong. In our conversation following the meeting, I learned that

27

his attitude toward me had changed. I had earned *his* respect! I felt both relieved and exhilarated.

Patterns in Lives

There is a form to human life. It is the form of narrative, or story. Like most stories, our lives have beginnings, middles, and endings. Our lives contain plots, scenes, characters, settings, and themes. We live through chapters in which events build up to a climax and then unfold to reveal the denouement. Early experiences sometimes foreshadow later ones; later episodes may contain flashbacks of the earliest scenes. As the philosopher Jean-Paul Sartre said, "a man is always a teller of tales, he lives surrounded by his stories and the stories of others, he sees everything that happens to him through them; and he tries to live his life as if he were telling a story."[29] A major goal in life— perhaps *the* major goal—is to discover or compose the right story for one's own life. The person who is able to do so understands who he or she was, is, and will be, integrating past, present, and future into a meaningful and unifying life narrative. The person who has found a story to unify life has found what psychologists call "identity."

In my book *Power, Intimacy, and the Life Story,* I argued that a person's identity is an integrative life story that he or she begins to compose, both consciously and unconsciously, as a young adult. At the end of adolescence, the young person in our society is faced with the problem of finding an appropriate "place" in the world of adults. In order to find it, he or she must answer a number of tough questions about occupation ("What do I want to do in my life?"), ideology ("What do I truly believe?"), and interpersonal relationships ("With whom do I want to live?"). The young person addresses these identity questions by experimenting with various possible scenarios—undertaking new lifestyles, trying new value systems, exploring new kinds of interpersonal relationships, meeting new people, and entertaining new ideas—until he or she finds some that seem to "fit."

The young person examines his or her own past, as well—old lifestyles, childhood values, family ties—and takes from the past what also seems to "fit." The result is a new view of self, a new identity, that integrates past, present, and anticipated future within a personalized story, providing the young person's life with a sense of unity and purpose.[30]

Within a person's self-defining life story, themes of intimacy and power organize the text. In my life-story model of identity, I call intimacy and power the two major "thematic lines" in the narrative. This means that a good deal of the basic content that makes up a person's life story is organized around strivings to be close, connected, and intimate on the one hand and to be masterful, separate, and powerful on the other. All life stories—all persons' identities—contain drives for both intimacy and power. Everybody seeks, in one way or another, to be both connected and separated, intimate and powerful, communal and agentic. Nonetheless, we can see striking differences in people with respect to how prominent each theme is in their lives. The differences yield fascinating insights into human uniqueness.

At the risk of oversimplifying people's lives, we can identify four general types of life stories. Some people construct stories that are highly intimate but not very powerful. A second group focuses on power but not intimacy. A third group expresses both strong intimacy and power, and a fourth group emphasizes neither intimacy nor power.

A key to determining the characteristic pattern of a person's life story is to consider the narrative dimension of *character*. Obviously, the "main character" in a person's life story is himself. But a person can be many things and represent many different sides or aspects of personality. For instance, I may see myself both as a learned professor who loves to read and entertain esoteric ideas, and as a rough-around-the-edges working-class boy who loves to mix it up on the basketball court. These are two different sides of me, two different selves within me that sometimes come into conflict. The "professor" takes center stage when I am in the classroom or when I am writing or doing research, but "he" serves to structure my life in other

29

ways as well, dictating what I prefer to do in my leisure time, the kinds of friends I care to be with, how I raise my children, how I relate to people. Similarly, the "working-class boy" often does "his" thing when I am with my brother and sister, when I go back to my college fraternity, when I play with my daughters in the backyard, when I am feeling especially excited, romantic, or frustrated. Neither of these two characters is the "real me." Rather, the real me is the story that unfolds as a result of the actions of these and other characters who play dominant roles in my life.

The dominant characters in a person's life story reveal the relative importance of intimacy and power in that person's life. A person with very high intimacy motivation but relatively low power motivation is likely to create a story in which the main character is loving, gentle, and compassionate. A good example is Sara N. While Sara is surely a very complex person with a number of different sides to her personality, her central character is "the lover." As a nun and as a counselor, in her work and in her relationships, Sara views herself as living a narrative of passionate love and care. Of course, she is not loving people every minute of the day. She does many things that have nothing to do with love, like taking the class in financial investment. But the overall pattern of her life is one in which we follow the development of a woman who lives in order to love others and to be loved.

The main characters in the life stories of people who are high in intimacy motivation and low in power motivation often appear in the guises of "the lover," "the loyal friend," and "the caregiver." In the mythology of ancient Greece, we find prototypes for these characters in the goddesses of Aphrodite, Hera, and Demeter. Aphrodite is the goddess of passionate love in both its noblest and most degraded forms. She is the inspiration for the amours of deities and mortals alike. She seeks to form loving and passionate unions, to delight others, to charm and enchant. She is especially affectionate, charming, dependent, emotional, sensitive, sincere, softhearted, and warm.

The loyal wife of Zeus and queen of Olympos, Hera is the faithful helpmate and friend. She is always appreciative, cooperative, friendly, loyal, praising, sociable, submissive, and trusting. Demeter is the devoted caregiver and goddess of the earth's fertility. She seeks to care for, to nurture, to cultivate, to provide warmth and support, to promote growth. She is gentle, kind, modest, moody, natural, self-denying, steady, and sympathetic. In the coming chapters, we will see reflections of all three of these intimate deities in the lives of women and men who are high in intimacy motivation.

A person with high power motivation and low intimacy motivation is likely to develop a life story in which the main character is strong, independent, and masterful. An example is Roberta K. The main character in her life story is "the swift traveler," an image of the self reflected in the ancient Greek god Hermes. Hermes was the traveling messenger of the gods, known for his quick wit and quick feet. Born the illegitimate son of Maia and Zeus, the precocious Hermes stole Apollo's cattle, invented the lyre, and kindled the first fire, all during his first day out of the womb! Needless to say, he worked fast. Indeed, throughout all of Greek mythology, Hermes is the one god constantly *on the move.* Likewise, for Roberta, "it is the journey that matters, not the arrival. I will not stop running; I refuse until I'm in a wheelchair." It is not that Roberta is a modern-day Hermes; rather, one very important character in Roberta's life story is Roberta-the-swift-traveler. But there are many different aspects of Roberta, and, like all human beings, she is more complex, and more interesting, than the Greek gods. Still, the Hermes within her shows us that her life story generally emphasizes power rather than intimacy.

After Hermes, two deities of ancient Greece that provide character models for people high in power motivation and low in intimacy motivation are Zeus and Ares. Zeus is the all-powerful ruler of Olympos, the king of the gods and goddesses. As the final judge in all controversies, he makes decisions that are absolute and irrevocable. As the ultimate seducer, he makes love, in a conquering way, to many goddesses and mortals. He is also the wisest sage, the most bountiful provider, and the greatest celebrity in all of creation. Overall, Zeus is forceful, dominant, dignified, intelligent, severe, stubborn, sophisticated, and wise. Equally agentic is Ares, the god of war. A furious and impetuous god, Ares fights many battles through which he exhibits matchless courage and rage. He is handsome and agile, but he loses many battles because of poor judgment. He is the ultimate "warrior," repeatedly described as aggressive, argumentative, bossy, daring, courageous, impulsive, uninhibited, and tough.

People who are high in both intimacy and power motivation tend to construct relatively complex life stories in which they strive to integrate their competing desires for connection and separateness, closeness and strength. Models for the main characters in their life stories include Apollo, Athene, and Prometheus. All three of these deities are extremely forceful beings, even by the exalted standards of Olympos, and yet all three frequently use their power to promote interpersonal relationships and the welfare of others. The versatile Apollo is "the healer," "the prophet," "the artist," and "the legislator." He is artistic, clear-thinking, imaginative, foresighted, planful, organized, progressive, and rational. Athene is "the peacemaker," "the teacher," and "the counselor," who works to resolve conflicts and find a common ground. She is fair-minded, honest, moderate, peaceable, patient, practical, stable, and understanding. Prometheus is "the humanist" and "the revolutionary," who always defends the underdog and seeks to promote and preserve the noblest achievements of humankind. He is generous, helpful, idealistic, inventive, persevering, outspoken, rebellious, and unconventional.

Finally, people who are low in both intimacy and power motivation tend to construct life stories that emphasize neither of these two general thematic lines. Their lives tend to be organized around the search for stability and security on the one hand or escape and diversion on the other. The main characters in their life stories are reminiscent of the Greek deities of Hestia, Hephaistos, and Dionysios. While Hestia tends house at Mount Olympos, Hephaistos works hard with his hands to make practical things and to accumulate wealth. The two embody something of the feminine and masculine stereotypes, respectively: Hestia the homemaker, Hephaistos the wage earner.

Neither personifies intimacy or power. The god of wine and merriment, Dionysios, is "the escapist" who wants only to play. He flees the drudgery of adult reponsibility epitomized in the lives of Hestia and Hephaistos, but like them he, too, eschews intimacy and power. In modern-day, middle-class terms, Dionysios lives for the weekends.[31]

In this book, we will be examining people who have high intimacy motivation, regardless of the level of their power motivation. We will concern ourselves with those men and women whose life stories present main characters in the guise of Aphrodite, Hera, and Demeter (high intimacy and low power) as well as Apollo, Athene, and Prometheus (high intimacy and high power). What are these people like? How do they act? How do they live? What do they want? Are they happy? Are they healthy? How did they become who they are?

CHAPTER 2

The Intimacy Motive

When I confront a human being as my Thou and speak the basic word I–Thou to him, then he is no thing among things nor does he consist of things. He is no longer He or She, a dot in the world grid of space and time, nor a condition to be experienced and described, a loose bundle of named qualities. Neighborless and seamless, he is Thou and fills the firmament. Not as if there were nothing but he; but everything else lives in his light.

> —Martin Buber, *I and Thou*

A thirty-six-year-old father of two, Dean K. has lived his entire life in a working-class neighborhood on the southwest side of Chicago. It is the same neighborhood in which his parents grew up, and their parents before them. Many of Dean's childhood friends still live on the same city block on which they were born. And that is where, he believes, most of them will die as well. There is no good reason to leave the neighborhood, Dean maintains. Where would a person go? Who would a person be after he left? Family, friends, neighborhood—these define who a person is. In Dean's life story, family, friends, and neighborhood merge into one. To abandon all of this would be to give up one's entire life.

At the outset of our interview, Dean describes in detail the neighborhood that provides the main setting for his life story. He stresses the continuity of generations. For Dean, childhood was an innocent and idyllic chapter in his life story. He and his younger sister were happy and comfortable and surrounded by people who cared. Dean's father worked as a mechanic, holding the same job for almost forty years. His mother was a housewife and part-time assembly worker. None of the families in the neighborhood had a lot of money, "so life wasn't awfully exciting—there wasn't any drugs, there wasn't any cars, not too many girls, because there just wasn't the money; so there were a lot of simple things—playing baseball in the streets and alley, jumping roofs, things like that. Friendships were the main thing."

Dean worked his way through a local university, receiving a degree in engineering. In his senior year, he married the girl he had dated since seventh grade. Their first child was born in 1968, a few days before Robert F. Kennedy was assassinated. Dean had worked hard on the Kennedy campaign in Illinois. Like many young people at the climax of the Civil Rights Movement and the Vietnam War, Dean was drawn by the charismatic candidate's emphasis on peace and global harmony. Dean was crushed when he learned of the death of his hero but was exhilarated by the recent birth of his son. The intense and conflicting emotional response ushered in a new chapter in Dean's life story—that of "building a family." If the world rejected peace and love, he would at least find it in his own family life, in the neighborhood in which peace and love had never died.

Dean describes the next ten years as "very even." He worked hard as an engineer and was moderately successful. He and his wife had another son. Dean volunteered some of his free time to be a Scoutmaster and a Little League coach. The chapter ended with a wonderful climax—the birth of a daughter. Dean describes this event as the highest point in his life:

A very special experience that recently happened was the birth of my last child, in 1978. She was born nine years after my second child and she was the first daughter after many years of waiting. Perhaps the greatest moment of my life was when she was born since, unlike the birth of my two sons, I was able to be in the delivery room at my wife's side. Her birth is a moment I will never forget, especially when she was placed on my wife's chest and she just stared at the two of us without crying. I found myself crying instead, out of pure joy and happiness.

Since that day three years ago, she has brought boundless love and happiness into my family life and has brought more love out of me than I thought existed.

In Dean's life story, however, beautiful moments have a way of fading into despair and confusion. Two days after his son was born, Robert Kennedy was killed. Shortly after his daughter was born, Dean's father died. Just as significant, Dean came to realize that his marriage itself seemed to be dying. He is not explicit about what has gone wrong, merely suggesting that he and his wife "no longer feel close." Shortly after the birth of his daughter and the death of his father, Dean began seeing another woman. The affair now seems to be over, and Dean and his wife have begun marriage counseling. In addition, both are involved in individual therapy with clinical psychologists. Dean expresses a strong desire to "save the marriage, for the children's sake." He feels that his life is now in great turmoil, and he is unable to predict how the marital situation will ultimately be resolved.

Dean believes that in his relations with his children he has created the kind of loving and supportive environment that he experienced as a child. He is very close to all three children, though he feels the strongest attachment to his daughter. He takes extremely seriously his role as teacher and guide for his children, always striving to promote the continuity of generations. He teaches his children painting and carpentry. He takes the neighborhood kids to museums. He feels it is very important that his two sons understand their parents' problems, so he has tried to explain to them what has gone wrong in the marriage. Throughout all of this, he has retained his very close friendships with neighbors. His best friends' children play daily with his own.

Dean's dream for the future is to make his marriage work and to have another child. This goal is consistent with his overall image of himself as a *caregiver*. Many people, both men and women, express a strong intimacy motive through the character of the caregiver. Kind, modest, sympathetic, caring, and mildly self-effacing, the caregiver is the main character throughout

37

Dean's life story. It is reflected in his reports of the greatest moments in his life, his greatest aspirations for the future, and his involvement as Scoutmaster, Little League coach, and the bearer of family and neighborhood traditions. The caregiver speaks most clearly in Dean's answer to the question, "What is the major theme of your life story?" He responds, "To be there for others." This image of himself is also reflected in Dean's statements that it is his children and his friends who provide for his life the most satisfaction.

Yet, all is not love and harmony in Dean's life. At one point in the interview, Dean interjects that he occasionally gets the urge to escape from his wife and indeed from the neighborhood as well, to live by himself in the Rocky Mountains, perhaps doing freelance photography. In the next breath, he says that such an idea is ridiculous, for friends and children will always be the center of his life. Whether we believe he will stay with his wife or end the marriage; whether he will stay in Chicago or escape to the mountains, or remain faithful in his marriage or have another affair, we must acknowledge that this is a man whose life is organized and directed by strong intimacy motivation. In many different life domains, Dean's behavior is structured by a strong appreciation and preference for close, warm, communicative interaction with others. More than anything else, Dean wants to be a part of a loving and supportive network of family and friends.

Forms of Loving

In Dean's life, we see that intimacy motivation wears many faces. It can play itself out in our relationships as lovers, parents, children, friends, neighbors, siblings, teachers, students, coworkers, and citizens. Different people express intimacy motivation through different channels. In Dean's case, it is a strong organizing force in his roles as father and friend. As a husband, however, he seems less able to find the warm, close, and communicative kind of relationship that he so desires. You might say that Dean is not a "perfect case" for strong intimacy motivation. But in human lives there are no perfect cases for anything; in the realm of human personality nothing is ever that simple. Dean's life is complexly determined by many different forces. A strong desire to be close to other people is but one. But even with respect to this single dimension of Dean's life, we encounter considerable complexity, for Dean, like all of us, is able to experience intimacy in many different ways, and at the same time there are many ways in which he is unable to experience intimacy.

What are the different ways in which we can be close to people? For over two thousand years, poets and philosophers have speculated about different forms of human love. In the last one hundred years or so, psychologists and other social scientists have gotten into the act. Some have argued, like the Chinese philosopher Confucius, that there is only one form of love. In the sixth century before Christ, Confucius called on his fellow Chinese to exhibit *jen* in their daily lives. For Confucius, *jen* is the fundamental virtue in human life, encompassing humaneness, love, fellowship, charity, and kindness. The gentle and loving attitude of *jen* begins in the family, argued Confucius, as sons and daughters who treat their elders with deference and affection will grow up to form loving bonds with many other people in their community. By contrast, Saint Augustine (A.D. 354–430) distinguished between two basic forms of human love. *Cupiditas* includes sexual love and other earthly affections that, Augustine maintained, must be short-lived. *Caritas*, by contrast, is the universal, true, and rational love that God expresses to humankind and which people may sometimes express to God when they have mature Christian faith.[1]

The distinction between viewing love as unitary and viewing it as having many different forms can be traced from the writings of antiquity to the present-day formulations of social scientists. Representing the view that there is only one kind of love is psychologist Robert Sternberg, whose statistical analyses of questionnaires administered to hundreds of people suggest that underneath the diversity in human experiences of love lies a single "factor" or quality. Sternberg writes that the factor "is well identified as one of interpersonal communication, sharing, and support. . . . Its aspects include especially (a) deep understanding of the other, (b) sharing of ideas and information, (c) sharing of deeply personal ideas and feelings, (d) receipt and provision of emotional support to the other, (e) personal growth through the relationship and helping the other in his or her personal growth, (f) giving help to the other, (g) making the other feel needed and needing the other, and (h) the giving and receiving of affection in the relationship."[2]

While Sternberg argues that there is one kind of love that cuts across romantic relationships, friendships, and even a person's relations with parents, children, and siblings, psychologists Clyde and Susan Hendrick focus on only one kind of relationship—that between romantic lovers—but argue that there are six different styles of loving. Like Sternberg, Hendrick and Hendrick rely on the administration of questionnaires. In their latest questionnaire, entitled "Attitudes About Love and Sex," they ask people to consider their "current love partner" or, if they are not "in love" at present, a love partner from the past. Their analysis of hundreds of responses yield six basic dimensions of romantic love: (1) *eros,* or passionate, sexual love; (2) *ludus,* or love as coy game-playing; (3) *storge,* which encompasses friendship and caring; (4) *pragma,* a practical and logical approach to love; (5) *mania,* or dependent and jealous love; and (6) *agape,* or selfless, altruistic love.[3] This breakdown is like a periodic table of loving. Each of our love affairs, they maintain, is like a chemical compound containing some proportion of each of the six love elements.

When it comes to understanding love, intimacy, and closeness to other people, I tend to adopt a compromise position between Sternberg and the Hendricks. Like Sternberg, I believe that there is a common quality to all relationships that we consider to be loving and close. It encompasses "interpersonal communication, sharing, and support," as he claims, but I would not call this common component "love" per se; I call it *intimacy.* All love relationships contain some intimacy, but love contains other things as well. These are tapped by the Hendricks in their six styles of romantic loving. Nonetheless, I think that the Hendricks' approach is focused too closely on romantic, generally heterosexual relationships. When identifying the different forms of loving, I prefer an older typology with broader significance that goes back to Aristotle and the ancient Greeks and is beautifully described by C. S. Lewis in his little book, *The Four Loves*.[4]

As Lewis sees it, the humblest and most widely diffused form of loving is *affection,* or what the ancient Greeks (along with Hendricks and Hendricks) called *storge.* This is the form of love that parents show their children and that all of us show to those things and people with whom we are most familiar. This gentle form of caring may be the most natural of loves, Lewis suggests. Epitomized in the bond between mother and baby, affection generally serves to protect the weak and defenseless and to assure security and trust. Affection tends to grow stronger with time, as that to which we feel affection becomes more familiar. Lewis writes, "Affection almost slinks or sleeps through our lives. It lives with humble, un-dress, private things; soft slippers, old clothes, old jokes, the thump of a sleepy dog's tail on the kitchen floor, the sound of a sewing machine, a gollywog left on the lawn." He adds, "the especial glory of Affection is that it can unite those who most emphatically, even comically, are not; people who, if they had not found themselves put down by fate in the same household or community, would have had nothing to do with each other."

Lewis clearly has a great deal of affection for the general idea of affection. He sees it as a natural and wonderful force that binds all kinds of people together by virtue of chance and shared history. Indeed, the affection I feel for my mother and for my daughters seems extremely natural and generally beyond my control. I did not choose any of these objects of affection; yet my extraordinary familiarity with them enhances the love I feel for them. Of course, there's more to that love than familiarity, but I would agree with Lewis that without the familiarity, the affection could not exist. We should never underestimate the power of affection, Lewis maintains, for it is probably responsible for "nine-tenths of whatever solid and durable happiness there is in our natural lives." Yet, we cannot live full and satisfying lives unless we experience other kinds of love.

A second form of love is *friendship*, or what Aristotle termed *philia*. Unlike affection, *philia* requires that friends be equals. Aristotle saw friendship as one of the highest human virtues. It is a rational and tranquil form of love whereby two people came together by virtue of a shared truth or common interest. As Lewis paints it, the portrait of friendship is two friends standing shoulder to shoulder, eyes fixed straight ahead on some third entity or quality to which both have committed themselves. Lewis sees friendship as the "least natural" of all the loves, the least necessary but one of the most valuable ways in which people can be close to each other:

> Hence (if you will not misunderstand me) the exquisite arbitrariness and irresponsibility of this love. I have no duty to be anyone's Friend and no man in the world has a duty to be mine. No claims, no shadow of necessity. Friendship is unnecessary, like philosophy, like art, like the universe itself (for God did not need to create). It has no survival value, rather it is one of those things which gives value to survival.[5]

But is it true that friendship has no survival value? Scholars who study human evolution have suggested that close, nonsexual bonds of friendship between adults likely increase group solidarity and make for the greater survival and ultimate reproductive capacity of the individual human being. In other words, we may have evolved to form natural friendship bonds because such bonds have, throughout the evolution of the human species, protected us from dangers and increased our chances of surviving and reproducing.[6] But I still like Lewis's portrait of two friends as freely choosing to distinguish themselves from the rest of humankind by virtue of their common focus or perspective. A major factor in friendship is that friends be alike in some fundamental way. Indeed, Aristotle viewed the love of one's friend as akin to self-love, in that the friend should embody good qualities that one sees in oneself.

42

A third form of love is *charity*, or what is often termed *agape*. As a Christian theologian, Lewis holds up as the perfect example of *agape* Christ's love for humankind. In the Christian story of crucifixion, Christ sacrifices himself on the cross to "save" or "redeem" all persons. His love is unconditional, and it is given to all persons, both familiar and unfamiliar. Unlike affection, therefore, *agape* does not require familiarity. In *agape*, the human being expresses unconditional love for all persons, and he or she may be willing to sacrifice the self in order to realize that love. In a different but related vein, psychotherapist Carl Rogers speaks of "unconditional positive regard" as a loving attitude of unqualified acceptance that good therapists should express to their patients and clients.[7] But Lewis underscores how radical *agape* can be, praising it as a "crazy, deviant, socially-inappropriate, revolutionary kind of love." Many of history's greatest proponents of *agape*—Jesus, Gandhi, Martin Luther King, Jr.—met early, violent deaths, so dangerous was their love, so deviant and reprehensible in the eyes of their contemporaries.

A fourth kind of love is *eros*. This is the romantic, sexual, passionate love of "lovers." It has been called everything from ultimate ecstasy to divine madness. Poets celebrate it as delicious consummation, glorious battle, ultimate transcendence. Scientists understand it as the key to the species' survival, for without sexual love men and women would not cleave to each other and reproduce their own kind. And it has been blamed for starting wars and ruining lives, called a sickness and a curse. One psychologist calls eros "the single greatest energy system in the Western psyche," having supplanted religion in contemporary Western culture as the primary "arena in which men and women seek meaning, transcendence, wholeness, and ecstasy."[8] Another warns that it is like an "addiction."[9]

Our understanding of eros has been shaped by some of the greatest stories in Western tradition. In Plato's *Symposium*, Socrates tells the story of the "myth of Aristophanes," concerning the origins of sexual love. According to this myth, the original inhabitants of the Earth were round creatures with four hands and feet and with back and sides forming a circle. These self-sufficient, sexless beings were quite arrogant, and they repeatedly attacked the gods. To punish them, Zeus hurled thunderbolts and split them apart. Each creature was now two, longing to merge with its other half. Eros is this ancient desire for fusion with the other half. Lovers seek to meld into each other, to eat each other up and be eaten. Bringing the myth of Aristophanes to the twentieth century, contemporary psychoanalysts like Margaret Mahler[10] and Lloyd Silverman[11] place great emphasis on a universal and unconscious human need to fuse with another. They argue that the need is rooted in the oneness experienced in the first months of life before the infant understands the distinction between self and other. Later in adulthood, the need permeates our private, unconscious fantasies.

Our understanding of eros is further enriched by the great stories of "courtly love" that come to us from the Middle Ages. In romantic myths, as with the story of Tristan and Iseult, a gallant knight on horseback swears his eternal love to a beautiful lady. She is perfect and pure; he is courageous and manly. Both lovers are *idealized:* they are perfections, and their love is also perfect. Yet, the two must generally worship each other from afar, for she is usually promised to another. While they may meet in an episode of ecstatic union, the lovers will not live together in happiness for long. The relationship invariably ends in tragedy, though both lovers reach ever nobler heights through their separation and death.

The troubadours of the twelfth and thirteenth centuries were love poets and singers who told the stories of courtly love. Their hymns to castle ladies paved the way for much of the love literature of future generations. Jealousy is an essential component of courtly love. Men vie for the honor of possessing that single, perfect maiden. The tug of courtly love is much stronger than the marriage bond. The beautiful princess may be married to a man she does not love. She may or may not give him her body. But she saves her soul for her lover.[12]

The themes of fusion, idealization, and jealousy are almost unique to eros, having virtually no part to play in affection, friendship, and charity. Modern psychoanalysts place them at the center of the experience of adult romantic love. Psychoanalyst Myron Weiner says that adult romantic love is psychodynamically characterized by the following eight qualities:

1. a wish to be united with one's beloved, both emotionally and sexually;

2. temporary "losses of boundaries" between lovers, which means that the two lovers may find their lives—indeed, their very identities or selves—to be inseparable;

3. idealization of one's beloved;

4. some reenactment of one's childhood experiences with parents and other love objects in one's adult relationships;

5. the ability to recognize the needs of the beloved and to differentiate them from one's own;

6. the desire to satisfy the beloved's needs, even at the expense of one's own;

7. "vigilance over one's beloved" to prevent his or her loss;

8. and a "narcissistic vulnerability to the beloved."[13]

In this list, points 1 and 2 suggest fusion; point 3 is idealization, or viewing the beloved as virtually perfect and ideal; and points 7 and 8 suggest jealousy and possessiveness.

What Is Intimacy?

Intimacy is not the same as love. It cannot be identified solely with any one of the four loves we have discussed—affection, friendship, charity, or eros. It is both more general and more specific than each of these. Intimacy cuts across all forms of love; it can be experienced in the contexts of any of them. It is more specific in the sense that any one of these four loves encompasses much more than just intimacy. For instance, intimacy is likely to be a central component of many erotic relationships. Yet, as we have seen, eros also includes fusion, idealization, and possessiveness.

45

In its basic sense, intimacy refers to the sharing of one's innermost being, or essence, as we saw in Chapter 1. When I desire to share with you that which is personally meaningful to me, I desire to get close to you through intimacy. This is but one of many different and sometimes conflicting desires that may operate in any particular relationship. Take an erotic love affair, for instance. I desire to share with my lover my innermost self and to receive the same from her in return. Thus, I desire intimacy. I also desire to worship her, however, to idealize her as the paragon of feminine virtue, as did the troubadours of courtly love. I desire to possess her, to keep her as my lover, lest I lose her to those many men who seek my prize. And I desire to fuse with her, to merge with her body and soul, so that, in the words of contemporary psychoanalysts, the "boundaries" between us no longer exist.

In simple terms, I want to open up to my lover; I want to worship my lover; I want to own my lover; and I want to be one with my lover. That is, I desire intimacy, idealization, possession, and fusion. Actually, I probably desire a lot more, too, but these four will do to illustrate the point. They are but four of many different desires that play themselves out in complex erotic relationships. It is essential that we realize, then, that any love relationship serves many motivational masters. As Sigmund Freud would put it, love is *overdetermined*. Like all complex human behavior and experience, it is a product of a wild collection of diverse and conflicting forces, many of which are outside our conscious awareness. The desires for intimacy, idealization, possession, and fusion are all very different from one another. Furthermore, *they do not get along with one another*, which is to say that they conflict, both logically and psychologically. I want to possess my lover, and I also want to open myself up to her. Yet, how can I do both to the fullest? To own her is to treat her like an object, which will likely ruin my intimacy with her, for I cannot share equally with an object that I own. To idealize her is to overlook many less than perfect qualities that are part of her essence, again undermining my desire to share that which is "innermost" through intimacy. And how can I worship her and "be" her at the same time, without falling into hopeless narcissism? No wonder eros can make us miserable. It asks us to accomplish the impossible![14]

Intimacy is one current in the torrential stream of any love relationship. Most psychologists contend, as do I, that it is a strong and vigorous current in the healthiest, most mature, and most fulfilling love relationships. But the myths of romantic love—like Aristophanes' ancient story and the legends of Tristan and Iseult, Romeo and Juliet, Antony and Cleopatra—are not myths of intimacy. They tend to celebrate idealization and possession at the expense of intimacy. And they substitute fusion for closeness, oneness for connection. We must understand that intimacy is not the same as fusion. The desire to be close through sharing one's essence is not the same as the desire to merge with another into undifferentiated unity. Although both of these desires may play themselves out in a relationship, they should not be confused with each other.

Intimacy involves *two persons relating to each other as two persons*. They are separate beings who seek to connect, to share, to become closer. But they do not seek oneness, for in oneness their uniqueness, their individuality, their very identity is annihilated. The philosopher Gabriel Marcel writes that in intimacy, "even if I cannot see you, if I cannot touch you, I feel that you are with me."[15] You do not exist inside me, or I in you. We do not blend into each other to become one. Rather, in intimacy, you are *with me*, and I apprehend you, as you apprehend me, in the fullness of individuality. As I see more and more of your essence—and you, mine—we grow closer, more richly connected, and we move nearer and nearer to sharing our *wholeness* with each other. Psychotherapist Warren Wilner defines intimacy as *the experience of another's wholeness.* The person who is capable of intimacy "must have the requisite proportions of solidity and openness in order to allow the experience of wholeness to form itself."[16] In other words, intimacy requires that two people exist as two people, each individuated enough to share the wholeness of the self with the other.

Our most intimate moments in life are viewed by the theologian Martin Buber as encounters of the I–Thou. This chapter's opening quotation relates Buber's intriguing sense of the

I–Thou encounter. I ask you to read again, slowly, Buber's wonderfully poetic passage. In the I–Thou, two persons focus unswervingly on each other, seeking to apprehend each other's unique wholeness. They confront each other as two subjects, not as a subject and an object—two unique human beings. Neither is a "thing" to the other, nor does he or she "consist of things."

Most of life involves relating to things, Buber maintains, even when these "things" are really people. In Buber's terms, human beings operate predominantly in the mode of the "I–It." We analyze, master, calculate, achieve, dismiss, and generally objectify our world and the things and people in it. We tend to treat things and people as "its." But in certain moments, moments both sublime and divine, we actually relate to the other as Thou. In such moments, the other is more than a "dot in the world grid of space and time," "a condition to be experienced and described, a loose bundle of named qualities." The other is instead "neighborless and seamless." I see the other for his or her own sake, as a unique and undivided being. I do not compare the person to his or her "neighbors." Neither do I analyze the person in terms of his or her various parts, features, characteristics, or aspects. Instead, I apprehend the Thou as a single totality. And the Thou does the same to me. We realize that we are not the only two people in the universe, but for the time being each of us "fills the firmament" for the other.

In the I–Thou encounter, two persons share their essence in a spontaneous and sometimes playful manner. The experience unfolds as the dialogue grows and deepens, becomes richer and more wide-ranging. Neither person can control the development of the I–Thou encounter. Rather, each person surrenders him- or herself to the larger flow of the exchange. Ralph Waldo Emerson described this intimate communication as requiring "a light touch," referring to intimacy as the atmosphere of something rather than its content: "the mere air of doing a thing."[17] The tone is gentle, spontaneous, playful, precious, and passive. Writes Abraham Maslow, intimacy is "gentle, delicate, unintruding, undemanding, able to fit itself passively to the nature of things as water gently soaks into crevices."[18] Adds

Buber, "the Thou encounters me by grace—it cannot be found by seeking."[19]

I cannot control the I–Thou encounter, and I cannot go out and actively find it. Rather, I remain open to the possibility of the I–Thou in daily life. One never knows when the possibility will arise—with a friend, a lover, a stranger, over candlelight, on a bus, in a bar, in a class. I cannot find intimacy by making a plan, devising a scheme. I cannot actively strive to have it, for in the striving to *have* intimacy I lose the capacity to *be* intimate. Instead, I must wait and be ready. A person who is high in intimacy motivation—a person like Sara in Chapter 1 or Dean in this chapter—is consistently ready for the experience of intimacy. Such a person is on the lookout for opportunities to share the inner self and to experience the wholeness of the other.

What Is a Motive? What Is Not a Motive?

The experience of intimacy, captured in Buber's vision of the I–Thou, requires the existence of two people who find themselves, if only for a moment, in a special kind of relationship. Therefore, intimacy exists *between* people. By contrast, the intimacy motive exists *within* a single person. The study of motivation is the study of what people "really want."

My own interest in the study of human motivation stems in part from my perceptions of my own life and the lives of others. What I invariably notice when I observe behavior is that people's lives generally appear to be organized and directed. In other words, people appear to strive toward desired ends. People seem to behave in accord with personal goals, desires, plans, wishes, concerns, and expectations. Although some of our behavior may seem random and chaotic, much of what we do suggests that we, in fact, want something! And whatever it is that we want appears to energize and direct our behavior across different situations and over time. In simple terms, human motives are recurrent "wants" that get us moving in certain directions in our lives. They are consistent desires for particular kinds of experience, and these desires provide our lives with a particular direction and organization.

In Chapter 1, I asserted that two important human motives are the power and the intimacy motives. These are certainly not the only two recurrent wants in daily life, but they do seem to carve up human experience in an initially satisfying, albeit very rough, way. They capture a fundamental distinction in human motivation that goes back to Empedocles and the ancient Greeks—the distinction between strife and love, or what psychologist David Bakan calls agency and communion. There are, however, many different theories of human motivation, ranging from highly biological views of instincts, drives, and brain functions on the one hand to highly cognitive approaches that emphasize human thinking itself as a motivational factor on the other.[20] The view I adopt tends to deemphasize biology and focus instead on thought and feeling, or what psychologists call cognition and affect. As we shall see, intimacy motivation speaks to the ways we think and feel about things, people, and experiences.

Motivation, however, is just one dimension of the person. This is one of the hardest lessons for professionals and laypersons to learn about human personality. People are extremely complex. Their lives are animated by an army of different factors, some within the person and some outside. Knowing about a person's intimacy motivation—like knowing about his or her intelligence, political attitudes, family history, ethnic group, neighborhood, or diet—tells you something about that person that may be useful in understanding who he or she is, and even in predicting what he or she will do in certain situations. But it only tells you one thing. In daily relationships and in professional practice, laypersons and psychologists repeatedly make the mistake of assuming that knowing one or two important things about a person provides the "key" to personality. Intimacy motivation is not *the* key to personality. Nothing is the sole key to personality. But intimacy motivation is one of a number of important things that can be known about a person —a basic component of personality.

What can be known about a person? What are the basic components of personality? Psychologists have provided many answers to these questions. One of the most scientifically and practically useful answers, though, comes from Harvard University psychologist David McClelland. McClelland argues that, at a minimum, we should try to know four things about a person, tapping into four basic features of personality: (1) what a person does well, (2) how he or she behaves, (3) how a person sees the self and the world, and (4) what he or she wants. These four correspond to the personality features of skills, traits, schemata, and motives.[21]

By virtue of heredity and learning, every person has different skills. My father was an outstanding salesman and, in his youth, a fine baseball pitcher. But he was terrible with babies and did not have a clue about what you should say and how you should behave when discussing a poem, or a tender feeling. Like all people, he was good at some things and not so good at others. His athletic prowess and his skills of persuasion were significant parts of his personality—things that you should know if you were to know him well. Psychologists have developed many different methods for measuring human skills. Many of these take the form of "tests," such as intelligence tests, which tap into general intellectual skills. Others involve directly observing the person perform in a situation that requires skillful behavior of some kind. Auditions, tryouts, examinations, interviews—these are some of the common situations we all encounter through which our skills are assessed.

Traits refer to behavioral style. They speak to the way a person typically behaves. Is a person generally outgoing and friendly or withdrawn and sullen? Is he or she usually anxious or calm? Active or passive? Dominant or submissive? Psychologists have done a tremendous amount of work on traits in the past fifty years. Current thinking has it that a person's overall behavioral style can be boiled down to between three and eight basic traits. One of these, for example, is extraversion–introversion. People who are extraverted tend to be outgoing, sociable, and impulsive; those who are introverted are somewhat withdrawn and introspective. Many people are a bit of both, falling in the midrange on a continuum. Traits such as extraversion–

introversion may be strongly influenced by our biological makeup and tend to be relatively stable over time. In other words, each of us is born with a certain predisposition to an extraverted or an introverted behavioral style. Further, the style does not appear to change much after childhood. People who are highly extraverted in their twenties tend to be highly extraverted in their fifties as well.[22]

People tend to know where they stand, relative to other people, on basic trait dimensions. Extremely outgoing and friendly people generally know that they are more outgoing and friendlier than most of their peers. Therefore, measuring traits is a relatively straightforward thing to do. We simply ask people about their traits, usually in the form of a self-report questionnaire. Psychologists have developed a number of reliable and valid questionnaires to measure such traits. One measure of extraversion–introversion asks people to answer "yes" or "no" to questions like the following:

Are you usually carefree?

Do other people think of you as very lively?

Are you mostly quiet when you are with other people?

Do you find it hard to enjoy yourself at a lively party?[23]

A third personality dimension is what McClelland calls "schema." In general, a schema is a characteristic pattern of understanding the world. Examples include beliefs, attitudes, values, and philosophy of life. A staunch conservative who almost always votes Republican and professes a strong Mormon faith sees the world very differently from the way a political liberal does, who votes Democrat and professes that he or she was once Catholic but now "isn't sure." In Chapter 1, we saw that Sara's beliefs about God and religion had been a central part of her personality at least since elementary school, shaping the content and structure of her life story. In order to know her well, it is imperative that we know that she wanted to be a Catholic in childhood, even when her parents disapproved, and that she believes that her counseling is a way of ministering to others and professing her faith, even though she is no longer a nun. As with traits, people usually know what their own beliefs and values are. Psychologists have developed a number of self-report questionnaires to assess beliefs, attitudes, values, and other dimensions of schema.[24]

Finally, there are motives. As we have seen, motives are recurrent "wants" or "desires." Motivation speaks to what we want to do, what we hope to experience; but it does not directly address questions of skill, style, or schema. If we say that a person is high in intimacy motivation, we cannot assume that his or her skills, traits, and schemata reinforce intimacy. You probably know people who have a strong desire for warm, close, and communicative relations with others—that is, a strong intimacy motive—but who also have few social skills. Even though they desire intimacy, they may not be able to experience it because they simply do not know how. People who are high in intimacy motivation are not necessarily outgoing and "people-oriented." They may be extraverted or introverted. Some very shy and retiring people have very strong intimacy motivation. And people may be high in intimacy motivation, yet they do not consciously profess highly intimate values and beliefs. You might expect a person who is high in intimacy motivation to believe strongly in world peace and global cooperation, in government social programs that help the poor, in equality, family, home. But research suggests that you would be wrong. Motives, skills, styles, and values do not relate to one another in a direct and consistent way. One of the reasons is that people do not always consciously know what they want. As Sigmund Freud taught us almost a century ago, motives are (at least partly) unconscious. While I may have a pretty clear and conscious understanding of what I do well, what my basic behavioral style is, and what I believe in, I am likely to be less than perfectly informed about my motives. As a result, measuring motives is tricky business. You cannot obtain a sensitive measure of intimacy motivation, for instance, by asking people directly how much they truly want intimacy, or the extent to which they enjoy engaging in I–Thou experiences. You need a more subtle and mildly devious technique.

How to Measure the Intimacy Motive

On the night of July 23, 1895, Sigmund Freud had a dream about an attractive and intelligent patient of his, a widow and hysteric named Irma. In the dream, the pale and puffy Irma appeared at a party being given by the Freuds and proceeded to engage her doctor in an argument about the origins of her neurosis, which of late had caused her great pain in her abdomen and throat. Undertaking a medical examination on the spot, Dr. Freud discovered whitish-gray scabs and remarkable curly structures (which reminded him of bones in the nose) in poor Irma's throat. One of Freud's colleagues, Dr. M., confirmed the observation, and another, Leopold, found an infection on Irma's shoulder after repeatedly and rudely pressing himself up against her body. Dr. M. believed that the infection, however, was nothing to worry about because the girl would soon develop diarrhea and thereby pass the poison out of her system while sitting on the toilet. All three doctors knew how Irma had contracted the infection. An untrustworthy physician named Otto had thoughtlessly given her an injection of a medicine known as propionic acid trimethylamin. And the syringe had probably not been clean.

In the second chapter of his masterpiece *The Interpretation of Dreams*, Freud provides a detailed analysis of his dream of Irma's injection.[25] Although the dream as he remembered it (what Freud termed the "manifest content" of the dream) is a short and unassuming story about a queer exchange between doctor and patient at a party, the "latent" or hidden content fills the entire second chapter of Freud's book, exposing powerful motivational forces shaping the life of the dreamer. To analyze the dream, Freud let his mind wander in response to each of the dream's elements, a process that he termed "free association." Free association led to a number of recurrent themes and concerns that connected to Freud's current life situation. He realized that the manifest figure of Irma, who in real life had a ruddy complexion, represented in the dream at least two latent characters: Irma herself and an intelligent female friend of

Irma's who also suffered from a neurosis. Freud had once wished Irma's friend would seek his therapeutic services, but she had rejected him.

Further analysis indicated that the clean-shaven Dr. M., who in real life sported a beard, represented a blend of Dr. M. and Freud's clean-shaven brother. Irma, Irma's friend, Dr. M., and Freud's brother had all recently disagreed with or rejected Freud. So had Otto, whose injection of medicine in the dream had smelled of fuel oil and reminded Freud of a foul liquor Otto had recently presented to him and his wife as a gift. The most trenchant manifest element in the entire dream, however, is the medicine. The chemical compound for this appeared in bold print in the dream. Freud's associations traced the chemical back to his current colleague and dear friend, Wilhelm Fliess, whose wild theory about the sexual significance of the nasal membrane is a latent motif underneath the curly structures in Irma's throat, which look like the bones of the nose.

Fliess, in fact, turns out to be almost everywhere in the dream, though he never explicitly appears. He lurks as part of the latent content, between the lines of the text as it were, disguised, hidden, and distorted. Unlike the other characters represented in the dream, Fliess in real life did not disagree with Freud. Quite the contrary. Fliess and Freud were soul mates. At this point in Freud's life and career, Fliess was one of the few scientists who endorsed Freud's controversial theories of personality. And Freud in turn was a big supporter of Fliess's theories, even though some of them, like the theory of noses, were quite outlandish. He and Freud, therefore, emerge victorious in the dream, as Irma, her friend, Dr. M., Otto, and Freud's brother are all punished, proved wrong, or made to look foolish: Irma and her friend get the injection; Otto proves to be a bad doctor, and by implication Freud's brother proves to be a bad brother; Dr. M. makes a ridiculous diagnosis about diarrhea. The motivation for the dream is the fulfillment of the dreamer's unconscious wishes. Freud discovered that a major wish behind his dream of Irma's injection was that Freud himself, in consort with his good friend Fliess, exact revenge on those who had rejected him.[26]

Freud's example of analyzing a dream illustrates three crucial assumptions about the psychology of human motivation:

1. Motives are (at least partly) unconscious.

2. Motives are revealed in stories, like the narratives of dreams.

3. Measuring motives involves the interpretation of these narrative texts.

Ninety years after the publication of *The Interpretation of Dreams,* psychoanalysts still interpret the texts of dreams in order to uncover their patients' unconscious motivations. While the same procedure has been utilized in scientific research, dream interpretation has generally proved unwieldy and unreliable when studying large numbers of people, many of whom have a difficult time remembering their dreams. An alternative is to ask people to tell imaginative stories. While such stories may not plumb the depths of a person's unconscious life to the extent that dreams do, like dreams they provide the psychologist with a rich narrative sample of the person's imagination.

More than fifty years ago, psychologist Henry Murray devised the Thematic Apperception Test (TAT) as a storytelling alternative to dream interpretation in the study of human motivation.[27] On the TAT, a person is presented with a series of ambiguous pictures and then asked to tell or write an imaginative story in response to each picture. The assumption behind the TAT is like Freud's assumption about dreams. People will project their own unconscious wishes, conflicts, and motives onto the text of the narrative. The innocent story they tell will tell something about them.

Like dreams, the imaginative stories that people create on the TAT can be analyzed in many different ways. From a Freudian standpoint, the most valuable method to follow on the TAT would be to ask the story's writer to engage in free association to each of the stories, as did Freud in his dream. By analyzing the associations, the psychoanalyst would be able to discern recurrent motivational themes. But this is virtually impossible to do in large-scale scientific research. Therefore, researchers tend to examine only the manifest content of the TAT stories in order to arrive at estimates of the relative strengths of various motivational concerns.[28]

So how are these stories analyzed? In the early 1950s, research psychologists David McClelland and John Atkinson developed a general procedure for devising ways of scoring TAT stories, and other narrative productions, for various human motives. They argued that it is not enough to adopt a "common-sense" perspective in analyzing stories for motives. In other words, simply deciding how much overall "love and intimacy" is in a person's stories, or dreams for that matter, is not a good scientific way of measuring intimacy motivation. Rather, an objective and rigorous method of measuring motives requires an empirical procedure by which a system of interpretation is derived and then validated before it is generally accepted as a good measure. The general procedure for doing so involves three steps: arousal, comparison, and cross-validation.[29]

In the first step, the psychologist must arouse the experience of interest and then sample stories written by "aroused" people and by people who are not aroused. Remember that a motive is a recurrent desire for a particular kind of experience. Intimacy motivation is a recurrent desire for warm, close, and communicative relations with other people. For intimacy motivation, then, the challenge of the first step is to arouse intimacy—to arouse feelings of desire for close relations—and to collect imaginative stories written by people who are aroused. These stories, then, would be compared to stories written by people who are *not* aroused—say, people who write TAT stories under "neutral" or "normal" conditions. The second step of comparison should reveal consistent differences in the "arousal" and the "neutral" stories. Those differences can then be checked out in the third step of cross-validation, when the researcher examines a new sample of stories. So much for the general procedure. How, specifically, might this be done?

As a first-year graduate student in psychology at Harvard University in 1976, I sat with David McClelland in his office and tried to figure out how we might arouse intimacy in people and then get them to write TAT stories. The problem was a thorny one. We would be asking people to do a very strange thing. In the middle of a friendly, intimate moment in their lives, we would be jumping into the scene, saying, "Hey! How about writing a few imaginative stories for me to these TAT pictures? Quick! Before the mood dies." Furthermore, how would we know that they were having a friendly and warm experience? Where would we find people having friendly and warm experiences? How might we induce them to write TAT stories?

I tried to think of times in my life in which I felt intimacy—the kind of warmth, openness, and communication described by Buber and Maslow. I could think of a number of very personal, private moments. But I really needed a group event, so that I might obtain stories from many people at the same time. I remembered a series of experiences in college. As a member of a fraternity at a small, midwestern university, I participated annually in the fraternity's initiation ceremony, through which new initiates were inducted into the membership. While I had many good times in my fraternity years, these particular events stand out as especially positive because of the feelings of closeness and friendliness that most of the men seemed to feel at these times. My friends in the fraternity often remarked that the initiation ceremonies were special, unlike the riotous parties and general chaos that we sometimes experienced. These events stood out as surprisingly gentle, friendly, open, relaxed, spontaneous, and "brotherly." Why not sample TAT stories written by fraternity men during these moments?

I made a deal with my old fraternity whereby Dr. McClelland and I would contribute money to the treasury in return for their cooperation in our research project. My old friends thought it was a weird but interesting idea, and they liked the idea of getting the money. I worked out a similar deal with a sorority on campus. The procedure worked beautifully. At the end of their spring initiation ceremonies and before the big parties that were to follow, about twenty members of the fraternity and twenty in the sorority (approximately half of the people attending the two ceremonies) took about thirty minutes to write imaginative stories in response to six TAT pictures. I administered the TAT procedure in the fraternity, and a member of the sorority did the same thing there. These results were then considered the "arousal stories"—TAT stories written under the intimacy arousal situation. A few weeks later, I showed the same six TAT pictures to the members of the fraternity and sorority who had not written stories under the arousal conditions. The resulting stories, written under neutral conditions in a university classroom, were then considered the "neutral stories."[30]

We later did three other kinds of arousal studies. In one we collected imaginative stories written by college students at a friendly dancing party. In another we induced feelings of warmth and spontaneity in a psychological laboratory with small groups of students who played games and had conversations. In another we obtained TAT stories written by young men and women who reported that they were intensely in love, stories written in the company of their lovers. In all three of these cases, contrasting sets of stories were obtained from similar kinds of people but under neutral, classroom conditions.[31]

Comparing the stories, we found a number of striking differences. The arousal stories contained a number of content themes that showed up only rarely in the stories written under neutral, classroom conditions. We did careful comparisons for selected participants in all four of our arousal studies and then checked our findings (cross-validation) on the rest of the stories. Analyzing more than a thousand imaginative stories written about TAT pictures, we derived and validated a set of ten specific themes that consistently appeared in the stories written by people under the arousal conditions, but appeared much less frequently in stories written by those in neutral conditions. These we considered to be the ten themes of intimacy motivation. To measure intimacy motivation in a person's imaginative stories, the psychologist determines the presence or absence of each of these ten themes. A person's total intimacy motivation score is the number of these themes present, added across the different stories that the person writes.[32]

Intimate Stories

There follow three of the imaginative stories[33] written by fraternity and sorority members who were given the TAT under the arousal condition of the initiation ceremony. The first two are written in response to a picture of two people sitting on a park bench. The third is in response to a silhouette of two people standing on a rooftop.

> This is a picture of two college students, a guy and a girl, who have a serious relationship. It is summer and the guy has come from his home, far away, to visit the girl. They decided to go for a walk by the river nearby, with her dog, and later sat down in the grass enjoying nature and the warm summer weather. As they sat they started chatting about each of their lives and got into a serious discussion about themselves and what will happen to them in the next two years. They are very much in love and she becomes very upset and cries because they are going to have to separate for some time and this is very hard on them both. They are not attending the same college but have been dating for two years. They each have their own lives but want each other too. It is all very difficult for them.

> The girl was sitting alone, quietly meditating, lost in thought on the bench of the river. She was watching the ripple of the wind on the water, mourning the absence of her love who was at sea in the Navy and would not be back for months. All of a sudden a young man came strolling along the river humming a simple tune enjoying the weather and scenery. He saw the lonely girl and chose to sit down beside her and then started a conversation about the weather, river, etc. She was slow to answer at first, responding in terse replies. But, he was so friendly that he made her open up and she found herself telling him all of the sorrows she had held in for so long.

The two people standing on the rooftop have lived in the same apartment building for a couple of years. On hot summer nights such as this one, they both enjoy ascending for a breath of fresh air. There they often encounter each other, and over the months they have developed an open, though not overly intimate, conversational relationship. Here the woman looks outward over the city, the man inward toward the roof, symbolically toward himself. They do not speak, each rapt in his own thoughts. Unwittingly, however, they have strayed very close to each other, and close to the edge of the roof. They will remain in their proximate, perhaps precarious, distinctness for a time before suddenly, probably spontaneously, recognizing each other's presence. After a bit of small talk, they will return to their separate abodes, mysteriously refreshed and united.

Let us briefly consider each of the ten themes of intimacy motivation as they appear in such stories.

1. *Positive affect.* The first and most common theme in intimacy motivation is "positive affect." A story contains positive affect when the characters experience some kind of positive emotional state that is a result of their interaction. Positive emotional states are always feelings, rather than thoughts, and include such things as joy, excitement, love, liking, happiness, and having "fun" together. In the first story, the two characters "are very much in love." Here are a few examples from other stories:

There is a true *affection* between the two, the feeling that exists between father and daughter.

Although it is raining outside and on the whole a very dreary day, Nancy is still in a *good mood.* There is no particular reason for her *happiness,* just that things are going well for her with her job and *with her relationships* with the important people in her life.

They're just sitting there *enjoying being together.*

61

2. *Dialogue.* In this common intimacy theme, two or more characters are engaged in conversation. The conversation must be reciprocal: all characters must be talking, not just one of them, as in a monologue. Furthermore, the conversation must be "noninstrumental." This means that the people are talking with each other for the sake of talking—as an end in itself. Such instrumental conversations as interviews, interrogations, and lectures would not count as dialogue. Also, arguments do not count, unless they are friendly or playful. All three of our sample stories contain dialogue. In the first, the two people are "chatting about each of their lives," eventually getting into a "serious discussion about themselves and what will happen to them in the next two years." In the second, two strangers have a conversation that starts slowly and then builds. In the third, the characters engage in "a bit of small talk."

Positive affect and dialogue are the two cardinal features of intimate stories. For people to experience intimacy, they must either be *feeling* good about each other or *sharing* thoughts and feelings through conversation. The remaining eight themes are less common and less central to the experience of intimacy, but they flesh out in greater detail the intricacies of interpersonal communion, as characters come to apprehend each other's "wholeness."

3. *Psychological growth.* A relationship between characters in the story promotes psychological growth, self-esteem, coping with problems, self-realization, psychological health, the search for self-knowledge, enlightenment, spiritual salvation, inspiration, creativity, maturity, or the like. Here story writers speak to the healing power of intimacy:

Bev is continually becoming better adjusted to everyday life and how to handle it because of Harry.

He feels that she has changed his life. He has finally come to realize that he loves mankind.

A warm relationship with another person can be very comforting when trouble comes up.

When he is with his wife, whom he loves very much, he will think of a new design and solve the crisis.

4. *Commitment or concern.* A character in the story feels a commitment to another person or shows his or her concern by helping the other or engaging in some form of humanitarian behavior, which sometimes involves personal sacrifice. In the second story above, the young man sees the lonely woman and takes the trouble to help her, cheering her with his friendly conversation and enabling her to open up and relate her sorrows. Some other examples:

She is devoted to her husband.

The old man left his fortune to the poor family in Harlem.

The youngest grandson has taken his ailing grandfather outside for a walk and some fresh air.

5. *Time-space.* A relationship transcends the usual limitations of time and/or space. This concept includes any explicit references to the enduring quality of a relationship over an extended period of time or in the face of physical separation. References to "timelessness," "time standing still," "the eternal moment," and so on also count when they refer to a relationship of characters in the story. In the first story, the college students have been dating for two years. In the third, the two people have repeatedly seen each other on the rooftop over the past few years.

6. *Union.* Characters in the story come together in union after being apart. The emphasis is on unity, reunion, togetherness, oneness, reconciliation, synthesis, or integration. In the words of E. M. Forster from Chapter 1, stories that embody the union theme suggest that human beings need "only connect." Often the characters who come together to connect in intimate stories represent contrasts or opposites. For example, an atheist might meet a priest; an old man might confront a young

woman; blacks and whites may find reconciliation. Some other examples:

> This is a father and daughter who have come together after a long time.

> They fought like cats and dogs. But then they kissed and made up.

7. *Harmony.* This relatively rare theme refers to characters' finding that they are "on the same wavelength," that their actions are in "synchrony," that they truly "understand" each other, or that they "find something in common." Some examples:

> The two people are discovering a problem that both of them share.

> Usually she does not listen to her father. He is saying the same thing again, but somehow she sees why this time.

> Their actions were in perfect harmony. She seemed to intuit his every move.

8. *Surrender.* This is my favorite theme in the intimacy system because it captures that gentleness and spontaneity, that passivity and loss of control which both Buber and Maslow affirm. Recall that "the Thou encounters me by grace—it cannot be found by seeking" (Buber). Intimacy is "gentle, unintruding, undemanding, able to fit itself passively to the nature of things as water gently soaks into crevices" (Maslow). In imaginative stories, the characters find that they cannot control relationships. They, in turn, surrender control to the relationship itself, "going with the flow" and experiencing the interaction in a spontaneous manner. In the third story above, the characters on the rooftop "unwittingly" stray close to each other and then "spontaneously" recognize each other's presence. Other examples of surrender include chance encounters (when people meet

accidentally, the writer is suggesting that relationships are, in some sense, beyond the individual's control), quirks of fate, and the unleashing of uncontrollable emotions:

A young couple *find themselves* deeply in love.

They *accidentally* meet on the road to Crown Point.

She *let herself go* and found that she enjoyed the party much more.

They are *helplessly* in love.

9. *Escape to intimacy.* In the third story, the two characters escape from their stifling apartments to catch a breath of fresh air, and ultimately to find a moment of intimacy on the rooftop. In escape, characters actively or mentally escape from a negative, nonintimate situation and move to a positive and intimate one. The characters may escape together, as in the case of a family leaving the city to take a vacation in the mountains or a group of meditators entering an altered state of consciousness together. Or a character may escape by him- or herself in order to think about a relationship. Some examples:

She is taking a walk to think out her problems with her boyfriend.

He is taking a break from his busy day to think about his family.

Her father wants her to remain chaste and pure. But she will run off with her lover, and they will become gypsies.

10. *Connection to the outside world.* In this last and rather surprising intimacy theme, characters in the story experience a relationship with some aspect of the nonhuman world, such as with nature, the cosmos, streets and skyscrapers, or God. The theme suggests that intimacy involves a willingness to open

oneself up to the universe at large. In the first story, the two characters were "enjoying nature and the warm summer weather." In the second, the young man was "enjoying the weather and scenery." In the third, the man and the woman "both enjoy ascending for a breath of fresh air." The connection to the outside world is usually positive, but it need not be. Examples of characters' becoming "depressed" because of the gray weather or feeling "alienated" because of the impersonal nature of a city environment would also count. The key here is that characters are open to and influenced by the outside world.

How Others See Us

A person who is high in intimacy motivation creates imaginative stories that emphasize the ten themes described here. As we have seen, these themes were derived by contrasting the stories written by people under intimate conditions (arousal stories) to those written under neutral conditions (neutral stories). The key assumption of my research, however, is a tricky one. I assume that *people who are generally high in intimacy motivation will naturally write the kinds of stories that almost all people write when they are temporarily aroused in an intimate way.* In other words, the ten themes that characterized as a whole those stories which were written under arousal conditions should also show up quite often in stories written by people who are naturally (characteristically, consistently) high in intimacy motivation, even when those stories are written under everyday, neutral conditions.

Indeed, the only way to estimate the true level of intimacy motivation in a person is to administer the TAT under neutral conditions. The stories written by the fraternity and sorority students who had attended the initiation, therefore, were not indicative themselves of the natural intimacy motivation levels of those persons. The intimacy imagery was highly inflated by virtue of the unusual arousal situations under which these students wrote their stories. This situation was necessary in order

66

to derive a valid scoring system for the intimacy motive as a whole. Now that we have done that, we may apply the system to all kinds of people under neutral conditions in order to measure individual differences in their characteristic levels of intimacy motivation.

In our first attempt to do so, we returned to the fraternity and sorority students, but this time we concentrated on those approximately forty students who wrote TAT stories under the neutral, classroom conditions. Based on the scoring system we devised from the arousal studies, some of these people scored naturally high in intimacy motivation and some low. A few months after the TAT stories were collected, we contacted the fraternity and sorority again. We solicited the cooperation of ten fraternity men and ten sorority women who (1) had *not* participated as story writers in the neutral condition and (2) were well acquainted with the members of their organization who had participated in that part of the study. We asked each of them to rate each of the twenty members of his or her fraternity or sorority who had written stories under the neutral conditions on a number of adjectives that describe personality. These twenty-five adjectives ranged from words such as "warm" and "loving" to "intelligent," "efficient," "active," and "conscientious." Virtually all of the adjectives were very positive.

The findings we obtained were repeated in a later study in which friends rated each other. People who score high on intimacy motivation, based on the imaginative stories they write under neutral conditions, are consistently seen by others as especially natural, warm, sincere, loving, and appreciative, compared to people who score low in intimacy motivation. Further, people high in intimacy motivation are seen by others as less dominant and less self-centered than people low in intimacy motivation.

Equally interesting is something we discovered later. People who are high in intimacy motivation are *no more likely* than those scoring low in intimacy motivation to see themselves as especially natural, warm, sincere, loving, and so on. Essentially, virtually everybody—regardless of his or her intimacy motive score—rates him- or herself as especially natural, warm, sincere, and loving. Self-ratings are not a good barometer of motivation, as Freud always maintained. Our desire to be close is better manifested in our imaginative fantasies than in our conscious self-descriptions. And in their perceptions of us, other people may be better judges of how strong our desire for intimacy is than are we ourselves.[34]

CHAPTER 3

Intimate Behavior, Intimate Lives

Something I want to communicate to you,
I keep my door open between us.
I am unable to say it,
I am happy only
with the door open between us.

—David Ignatow, "With the Door Open"[1]

Imagine that you are a college student. In order to earn a little spending money, or to gain a few extra credits for your Psychology 101 class, or perhaps just out of the kindness of your heart, you have volunteered to participate in a "psychological experiment." It will take only a couple of hours and it concerns "people in groups." At the first experimental session, you fill out questionnaires and write six imaginative stories in response to pictures. You have participated in these kinds of studies before. So far, this one is nothing out of the ordinary. The experimenters promise that the second part of the study will be "interesting" and "fun."

You show up at the appointed time for the second part: around 7:00 P.M. in one of the laboratory rooms in the psychology building. The room is carpeted and surprisingly comfortable for a "laboratory," with chairs, sofas, pillows, and tables. One of the walls is made of reflecting glass. Behind the glass, you learn, sit technicians who will videotape the proceedings. You cannot see them, but they can see you. Eight or nine other college students have congregated in the room. Although you have observed a couple of these students on campus before, you are not personally acquainted with any of them. Indeed, all of the students in the group are strangers. Everybody seems mildly nervous. But the situation is really not all that strange and fearsome. Virtually all of the students in the room have participated in psychology experiments before. This participation is almost a routine part of undergraduate life, especially for students enrolled in entry-level classes in the behavioral sciences.

The group leader introduces himself. He is a therapist who has been trained in the technique of psychodrama, a method of group therapy in which people meet regularly to resolve personal problems through theater. In a classic psychodrama session, one person would be designated the protagonist—he or she would play the roles of main actor, director, and screenwriter for a dramatic story that all of the group members would enact. The drama would illustrate a major psychological issue or conflict in the protagonist's life. For example, a man who finds it difficult to talk to his mother might enact a typical conversation with her, designating one of the other group members to be his mother. Or a woman who feels that she is afraid of men might relive a childhood scene in which she was abused by her father, as various group members play different roles in her family and other members serve as audience for the drama. After the scene had been enacted, group members would then share similar experiences from their own lives. The theory is that such dramatic action and subsequent sharing encourage people to reexperience and master difficult life events and to learn new ways of responding to personal problems.[2]

There are two purposes for tonight's session, the group leader says. The first is to teach you a little bit about psychodrama. The second purpose is a scientific one, aimed at exploring individual differences in interpersonal behavior under rather unusual laboratory conditions. The group leader gives a brief lecture on the history and current uses of psychodrama. Then he illustrates some of the favorite methods of promoting creativity and spontaneity in psychodrama groups. For almost an hour, you play games and engage in conversations that are designed to relieve anxieties and to get you to open up to other group members. In one of the games, you pair off with another member in the group, and the two of you choose a two-syllable word as your "name," one syllable for you and the other for your partner. Your partner goes to the other side of the room. The group leader then turns down the lights in the room and asks everybody to close their eyes and try to find their partners by crawling on the ground and shouting out the designated name. You are "base" and your partner is "ball." After a few minutes, you finally find your partner. It is all a little silly, but a lot of fun, too.

Forty-five minutes have passed, and you are now feeling pretty comfortable. The other students in the room seem friendly and enthusiastic, and the group leader is warm and encouraging. By this time, you are on a first-name basis with everybody—and you have learned something about each person. It is now time to begin the psychodramas themselves. The group leader explains that he does not want to turn this session into a full-blown, psychotherapeutic psychodrama. Instead, he would like each person in the group to put on a five-minute psychodrama skit, illustrating any "theme or event" that occurs to him or her. Your skit need not delve into serious issues, but it should be meaningful in some sense to you. The room will serve as the stage for the drama, and various objects can be used as props. The other group members may play roles as actors and actresses in the skit, or they may serve as the audience.

A young man sitting next to you volunteers to be first. He sets up a scene in a forest in which a man and woman are having a picnic. While he plays the leading man in the story, he chooses one group member to play his girlfriend and another to play his dog, Spot, who has come along for the fun. Two other group members play the roles of trees in the forest, offering shade from the hot sun. Everybody else is part of the audience. The man and woman in the skit pass around a bottle of wine, in the form of a pillow, and eat make-believe food. After a few minutes of drinking, eating, and enjoying the scenery, they go home. A simple, happy scene. Modestly intimate, though the

71

characters do not express much emotion beyond a general sense of pleasantness, and they do not talk to each other.

You are next. You have five minutes to put on your skit. What would you like to do?[3]

Intimacy on Stage

In one of the first studies we conducted of the relation between intimacy motivation and social behavior, college students met in small groups to enact psychodrama skits. The skits were videotaped and analyzed for themes and characteristics of intimacy. In a previous session, all of the students were given the Thematic Apperception Test (TAT), for which they wrote six imaginative stories in response to ambiguous pictures. The stories were scored for intimacy motivation according to the scoring system described in Chapter 2. Analyzing skits performed by forty-three students in five different psychodrama groups, we found that intimacy motivation was strongly associated with certain ways of expressing oneself in the skits. In this unusual opportunity to act out a personal fantasy and express oneself in an artful manner, the intimacy motive proved to be a powerful influence on behavior—so powerful that one could frequently guess the strength of a person's intimacy motivation solely by the way he or she responded to the psychodrama challenge.

A young man in our first psychodrama session—let us call him Simon—enacted a scene of solitude and alienation. Simon directed everybody to sit together in one corner while he sat on the floor by himself in another part of the room. As the skit begins, the group and he face each other. But after a few seconds, Simon turns his body slightly so that he is positioned at a forty-five degree angle to the group. He stares off into the distance while the people in the corner make buzzing sounds. Over the course of this eerie scenario, Simon occasionally comments on his own emotional state: "I am just sitting here lost in thought . . . it is hard to explain what I am experiencing— boredom, angst, perseverence—these are what I feel." The drama ends when Simon rises to his feet and thanks everybody for their participation. He smiles—surprisingly warmly—and remarks, "Hey! I was really into it."

It probably comes as no surprise that Simon's TAT stories indicated fairly low intimacy motivation. He chose to separate himself from everybody else in the group, pondering his aloneness as the rest of humanity droned on in a taunting buzz. No communication, save Simon's existential commentary, bridged the gap between him and the rest of the people. Neither did the group members communicate with one another. Simon had instructed them to create for him a uniform tableau. *They* were to buzz so that *he* could feel "really into it." But that is all they could do. And they must all do the same thing, each person sacrificing his or her individuality in order to create an effect.

Yet, this drama was not devoid of a kind of intimacy. Simon graciously thanked the group members at the end of the scene. His big smile indicates that he was genuinely pleased with their performance. And, more importantly, Simon chose to show them a rather personal experience. As one of the group members, you do not have to be Sigmund Freud to realize that Simon was telling you that he sometimes feels alienated and alone. He did not have to reveal this; he could have chosen something light and breezy, like the picnic in the forest with Spot. Instead, he made himself vulnerable, trusting the group to affirm that part of his innermost self which he has chosen to expose. Still, you may point out, he chose to *expose* himself, but did he really *share*? You are right. There is no sharing here. Simon may be seeking a kind of intimacy, but he is doing it, as Martin Buber would say, through the mode of the "I–It." He, the subject, chooses to express some of his own feelings to the group, the object of his exposition. Yet you can only watch, and buzz.

The first two things you notice about Sally, when she begins her psychodrama skit, are that she is extremely well dressed and that she speaks with a charming Southern accent. The psychodrama sessions are being conducted in the late winter and early spring of 1978, when blue jeans and flannel shirts are still what fashion dictates. But Sally is wearing a pretty, pastel, cotton dress, knee-length and very feminine in an innocent and down-home way. Her southern accent is a pleasant departure from the clipped Eastern tones you are likely to hear on this Ivy League campus. Sally is extremely friendly and outgoing. She immediately takes charge in her skit, laughing and joking as she tells the group members exactly what they should do. "I'm going to be the director, not the star," she proclaims. "You two people are going to be flowers—beautiful flowers—let's say poinsettias, or something like that." She points to one of the men in the group: "And you are going to be the wind." The rest of the group sits and watches.

Sally instructs the flowers to grow and blossom as the wind glides in and out between them as a gentle, teasing zephyr. The graceful scene is carefully choreographed. Both flowers do a masterful job of translating Sally's words into action. And although the wind is repeatedly chastised for blowing too hard (Sally insists that he not be a "hurricane," but her actor keeps getting carried away), he ends up fitting nicely into the scene, and all congratulate him afterward for a stellar performance. As the flowers move in harmony, they gaze intensely into each other's eyes. Although Sally does not instruct them to do so, you get the feeling that they are supposed to be falling in love. The scene is mildly sensual and rhythmic. The two flowers come together and touch, but then they are gently blown apart by the wind. They come together again. And the wind separates them once more. Together, apart. In, and then out. It seems very natural and intimate. Yet, with her relentless commentary, Sally controls every move.

Despite the tender touching and the gentle harmony of two flowers growing together in the sunshine, this particular drama was structured in such a way that the protagonist stands outside the beautiful scene, as the conscientious but aloof director. Sally could have been one of the flowers herself. But she preferred to observe and instruct, and from a distance at that. Her role was to tell others how to act out an intimate scene, but she did not share in that intimacy. Throughout the scenario, Sally was always friendly and outgoing. In general, she seems to be an extremely sociable and relatively assertive person. In the terms of

Chapter 2, she probably scores very high on the personality trait of "extraversion." But as we saw in Chapter 2, traits are concerned with interpersonal style. Motives, instead, concern desire. In assuming the role of director, Sally passed up an opportunity to engage in warm, close, and communicative interaction with her peers, implying that, for whatever reasons, she did not desire intimacy at this particular moment. Unlike Simon, she did not create a scene of alienation and loneliness. But she did separate herself from the group, keeping her distance both physically and emotionally in the scene. And like Simon she told the actors and actresses *exactly what to do.*

Sally's rather low intimacy motivation, as manifested on the TAT, is probably best reflected in her style of directing the psychodrama. While all of the students who put on skits had to set up an explicit scene and give general instructions to their peers, Sally and a number of other students who were low in intimacy motivation adopted the director's pose throughout the drama, never relinquishing control of the action. We see this tendency even in the first drama described, in which the man and woman enjoyed a picnic in the forest with the dog, Spot. In this scenario, the protagonist told the actors and actresses—his girlfriend, the dog, and the trees—precisely what to do not only at the beginning, but even as the plot unfolds. He told the woman when to pass the bottle of wine. He told Spot that even he could have a drink. He instructed the trees to move slightly so that they would provide more shade. And he repeatedly told everybody what they should be feeling in the scene—how the natural beauty and the good food and wine should make everybody happy. And indeed everybody seemed relatively happy. But none of the roles he created for the actors and actresses allowed them to go beyond his tightly controlled script. Like Sally, he did not choose to surrender control of the scene.

Mike offers a contrasting psychodrama. He is tall and has curly dark hair that, for the fashions of the mid 1970s, is surprisingly short. He seems as friendly and as outgoing as Sally. But at the outset, Mike seems to be more in a hurry. He introduces his idea for a psychodrama quickly, talking too fast for some of his listeners, who twice must ask him to repeat what he has said.

It is as if Mike wants to dispense quickly with the introduction and get right down to the fun of doing the skit. He explains that everybody will be involved in this drama—no audience. It is the last night of summer camp. Over the summer, all of the people in the skit have become close friends. The camp counselor has told them that they should go to bed, but after he falls asleep, they all escape from their bunks to sit out under the stars, together for one last time. Mike instructs everybody to lie in a circle, each body positioned like a spoke in a big wheel, feet touching in the hub. Everybody is to gaze up at the stars. And that's it.

With considerable enthusiasm, the group members enact Mike's sketchy plot. Lying on the ground, one young man remarks that something very much like this happened to him once, when he was a child at camp. One of the women in the group exclaims spontaneously, "I wish this could last forever." Other people make small talk; others comment on the beauty of the stars; some say nothing at all. Within the structure of the drama, the characters are given free rein to express themselves in any way they wish. Once he has introduced the scene, Mike interjects no further instructions. He remarks, "We are all equals in this thing." The spontaneity and lack of control in Mike's drama make for some awkward silences and nervous moments. The scene he creates has nothing of the harmony and smoothness we witness in Sally's story of the flowers. Mike's drama is rough and baggy, like life itself, a far cry from Sally's choreographed ballet, Simon's carefully hewn portrait of angst, and the pastoral picnic scene with Spot.

Mike's drama contained many of the features common to those scenarios created by the students who were high in intimacy motivation. In general, people with strong intimacy motivation, based on their TAT stories, created relatively warm and happy scenes in which characters spoke with each other in a reciprocal manner. The protagonist participated with the other characters as one among equals, instead of directing from afar, and he or she was willing to let the other characters develop their own roles according to their own wishes. These scenarios often involved tender, nonthreatening touching, as when the characters at summer camp touched feet in the center of the wheel. And the protagonists often portrayed issues or concerns that they said were of crucial personal significance. Ironically, an example of this last can be seen in Simon's scenario. Such references were more common, however, among protagonists high in intimacy motivation.

In one especially moving drama, a young woman sets up an elaborate scene in which she engages in a tense conversation with a music teacher who is counseling her to give up her family life and dedicate herself to music. Large walls, played by three of the students, slowly close in around them. On the periphery, a man stands alone—her husband, listening intently to the conversation. In another part of the room, a woman hops up and down, sucking her thumb. She represents the baby that the protagonist wants to have in the future. At the end of the scene, the protagonist's father enters slowly, creeping between the walls. He says simply, "Honey, life involves people." At that moment, the baby sighs, and the walls move gently but swiftly away.

On a more concrete behavioral level, we found that the psychodramas of students high in intimacy motivation differed significantly from those created by students low in it. Carefully measuring the physical distance between the protagonist and the other characters at various points in the skits, we found that "high" protagonists positioned themselves in close physical proximity to the others. They tended to stay within four feet of the nearest other participant, while "low" people often stood between four and ten feet away, or even farther, as in the case of Simon. Compared to "low" people, those high in intimacy motive issued fewer commands, made more references to "we" and "us," and elicited more outbursts of laughter.[4]

In general, the psychodramas show us that people will translate their desire for intimacy into observable behavior when asked to create and then enact a fantasy on stage. Themes of intimacy in TAT stories, therefore, are readily observed in behavior, too, when the behavior is displayed in a warm and supportive group. "High" people seize these opportunities for sharing their innermost beliefs and feelings and for creating scenarios in which characters are free to engage each other in warm, close, and communicative interaction. Instead of directing the actions of their peers in the I–It manner of Simon's scenario, they appear open to the possibility of the I–Thou in psychodrama. They are willing to surrender control and thereby provide the freedom through which others can express their own individuality, valuing that spontaneous experience of the other's wholeness which is at the heart of human intimacy.

A Day in the Life

Perhaps, at this point, you are protesting: Who cares about behavior in a psychodrama? The study is interesting, certainly, but what about real life? The study merely shows that people's behavioral fantasies are similar to those they compose when asked to write imaginative stories in response to pictures.

It is a lot more difficult to study daily life in a rigorous scientific manner than it is to examine behavior under controlled laboratory conditions. Still, as psychologists, we have to try, realizing that our humble attempts to tap real life will probably always be criticized as not representative enough of what life is truly about.

One of the most promising methods for studying daily life relies on a rather new technological advance with which you are probably acquainted. This is the beeper—yes, the gadget that doctors traditionally wear in hospitals and sometimes when they are on call. More and more business executives are wearing them these days, lest they miss some key communication signaling another million-dollar deal.

Social scientists have employed the beeper as a way of sampling the ordinary thoughts, feelings, desires, and behaviors of a normal person. In a typical study, a person agrees to wear a beeper during waking hours and to carry with him or her a response sheet that monitors daily experience. The person may be beeped at random intervals by a computer, say, seven or eight times over the course of a day. As soon as the person is beeped, he or she is to pull out the response pad and answer a series of quick questions about what he or she was feeling, thinking, and doing at that precise moment. Of course, it is not always possible to drop everything and respond to the beeper. And sometimes participants write, "None of your damn business." Yet the beeper has proved to be a surprisingly valuable tool for tapping into the stream of everyday behavior. People report that they get used to wearing the beeper after a day or two, and that it generally does not seem to interfere too much with their daily lives.[5]

As part of her doctoral dissertation, psychologist Carol Constantian conducted an ambitious study in 1980 in which fifty students wore beepers for a week while attending summer school. The students ranged from high school juniors and seniors who were taking classes for college credit, to graduate students working on theses and dissertations. All lived in campus dormitories or in apartments close to campus. Six of the students reported that they were married or "living with someone," while the rest (88 percent) were single. All of the students were administered the TAT at the beginning of the study, which was scored for intimacy motivation.

Between the hours of 9:00 A.M. and 11:00 P.M. each student was beeped seven times, once during each of seven 2-hour intervals. There was no way to anticipate exactly when the beep would happen, for a computer generated a random sequence of beepings. Over the course of the week, each student was beeped forty-nine times. For each beep, the student was to fill out a single sheet on the response pad, each generally requiring a minute or two of time. The person was asked to write a phrase or sentence describing, in turn, (1) What were you thinking about when beeped? (2) What was the main thing you were doing? and (3) What other things were you doing? In addition, the student was to rate his or her current mood or emotional state according to thirty different adjectives listed, such as "happy" and "irritable." And the student was to indicate which of the following three possibilities accurately described the interpersonal situation at the time of the beep: (1) completely alone (no one else in view, in communication with no one);

(2) alone but with other people present (in the presence of others but not interacting with them); or (3) with people and interacting with them. Finally, the student was asked: "Given your present activity, which of these three situations would you most like to be in? Choose one: completely alone, alone but with other people present, or with people and interacting with them."

Constantian and I analyzed the data in order to discover what characteristic thoughts, behaviors, and feelings differentiated people high in intimacy motivation from those scoring low. Our findings were clear-cut and very convincing.

First, people high in intimacy motivation, measured on a prior administration of the TAT, reported more thoughts about other people and their relations with them. We examined each of the responses to the question "What were you thinking about when beeped?" and determined whether the person was thinking about interpersonal or noninterpersonal matters. Interpersonal thoughts were indicated by such answers as "my boyfriend," "a friendship," "the obnoxious guy sitting next to me in class," "whether to have lunch with my roommate or alone," "people around me at the party." Whereas no student reported a total absence of interpersonal thoughts over the course of the forty-nine beepings, "high" people were much more likely than "low" to report these kinds of thoughts. As an interesting addition to which we will return in Chapter 6, women were almost twice as likely as men to report thinking about people and relationships, regardless of intimacy motivation scores. On the average, women reported interpersonal thoughts about 25 percent of the time (on one out of every four beeper responses); men, 13.5 percent of the time.

Second, "high" people engaged in more conversations over the course of the week and wrote more personal letters compared to "low" people. It is interesting to note that high intimacy motivation was not associated with spending more time with people, or less time alone. Rather, people high and low on intimacy motivation differed markedly in what they did when in the presence of others. The number of responses that mentioned conversation or letter writing ranged from 0 to 81 percent. In general, those scoring low tended toward the lower end on this continuum, revealing relatively low levels of conversation and letter writing. "High" people tended toward the higher end.

The third discovery we made was that, when in the presence of others, "high" students reported greater levels of *good feelings*, indicated by such self-ratings as "alert," "happy," and "care-free," compared to "low" students. By contrast, when alone, students high in intimacy motivation were no more likely than low to report greater levels of bad feelings, indicated by such self-ratings as "irritable," "bored," and "hostile." In other words, people high in intimacy motivation tend to enjoy other people more but experience no more distress when alone.

That high intimacy motivation should be associated with feeling good when one is with other people is not surprising. Most people, regardless of intimacy motivation level, report that in general they feel better when they are with others than when they are alone. People high in intimacy motivation report even greater levels of good feeling with others than the "average" person might. By the same token, you might expect that a strong desire for intimacy would lead one to feel great despair and sadness when alone. Yet this does not seem to be true. "High" people report no more negative emotion when alone than do "low." "High" people do not need to be with others every minute of the day. They are more open to opportunities for sharing and good feeling in the presence of others, but when others are not present they are not necessarily miserable. High intimacy motivation is not the same as a fear of loneliness. Although we all may fear loneliness to some degree, people high in intimacy motivation do not seem to fear it any more than anybody else.

Finally, we noted that, when in the presence of others, "high" people were less likely to report that they wished they were alone. Although they find solitude no more aversive than do others, they are not likely to wish they were by themselves when in the presence of friends, acquaintances, and other people in general. They are more likely to make the most of daily opportunities for warmth and sharing. "Low" people, by contrast, are more likely to find themselves wishing they were alone when in the presence of others. Daily interpersonal relations seem to be less satisfactory for the person low in intimacy motivation. While these people do not in general enjoy being alone for significant periods of time, they find that being with others is not as pleasurable as they would like, and they sometimes find themselves wishing they could escape.[6]

The beeper study provides powerful evidence that intimacy motivation helps shape the contour and content of everyday life. Although many different factors determine what we do, think, and feel in the course of a normal day, intimacy motivation exerts a surprisingly robust influence. It motivates us, if you will, to think about others and our relations with them, to engage others in mutual conversations and keep in touch through personal letters, to feel especially good when we are with others, and to feel that our daily relations with others provide us with enough satisfaction that we can immerse ourselves in those relationships, instead of feeling distracted to the point of continually wishing we were somewhere else.

The Intimate Face

Let us look more closely at people with a strong intimacy motive, at subtle ways in which they express warmth and tenderness in their relationships. People engage each other in the intimate I–Thou encounter through many different "channels." Verbally, they may share hidden treasures from their own lives, giving and receiving that which is innermost in reciprocal disclosures of the self. Behaviorally, they may touch each other, position themselves in close physical proximity to each other, speak of each other in terms of "we" and "us" rather than "I" and "me," and generally promote sharing, warmth, and concern for each other. In the I–Thou encounter, two people focus unswervingly on each other, committing their attention to the here-and-now interplay in which they find themselves. One of the most basic channels through which this commitment is made is the face, through smiling, laughter, and eye contact.

Many psychologists view the human face as the "organ of emotion," the mechanism through which we display, from infancy onward, the most basic feelings of joy, excitement, fear, anger, sadness, shame, and disgust.[7] Careful cross-cultural research conducted by such psychologists as Paul Ekman and Carroll Izard has provided strong evidence for a claim made more than a century ago by Charles Darwin: human beings appear to have evolved with specific facial expressions that signify basic emotional states. In virtually all human cultures studied, people show joy with a smile, surprise and interest with raised eyes and a focused stance, sadness by a drooping mouth and slackening jaw muscles, disgust by tightened muscles beneath the nose and the wrinkling of the nose, anger by clenched and exposed teeth and a flushed complexion, fear by widened eyes frozen open. We do not appear to learn these responses, though cultural "display rules" may dictate when and where we express certain kinds of emotions in facial behavior. The connection between basic emotions and the subtle behavior of the face appears to be innate—biologically "wired" in the human nervous system as a universal code for emotional experience and expression.[8]

Two key emotions in the experience of intimacy are joy and excitement/interest, and the facial manifestations most directly involved are eye contact and smiling. As we shall see in Chapter 5, these are considered two of the most evocative signals in the developing bond of love between mother and infant in the first year of life. Some ethologists have suggested that when an infant smiles at the caregiver or looks directly into the caregiver's eyes the infant is following a deeply ingrained biological blueprint, instinctively "releasing" tender behaviors from the caregiver, who is obeying an equally compelling instinctual mandate that says, "Love those who look you directly in the eye; care for those who smile at your face." For reasons that may be both biological and spiritual, we cannot resist the baby's smile, and we cannot help but be moved when an infant gazes directly into our eyes.[9]

Extensive psychological research along with our own experience strongly suggests that people of all ages show more eye contact and smiling—and they laugh more, too—in situations in which they feel love, liking, happiness, attraction, and/or interest. Along with other nonverbal behaviors such as forward body leaning, open posture, gentle tone of voice, and tender touch, the facial expressions of looking, laughing, and smiling have been classified by psychologists such as Michael Argyle, Miles Patterson, and Albert Mehrabian as cues of "immediacy," "intimacy," and "interpersonal arousal."[10] These behaviors "warm up" interpersonal relations and promote the kind of mutual sharing that leads to encounters of the I–Thou. Indeed, Jean-Paul Sartre wrote that it is through the perception of the gaze of another person upon oneself that we most directly apprehend the other person as an integral being like ourselves—a "Thou" endowed with consciousness and intention of his or her own.[11] Of course, we may stare menacingly at an enemy or laugh in disdain at a fool. A smile can be supercilious rather than sincere. Nonetheless, while eye contact, smiling, and laughter can serve other masters, more often than not they are considered to be primary signals of intimacy and warmth in human relationships.

Carol Kirshnit, Jeffrey Jackson, and I conducted a study in which we monitored the facial behavior of college undergraduates as each was individually interviewed by a fellow student. Male students were interviewed by a male; female students by a female. Each student was asked to relate seven personal experiences from his or her past, including his or her earliest memory and past experiences of joy, excitement, and sadness. In half of the interviews, the interviewer simply asked the questions and listened cordially to the responses. In the other half, the interviewer shared three experiences of his or her own, turning the interview into a mutual conversation in which both partners shared experiences. A videotape camera recorded the facial behavior of the students so that we could later analyze the tapes for the amount of eye contact, smiling, and laughter.

Overall, students scoring high in intimacy motivation engaged in more eye contact and smiling, and laughed more often.

Although these differences were more striking in the mutual-conversation interviews, the results of the two kinds of interviews paralleled each other. On the average, students high in intimacy motivation smiled about 15 percent of the time while they were speaking to the interviewer, compared to 9 percent for "low." They looked the interviewer in the eye for about 44 percent of the time they were speaking, compared to 35 percent for "low" students. And they laughed approximately once every minute, while "low" students virtually never laughed. These findings applied equally to men and women. Women tended to show higher levels of smiling, laughter, and eye contact overall, however, which is an important sex difference to which we will return in Chapter 6.[12]

The results of this study strongly support the idea that people high in intimacy motivation open themselves up to others by smiling, laughing, and looking at the other person to a greater extent than do people low in intimacy motivation. With our eyes and our faces, we can subtly tune our encounters with others, turning up the intimacy volume with eye contact and smiling, turning it down when we look away or frown. What might be muffled and indiscernible becomes a clear and crisp signal, an audible message that says, "I am listening to you and I hope that you are listening to me. . . . I am interested in sharing a bit of myself. . . . Let us see where this will take us."

Hera: The Friend

In his poem "Two Friends," David Ignatow captures a poignant moment of intersection between two separate lives:

I have something to tell you.
I'm listening.
I'm dying.
I'm sorry to hear.
I'm growing old.
It's terrible.

It is, I thought you should know.
Of course and I'm sorry. Keep in touch.
I will and you too.
And let know what's new.
Certainly, though it can't be much.
And stay well.
And you too.
And go slow.
And you too.[13]

This dialogue of friendship is ambiguous and troubling. On the one hand, two friends have met to share that which is innermost. One says he is growing old and dying. The other listens and expresses sympathy. But the dialogue is terse and perfunctory. While the one friend affirms the other's experience, we wonder how genuine his concern is, considering that he exits so quickly, without asking or giving more. In addition, what can we make of his admonition to "stay well"? *His friend is dying*—he's not "well" to begin with! Hasn't he been listening? Yet, he seems gentler in the next line, when he urges his friend to "go slow." Perhaps he means "take it easy" or "don't hurry too much, enjoy life while you can." "Go" may also mean "die," as in "he's dead and *gone.*" The one friend may be urging the other to stave off death for as long as possible, even to "die slowly."

The poet has stripped away the niceties of interpersonal relations and exposed a common dialogue of friendship in its bare bones. When the friend says he is dying, he may be expressing something closer to a universal truth than a specific personal revelation. We are all growing old and dying. Death is the ultimate vulnerability in every human life. By telling another something that is so obvious and universal on the one hand and so personal on the other, one friend is sharing something from within that indeed resides in the hearts of every man and woman. By affirming the truth—"it's terrible"—the other friend indicates that he has received his friend's offering of that which is innermost, and that he understands it completely. Yet we are left longing, aching for more at the end of this poem. We want the friends to say more, to love more.

The psychiatrist Harry Stack Sullivan believed that there was nothing more wonderful in the world than a close friendship. The intimacy experienced by two "chums" represented the pinnacle of human experience. Yet we are very fortunate, Sullivan lamented, if we experience such intimacy more than once or twice in our lives, especially as adults. As we shall see in Chapter 5, Sullivan believed that a person is most likely to experience the beauty of intimate friendship in the years just before puberty, as a preadolescent whose sexuality has yet to be awakened. For many reasons, however, life gets more complicated afterward, Sullivan maintained, and true friendship in adolescence and adulthood is very difficult to find. Like the friends in Ignatow's verse, we are left groping for connections with other people, ever longing and ever frustrated by the limitations of human communion.

Yet, there are differences among us. Some people seem to be much more optimistic about friendship, reporting many close and satisfying relations with friends throughout their adult years. Although they too may experience loneliness and alienation from time to time, these people also celebrate the possibilities of close friendship in human life. They may even understand their own life stories as primarily tales of friendship, as they envision their central life roles in terms that echo the closing words in that most intimate psychodrama: "Honey, life involves people."

Research suggests that a small but important minority of adults define themselves as living the central role of *the friend* in their own life stories. In the mythology of ancient Greece, the goddess Hera personified many features of the good friend. Wife and helpmate to Zeus and queen of Olympos, Hera repeatedly proved to be loyal, cooperative, and friendly. Her steadfastness and loyalty to Zeus distinguished her from all other deities in the Greek pantheon. Hera—a prototype of the friend—is the main character in the life stories of Marty N. and Susan T.

Marty is a forty-one-year-old mother of two who is enrolled full-time in a doctoral level program in counseling psychology.[14] At the beginning of every chapter in her life story, Marty highlights the status of the most important relationships in her

life during that period. Following a happy and relatively un-
eventful first eleven years, Marty moved from one part of Chicago to another in sixth grade and began to "feel really popular
for the first time." Through high school, her friendships with
other girls were numerous and lasting, though relations with
boys remained awkward until the middle of college. After college, she married a man sixteen years her senior. He was a Lutheran; she, a Jew. The relationship has been extremely rocky
ever since, but she remains faithful to him, committed to making the marriage work no matter how frustrated she feels. Raising two children has entailed more sacrifices than she expected
in that she felt compelled to give up full-time employment until
the children became teenagers. Nonetheless, a couple of part-
time jobs as a market research interviewer buoyed her self-esteem and convinced her that she has a genuine talent for working with people and listening to their concerns.

In 1979, Marty enrolled in the counseling program at a major university. Instrumental in her decision to go back to school
were her sessions with a therapist who serves as the most significant exemplar of "Hera-the-friend" in her life. Like her therapist, Marty hopes she can be an effective and caring friend to
others in her career as a counselor. Her two major goals for the
future are to become a counselor and to "have lasting and caring relationships."

Married for twenty years, Susan is a part-time speech therapist and mother of two teenagers. She divides her life story into
ten chapters—beginning with "Infancy" and ending in the
present with what she entitles "Midlife Crisis." Each chapter
centers on her description of an important person in her life at
that time, either a family member or a friend. Chapter 1 emphasizes how her father doted on her as a baby. She still thinks it
remarkable that, in her first year of life, he regularly rolled out
of bed to provide her with the 2:00 and 6:00 A.M. feedings. Chapter 2 centers on her description of her mother, cast in the form
of a rigid taskmaster who kept order in the home. What Susan
sees as most remarkable about this chapter is that in spite of her
mother's coldness, little Susan was still able to make many good
friends as a preschooler. Chapter 3 encompasses her very happy

years in elementary school, filled with fun and friendship. Chapter 4 begins with an incident in fourth grade. On the first day of class, she met a new girl, and they became best friends. Like many of the friends she has made over the years, her fourth-grade chum has remained a life-long friend.

Susan states, "If you have one best friend, you can survive everything else." Indeed, the proposition may be put to the test in her current career crisis. As the children go off to college, Susan hopes to shed her primary role as mother, quit her part-time job, and begin afresh. She hopes to start a business of her own and to do more traveling with her husband. Because of the uncertainty surrounding her future, however, Susan feels that these are very trying times. Without the children at home, how will she spend the next thirty years of her life? Some of Susan's friends, whose children are about the same age as hers, are also facing this challenge. Susan occasionally talks with her friends about these problems, and she looks to their lives for answers to the problems in her own. All in all, loyal and long-term friendship is a major theme in Susan's life story. Even though children leave, jobs change and people grow older, Susan's friendships endure as the one constant amidst the many variables of life.

Our research has shown that people with high intimacy motivation, like Marty and Susan, have richer and more rewarding friendship lives. In interviews with fifty men and women between the ages of thirty-five and fifty, we asked each adult to describe the most significant friendships in his or her life, to indicate how close these friendships are, how important they are, and how satisfied he or she is with them. Persons high in intimacy motivation consistently described extremely close relationships with a few friends and a rich network of other friends and acquaintances with whom they interacted regularly. They often reported that they were highly satisfied with their friendships and, in some cases, that friendship was the paramount source of meaning and fulfillment in their lives. People high in intimacy motivation do not necessarily have more friends. But we see in this study that the *quality* of their friendships appears to be especially high.[15]

Two Styles of Friendship

Consider the best friend you ever had. Perhaps it was a little girl with whom you played in first grade. Or a best buddy in junior high school. Or maybe it is a man or woman in your current life to whom you feel especially close but with whom you are not romantically involved. Think about the history of that friendship—how it started, how it developed, the high and low points, and how, if it is a friendship from the past, it ended. Think of a moment in the history of that friendship in which you and your friend felt that the friendship bond was strengthened or reinforced. In an intensive study of the experience of friendship, we asked college students to think about these things. Two students—the first female, the second male, and both high in intimacy motivation—described these two moments with their best friends in which they felt that the bond between them had been strengthened:

In junior year in high school, I went on a class trip to California and I roomed with Sandy and two other girls. Sandy and I paired up together for most of the activities, and during that time we became rather close, each of us telling each other boyfriend troubles. I was glad that I found someone who was interested in what I had to say and was sincere and honest in her replies. At the same time I was very interested in listening to her and trying to understand her.

This is not really dramatic. I think that what got us together so that we understood each other and laughed and yelled about the world and our feelings was not one particular thing but something that happened on several different occasions. These occasions were when we started writing crazy sayings—poems—of our day's events. We kept a diary-type journal in this class and we each felt confident enough to share the journals with each other. During the course of this year, we would exchange these notes—even up until our graduation we made it a weekly kind of thing to read each other's poems. I guess this is a silly and strange thing to do, but I never grew so close to anyone else.

These accounts provide windows into a particular pattern of friendship experience characteristic of people who are high in intimacy motivation. It is a communal style of friendship, and one of its major themes is *self-disclosure*. In each of these accounts, the student states that the friends grew closer by virtue of telling each other important things about themselves, disclosing previously hidden aspects of the self while receiving the reciprocal disclosure from the friend. In recounting high points from the histories of their best friendships, students high in intimacy motivation overwhelmingly cite examples of self-disclosure, suggesting that sharing the secrets of one's soul is the essence of being a friend.

But friendship involves other experiences, too. Consider these two accounts from college students—the first female, the second male—who are high in power motivation:

One incident where my friend and I grew closer was when I became ill and began to lose a great deal of weight. I had no appetite and went a long time without eating. It did not happen in a specific event, but rather I began to feel sick and she noticed how much I was changing and tried to console me. Others noticed that I began to look thinner and act a bit different than I normally did, but they really did not say much to me and acted just the way they did before (these were other classmates). This incident occurred when I was a sophomore in high school. I really was not aware of the changes at the time.

I was working at a restaurant as a waiter. A lunch rush hit and the cook (my friend) was in trouble. He and I figured out the situation and took on the problem. Within forty-five minutes we were able to serve lunch to seventy-five people. The best part was that we handled it so smoothly that there were no complaints.

These two accounts illustrate a contrasting pattern of friendship that we often see in people who are high in power motivation, what may be termed an agentic friendship style. The key theme in these experiences is *helping*. Friends are viewed as powerful agents who come to the rescue of each other in times of need. In the first instance, a good friend is the only person who cares enough to console the young woman when she gets sick. In the second, the waiter helps his buddy, the cook, stave off the wrath, and satisfy the hunger, of a restaurant mob.[16]

Friends are generally expected to come to each other's aid during times of distress. Some of the great stories of friendship —Damon and Pythias, David and Jonathan—dramatize this theme of helping as it manifests itself in prodigious valor and sacrifice. Helping—whether a heroic act or quiet counsel—is an active assertion of the self; it intervenes in the environment and effects a significant change. Helping temporarily transforms a relationship into one between relative unequals. For the moment, the helper is dominant; the helped is submissive. Yet, it is expected that the roles may be exchanged in the future.

In a survey of students' "friendship episodes," Sheila Healy, Steven Krause, and I explored further the roles of self-disclosure and helping in the experience of friendship, and the relations between self-disclosure and helping on the one hand and motives of intimacy and power on the other.[17] We administered the TAT and a lengthy friendship questionnaire to more than one hundred college men and women. The friendship questionnaire asked each student to describe in detail ten specific friendship episodes that had occurred in his or her life during the past two weeks. We defined a friendship episode as any interaction with a friend that lasted at least fifteen minutes. For each episode, the student was to describe the time and place of the occurrence, how many people were involved, the major activity of the episode, the contents of the conversations occurring, the major role the student played, and the feelings the student experienced.

The results strongly supported the existence of two distinct styles of friendship, one related to intimacy motivation and the other to the power motive. Students high in intimacy motivation described more episodes in which they engaged in self-disclosure and in which they played the role of "listener." They consistently reported that when they got together with friends they spent a good deal of time talking about relatively personal issues, such as feelings, emotions, needs, wants, fantasies, strivings, dreams, hopes, plans for the future, fears, and self-awareness. Students high in power motivation, by contrast, were more likely to engage in helping and other forms of "agentic striving" when with their friends. Examples included taking charge of a situation, assuming responsibility, making a point in a debate or argument, helping another, giving advice, making plans, organizing activities, and attempting to persuade others. In these episodes the students perceived their roles as dominant, guiding ones. They were actively doing something, behaving as powerful agents.

While people high in power motivation tend to *do* things in their friendships, people high in intimacy motivation appear content to *be*, connecting with the friend through the mutual self-disclosure of the I–Thou. Interestingly, people high in both power and intimacy motivation appear to blend these two orientations, emphasizing both doing and being, agency and communion, in their friendship experiences. The contrast between agentic and communal styles, however, has been fleshed out in a number of other dimensions of friendship experience.

We have found, for instance, that people high in power motivation prefer to interact with large groups of friends rather than one on one, that they find particularly repugnant any experiences in which a friend embarrasses him- or herself in public, and that they greatly fear the eruption of conflict in friendships. In the agentic style of friendship, friends are active, assertive, and expansive. But each friend is expected to appreciate and applaud the others' powerful displays. Any publicly humiliating or boorish act on the part of one friend, therefore, may be seen as lowering the prestige of all involved. Friends may be powerful, but they must be careful as well, lest they make fools of everybody. Further, friends should be careful not to come into conflict with each other. The clash of powerful agents threatens to undermine the equilibrium of the agentic friendship and destroy each friend's opportunity to display and expand the self in the presence of a friendly audience that knows when to cheer.

People high in intimacy motivation prefer to interact with one friend at a time, find particularly problematic experiences in which one friend privately betrays the trust of another, and greatly fear separation in their friendships. In describing the "lowest points" in the histories of their best friendships, students high in intimacy motivation frequently related incidents in which one friend broke a promise, disclosed a secret to a third person, or failed to show warmth and understanding at a particularly crucial time. In a number of cases, the violation involved a failure in candor, suggesting that honesty and confidentiality in self-disclosure were major concerns. Individuals high in intimacy motivation were more likely, furthermore, to accept at least partial blame for the friendship low point and to indicate that the two friends subsequently worked out a resolution to their problems. While people displaying the communal friendship style appear confident that they can work out their conflicts, they worry much more about situations beyond their control that might threaten to separate friends from each other. One friend might move to another part of the country. Two friends might unwittingly grow apart. Friendships might end because of sickness or injury. And friends die.[18]

Athene: The Peacemaker[19]

In my discussion of two friendship styles and in Chapter 1, I have distinguished between the intimacy and the power motives. We must keep in mind, however, the appropriate reference points for our conclusions about intimacy and power motivation. When we characterize people high in intimacy motivation, we are usually contrasting them to people low in intimacy motivation, rather than to people high in power. Similarly, when we characterize people high in power motivation, we implicitly compare them to people who are low on that same motive, rather than to people high in intimacy. Strong intimacy motivation does not imply weak power motivation; strong power motivation does not imply weak intimacy motivation. Indeed, some people score relatively high on both of these motives. And some score low on both, too.[20]

Psychologists know very little about how the desire to be close and the desire to feel strong may work together in human lives. As we shall see in Chapter 4, one study suggests that having both high intimacy and high power motivation can breed misery in the lives of some young people. At the same time, scoring high on both motives has been related to productive contributions in the lives of men and women in their thirties and forties, as we shall see in Chapter 5. Having high intimacy motivation may "soften" and "socialize" strong power motivation, motivating assertive behavior for the benefit of others. And being high in power motivation may invigorate intimacy motivation, energizing and selecting compassionate behavior that is bold and powerful. In my research and in my personal experience, I have witnessed the creative and beneficial merger of intimacy and power motivation in a few life stories, self-defining narratives that present main characters who are both warm and strong, communal and agentic. One of these main characters is represented by the ancient Greek goddess, Athene. She is the intimate and powerful *peacemaker*.

In Greek mythology, Athene is a very complex goddess representing many different aspects of human nature. She is Zeus's favorite of all of the deities, in part because she personifies both strength and gentleness. Striking traits of both masculinity and femininity are repeatedly observed in the exploits of this most androgynous of goddesses. Athene is the goddess of storms and lightning, who knows how to make war but longs for peace. She engages the powerful Ares in numerous battles, usually winning by outwitting and outmaneuvering the man of war. Yet she is also skilled in the arts of peacemaking, drawing on her prudent intelligence to solve conflicts among gods and goddesses and among mortals, too. Patron of architects, sculptors, spinners, and weavers, she serves as a counselor for many, protecting Odysseus after the Trojan War and guiding Telemachus in the search for his father.

In sum, the character of Athene emphasizes the interlocking themes of peacemaking, androgyny, counseling, and teaching. Athene is the main character in the life story of Richard W., a thirty-six-year-old father of two whose TAT stories indicate high power and high intimacy motivation. Richard is a professor of music at a major university in the midwestern United States. Throughout his life story, Richard describes himself as the consummate teacher who believes it his mission to "put back into life what you have taken out." By "taking out," Richard is referring to the many valuable lessons he has learned and the many breaks from which he has benefited through fortuitous meetings and relationships with other teachers, guides, and "mentors." Richard sees himself as a teacher most in his job at the university, but also in his family life, in his relations with friends, and in his outside commitments to such groups as a music society, blood donation organization, and youth orchestra.

At the center of his role as a teacher, Richard believes, is solving conflicts between people and bringing together diverse elements that have previously been apart. Richard believes that his greatest creative powers reside in his ability to "bring people and things together." Indeed, his life motto might be that of E. M. Forster, whose words at the beginning of Chapter 1 demand that we "only connect." Richard is busy resolving conflicts and bringing things together in his personal life and in his work. Listing the many conflicts in his own life and in the lives of others with which he is confronted on a regular basis, Richard frames his life story as one of alternating periods of conflict and peace. At present, he sees himself in the midst of a tumultuous life chapter and is actively working to produce peaceful ~olutions to conflicts between two different factions within the university, between his wife and himself, and between two different life goals of his own.

Moving from the private life of one ordinary man to the international stage, we see Athene as the guiding peacemaker in the life and work of India's Mahatma Gandhi. In his stunning psychobiography, entitled *Gandhi's Truth*, psychologist Erik Erikson characterizes Gandhi as a representative of a uniquely Indian kind of dual sexuality, in part a function of the enormous cultural influence of traditional Indian mother goddesses, which combine "autocratic malehood and enveloping maternalism."[21] The blending of agency and communion in the life story of Gandhi mirrors the psychological androgyny apparent in the myths of Athene. Although he pioneered a social movement based on principles of nonviolence, Gandhi, like Athene, deplored timidity in the face of threat. Gandhi argued that a human being does better to strike out violently against an aggressor than to flee in cowardice. Supremely superior to both options, of course, is a militant pacifism (*not* passivity) whereby an individual actively renounces harmful retaliation and suffers the blows of the aggressor without flinching. "Suffering convinces the enemy to use reason," wrote Gandhi, and "nonviolence is the law of the human race and is infinitely greater than and superior to brute force."[22]

In the ancient Homeric hymns, the muses sing of Athene's wisdom and prudence. Unlike the more abstract and systematic Apollo, Athene exhibits a more practical, down-to-earth form of wisdom, a "bright-eyed intelligence capable of discerning the decisive element at every juncture and of supplying the most effective instrumentality."[23] The Jungian scholar James Hillman writes that Athene excels in understanding the intricacies of concrete relationships, acting as the goddess who "grants *topos,* judging where each event belongs in relation to all other events."[24] Like Athene, Gandhi was no grand systematizer in his thinking about peace. Rather, he fashioned a patchwork of peace strategies, loosely tied to traditional Hindu and Buddhist conceptions and partially bolstered by his reading of the New Testament (especially the Sermon on the Mount), Emerson, Thoreau, and Tolstoy. These strategies were ultimately justified, however, by their effectiveness in social action. One biographer contends that Gandhi's Indian background and his Western education supplied him with the "vocabulary and the symbols of his nonviolence philosophy" but that Gandhi's translation of these abstractions into social action was an ingenious pragmatic achievement. The idea of *ahimsa*, for instance, or noninjury to any living organism, goes back thousands of years in Indian tradition. Gandhi reinterpreted this primarily personal duty into a social imperative that could be employed strategically to coerce the British into, ultimately, granting self-rule to India.[25]

Another public figure whose peacemaking efforts recall Athene and the creative blending of power and intimacy motivation is Vera Brittain (1893–1970).[26] Raised in middle-class and provincial comfort in northern England, Brittain abandoned her studies at Oxford in 1915 to enlist as a nurse in the armed forces. Throughout World War I, she treated the wounded and dying in London, Malta, and at the front in France. After the war, she devoted her life to the causes of peace and feminism, ultimately writing twenty-nine books dealing with these themes. Her most famous work is *Testament of Youth*, an autobiographical account of her first thirty years. In writing *Testament*, Brittain sought to "rescue something that might be of value, some element of truth and hope and usefulness, from the smashing up of my youth by the War."[27] Always the peace-loving pragmatist, Brittain justified the writing of her life story as a potentially *useful* contribution to the understanding of war and peace in modern times: "I knew that until I tried to contribute to this understanding, I could never write anything in the least worthwhile."[28]

From an early age, Brittain appears to have been preoccupied with war and peace. She writes that her early memories are tied up with dramatic national events and "the songs, the battles and the sudden terminations of suspense in a struggle more distant and more restricted than that which was destined to engulf us. Like the rest of my contemporaries, I began to distinguish real occurrence from fables and fantasies about the time that the South African War broke out at the end of 1899."[29]

The conflagration that was to "engulf" Brittain's generation, of course, was World War I. Brittain's experience of that war reflects in her individual life story the harrowing collective narrative of her generation: this is a major message of *Testament.* Youthful, vibrant, patriotic, and idealistic in 1914, Brittain and her surviving peers emerged from the war broken and disillusioned. Lovers, friends, and brothers were dead in the trenches, and very little moral or political justification could be dredged forth to make sense of the slaughter.

Brittain became a pacifist. During the 1920s, she worked in England as an advocate and a "teacher" for the League of Nations. She made speeches and led discussions on the league throughout England, and eventually incorporated themes of peacemaking into her novels, poetry, articles, and other nonfiction. By the time she was thirty (at the end of *Testament*), she had come to realize that her life story was defined in terms of peace and war:

> In one sense I was my war; my war was I; without it I should do nothing. If marriage made the whole fight harder, so much the better; it would become part of my war and as this I would face it, and show that, however stubborn any domestic problem, a lasting solution could be found if only men and women would seek it together.[30]

Brittain's central vision for the rest of her life was *men and women making peace together.* Her understanding of her own life as born from war and dedicated to peace reminds us of Richard's view of himself as a man dedicated to resolving warlike conflicts in his personal life and in his immediate surroundings. Both Vera Brittain and Richard, furthermore, see peacemaking and teaching as two sides of the same coin. Brittain's final vision of men and women making peace together—peace between males and females as equals and peace among nations in the world—blends her passions of pacifism and feminism and reminds us of Erikson's characterization of Gandhi's dual sexuality and of the androgyny of Athene. Resolving conflicts between warring factions in our personal lives and on the international stage, forging connections between disparate parts—these challenges call upon us to be both powerful and intimate. Peacemaking, in all its forms, asks us to bring together our sometimes conflicting desires to be close and to be strong— to find peace, in all strength and gentleness, within ourselves.

CHAPTER 4

Health and Happiness

Ah, happy, happy boughs! that cannot shed
Your leaves, nor ever bid the Spring adieu;
And, happy melodist, unwearied,
Forever piping songs forever new;
More happy love! more happy, happy love!

—John Keats, "Ode on a Grecian Urn"[1]

Sandy's life is full of laughter—always has been.[2] She grew up on a farm in central Iowa, immersed in what she now describes as the pure and simple joys of rural life. There were hayrides, nature hikes, ice-cream socials, church picnics, and lots of games. In elementary school, she was a tomboy who could out-run the boys, and she was the most popular girl in the class. In high school, she played sports, joined clubs, and enjoyed many other extracurricular activities. It was about this time that she discovered her talent for making people laugh. "I was always 'the clown' during these years, and I guess I still am," she re-marks. Her comic improvisations made her even more popular with her peers. When friends disagreed and tempers flared, they could count on Sandy to crack a joke to relieve the tension.

College was a little rougher, however. Sandy wanted to be a nurse, but she did not want to study. After a difficult year, her discipline improved, and she eventually succeeded in gaining her nursing degree. In her interview, Sandy underscores the fact that despite tough times in college, she virtually never felt anxious or depressed. And she never lost her sense of humor.

101

Shortly after she completed college, she fell in love with a graduate student. They planned to marry in a year. But his studies required more years of schooling than either of them had expected, and eventually he broke off the engagement, suggesting to Sandy that she "go travel around the world" because "you will never be completely happy if you don't." She took his advice.

Sandy claims she was "crushed" after the breakup. But you would never know it from the way she describes the next ten years of her life—a long and wonderfully happy chapter of continuous travel. During this period, Sandy financed her travels by taking on a series of nursing jobs in the United States, Europe, and the Orient. She reports having more fun during this time in her life than during her early golden years in Iowa. She chose as the "peak experience" of her entire life a 4,300-mile boat trip across the Atlantic, in which she became very close friends with four men—a German, a South African, an Englishman, and an American.

Sandy feels a strong need to help other people who are less fortunate than she. Her many attempts to put this desire into action include volunteer nursing in Vietnam and a one-year tenure with the "Hope Ship." In both, she reports, she had more fun than she ever dreamed possible and even came to feel a little guilty about not experiencing more hardship herself in situations in which so many others were in pain. Now that she has settled down in the Midwest again, she is finding her profession and her relations with many friends rich sources of satisfaction. With respect to friendship, it is amazing to note that Sandy regularly corresponds with every roommate she has ever had—at least twenty-five in all! Although a number of her peers in the nursing profession claim that they experience "burnout" after a few years, Sandy maintains that she still loves her job and "would not trade it for the world."

Unflagging optimism and affirmation of life are celebrated on every page of Sandy's life story. As the clown who makes people laugh, Sandy ends up having more fun than her adoring audience. In the best sense of the term, Sandy's life is a "comedy." Like the sitcoms of contemporary television and the high comedy of Shakespearean theater, Sandy tells an optimistic story about people having fun, even in the face of adversity. While tragedy finds great heroes confronting implacable fate and romance presents extraordinary adventures and exotic quests, comedy affirms the simple and pure pleasures of ordinary people who laugh, sing, and play together, and who find each other after being apart. Comedy is a narrative of love and intimacy; tragedy and romance speak the language of power.[3]

At the end of classic comedies, characters who have been trying to get together throughout the story finally succeed. The literal and figurative coming together is often marked by a wedding. A foreshadowing of comedy's "happy ending" is evident in Sandy's life story. Through an unlikely, even comic, set of circumstances, Sandy and her former fiancé have resumed their relationship and are now living together. As she tells it, he is the brooding intellectual; she, the carefree clown. While he is the thinker, she is the doer. She feels they are two opposites who, after many years apart, have now come together in harmony. At age thirty-nine, Sandy's plans for the future are to get married, travel, buy a larger condominium, and "do something for others." Throughout it all, she fully expects to have fun.

Is Sandy really as happy as she says she is? Although we cannot know for sure, she certainly seems convincing. Problems and conflicts probably lurk beneath the surface in Sandy's life. She may be troubled by unconscious complexes, defenses, or unresolved psychosexual issues. But all in all, I believe Sandy when she says that she is generally happier than many, if not most, people. And I would rate her psychological adjustment to be quite good as well. It is difficult to point to any single factor as primarily responsible for Sandy's happiness. Blessed with a comfortable home and a natural comic wit, confronted with no overwhelming personal tragedy to darken her sunny optimism, well-off and well educated enough to be able to travel around the world, Sandy is more fortunate than many thirty-nine-year-old women. At the same time, many of us probably know people who are equally fortunate but generally miserable.

To hear Sandy tell it, the key to her happiness is warm personal relationships. Friendship, love, and intimacy blend together to make a radiant glow. For hundreds of years, poets, philosophers, healers, teachers, gurus, counselors, therapists, and theologians—many wise men and women—have been affirming the power of loving and sharing for human happiness and health. Loving and intimate relationships with other people have been characterized as one of the key elements in happiness and well-being, psychological adjustment and adaptation to the world, and even physical health and healing. Warm relationships with others are thought to make us feel happy and fulfilled, to help us through times of stress, to promote the resolution of our conflicts, to bolster our health, to cure our sicknesses, to make us better people, and to promote the social good. Without love and intimacy, we are depressed, unfulfilled, lonely, alienated, anxious, conflicted, and sick. When we are unable to connect to others we may experience, in the words of Sören Kierkegaard, "fear and trembling" and "sickness unto death."

But is this all true? Do we have good evidence to support those who believe that love, friendship, and intimacy contribute significantly to our health and happiness? The question is complicated and difficult to evaluate in its entirety. But we do have some interesting answers to different parts of the question. Psychologists and other social scientists have explored the link between love and intimacy on the one hand, and health and happiness on the other. We still have a lot to learn in this regard, but recent research has been illuminating, teaching us some new lessons about the meaning of intimacy in human lives.

Broken Hearts, Empty Lives

If college students remember anything from Introductory Psychology, it is likely to be Harlow's monkeys. Many undergraduates have heard the story of Harry Harlow's legendary studies of infant rhesus monkeys raised in isolation, and many have even seen some of the touching photographs of these monkeys splashed across the pages of their textbooks. In the 1950s and

1960s, Harlow and his students at the University of Wisconsin undertook an ambitious research project to explore what happens to healthy baby monkeys who grow up under extraordinary conditions. Because rhesus monkeys closely resemble human beings in certain biological and behavioral ways, the implications of Harlow's research for normal and abnormal human development have been drawn time and again.

Harlow did many different kinds of studies in which he separated healthy newborn rhesus monkeys from their biological mothers and raised them in unique artificial environments.[4] In one series of studies, Harlow raised monkeys in complete isolation in stainless steel cages. The monkeys were provided with a clean and warm environment that was designed to meet all of their basic biological needs. They were fed well and given adequate care by the experimenters. But once they were separated from their mothers, the monkeys grew up completely alone, without the company of adult monkeys or peers. Within a few months, significant developmental differences could be noted between the isolated and normal monkeys raised with their mothers. After about six months, the pervasive effects of isolation appeared to be irreversible.

What were these effects? In short, they were overwhelmingly negative. Isolated monkeys repeatedly hit themselves, rocked back and forth for hours on end, and stared into space. Removed from their lonely worlds at the age of six months and introduced to agemates and elders for the first time since birth, isolated monkeys reacted with emotional shock and withdrawal, desperately clutching themselves and rocking back and forth, sometimes even refusing to eat. At this point, some of the isolated monkeys had to be force-fed, to prevent starvation.

In the company of other monkeys, the formerly isolated monkeys proved to be social misfits. They either withdrew from any contact with other monkeys or ferociously attacked their peers. They were unable to engage in normal monkey play. They abused younger infant monkeys. They were sexually inept, rejecting the sexual advances of other monkeys or acting out sexually in bizarre ways. The experimenters had a particularly difficult time getting the female isolates to mate.

Finally, through the herculean efforts of an experienced Don Juan monkey, a few female isolates were impregnated. When their babies were born, these mothers, who were never nurtured by mothers of their own, neglected or attacked their own babies. Experimenters had to intervene to keep some of the mothers from killing their infants.

In the simplest and most general terms, Harlow's studies show us that rhesus monkeys raised alone, unable to experience the warm and supportive relations provided by mother, invariably grow up to become social and emotional cripples. That such a result might occur if human babies were to suffer a similar fate is a possibility that cannot, for obvious ethical reasons, be tested with the same empirical certitude of Harlow's studies. Still, psychologists point to many tragic "natural experiments" in which children have been abandoned or separated from their parents at birth and raised under deprived circumstances. It is difficult to interpret the many different outcomes of these various situations.[5] While extreme deprivation can have long-term negative effects on development, some human babies are also quite resilient and able to bounce back from early interpersonal deficits. Furthermore, it is difficult to separate deficits in loving relationships on the one hand from other sorts of deprivation on the other, such as inadequate stimulation and nourishment.

The consensus among prominent researchers, such as psychiatrist John Bowlby, is that children and adults react to disruption and loss in their closest and warmest interpersonal relationships through a process of mourning.[6] The grief reactions of one-year-old infants to brief separations from their caregivers mirror the reactions of children to losing their parents and the reactions of adults to the loss, usually through death or divorce, of lovers and dear friends. The bereaved person may react initially with disbelief and denial and then with angry protest. Protest is followed by deep sadness and despair. Finally, there is detachment, signaling the emotional acceptance of the loss as a permanent reality. According to psychoanalysts, the lost lover, friend, or caregiver may live on in the unconscious mind of the bereaved, maintaining a kind of intrapsychic relationship that takes the place of something that was once interpersonal. Furthermore, repeated or especially devastating experiences of loss, especially in the early years of development, are the stuff of which psychopathology is made, some therapists suggest. Children whose love is repeatedly rejected or proves useless in the face of loss may find that, as they grow older, they are unable to love any more, even unable to feel strong human emotions. Extreme withdrawal, narcissism, neurosis, pervasive misery— these are a few of the possible outcomes. Although we can repair the damage in many instances, broken hearts still have the power to destroy our mental health and to ruin our lives.

There is considerable research evidence to show that poor health and well-being in the adult years may result from disruptions in personal relationships and failures in intimacy. For instance, widowered men have a higher mortality rate, greater incidence of mental illness, and a higher tendency to suicide than other men.[7] Women whose husbands have died are likely to complain of more health problems during the year following bereavement than other women.[8] Married men who are going through divorce or separation from their wives are much more likely to suffer from stress-related illnesses. Such men are also likely to become the victims of homicidal assaults.[9] Greater levels of depression and psychosomatic illnesses are reported by men and women who are dissatisfied with their marriages.[10] Lack of intimacy with both friends and lovers is consistently related to depression, especially in women.[11] Lonely people are more likely to suffer depression, to have general medical complaints, and to attempt suicide.[12]

A study of 1,300 medical students examined relations between psychiatric and physical illness on the one hand, and the depth of interpersonal relations on the other. Those students who reported superficial and unsatisfying relations with their parents throughout childhood were more likely to be afflicted with psychiatric illnesses and even cancer in their young adult years.[13] Summarizing these and other studies like them, psychologist Steve Duck concludes, "Taken generally, several sets of results indicate that persons in disturbed relationships have higher incidence of: low self-esteem, depression, headaches, tonsilitis, tuberculosis, coronaries, sleep disorders, alcoholism, drug dependence, cancer, and admissions to medical hospitals."[14]

The costs of disruptions in relationships and failures to form close bonds with other people extend beyond individual lives and take their toll on society at large. The sociologist Emile Durkheim pioneered the study of social integration in human societies. According to Durkheim, societies are socially integrated to the extent that members engage one another in regular social interaction, form close ties to socially cohesive groups, and develop strong collective sentiments.[15]

People who are not well integrated into society are isolated from supportive networks and cohesive social groups for long periods of time. They form few if any intimate relationships and tend not to commit themselves to social pursuits. They reject or are rejected by families, neighbors, churches, clubs, schools, community groups, and other social organizations and institutions. Far outside the mainstream of society, these people are alienated, not just lonely, and they are more likely to behave in ways that undermine what society deems to be "the good." They become misfits, criminals—wards of the state and dangers to the citizenry. Social integration therefore serves to maintain social order and restrain deviant behavior. It is not farfetched to conclude that problems in intimacy lie at the root of some of society's larger woes. Loss, loneliness, and alienation feed on one another. Together, they can eat away all that is good and healthy in individual lives and in society as a whole.

What We Give and Receive

Close and warm relationships with others serve as both ends and means in our lives. As ends, they are good in and of themselves. Our friendships, love affairs, and relations with family members are validated simply for the joy and fulfillment we experience when we place ourselves in the midst of them. As Buber maintained, the I–Thou encounter needs no outside justification. The divine process of meeting another person as Thou is good all by itself, even if it provides no other benefit beyond the wonderfulness of relating to another. A person should not try to justify his or her relationships in terms of what he or she can "get out of them," Buber believed. To conceive of relationships in terms of means rather than ends is to undermine the integrity of the Thou.

By contrast, contemporary psychologists suggest that there *are* indeed many other benefits of such relating. Relationships function quite powerfully as means to important external ends. For example, psychologist Robert Weiss lists six social provisions that we give and receive in close and warm relations with other people:

1. *attachment*, from which we derive a sense of security and commitment, particularly in an intimate relationship with a spouse or lover;

2. *social integration*, or a feeling of shared activities and concerns that we often derive from friendships;

3. *opportunities for nurturance*, in which we take responsibility for the welfare of another person, such as a child or elderly person;

4. *reassurance of worth*, or the validation of our competence in a set of social roles, provided mainly by family members, from whom we usually receive assistance and cooperation regardless of the nature of our relations with them;

5. *sense of reliable alliance*, or the expectation of continued assistance in the future, again usually provided by family members;

6. *guidance*, or help during times of stress and support for solving problems.[16]

Many psychologists are especially interested in the ways in which close relationships provide us with social support. Relationships lift us up and sustain us; they maintain, especially during times of considerable stress. Stress can arrive on the scene in virtually any form. It may show up as a financial burden, a bad investment, a major business loss, too many bills. Or it may be in the form of interpersonal stress—divorce, discord in the home, arguments with friends, competition with coworkers. Stress shows up at parties, in church, on airplanes, in the doctor's office, on the golf course, in the classroom, in front of the television set, in the middle of the night when we wake up from a dream, when we cannot sleep, when we sleep and sleep because we do not want to face the world. In all of these and millions of other confrontations with stress, we find it daunting to stand up tall and face the foe alone. As our knees buckle and we begin to fall back, relationships push us upward with renewed strength and confidence.

There are many ways in which our relationships can support us during times of stress, depending on the kind of stress we experience and the kinds of relationships on which we can call.[17] By listening to our problems and showing us sympathy and concern, other people may provide us with emotional support during difficult times. As a college student, I was perennially absorbed in one or another troubling nuance of my relations with my girlfriend. One of my roommates had similar problems. He and I would occasionally lie around on a weekday night, listen to the stereo, and commiserate about how awful these women in our lives made us feel. We did not really resolve anything by doing this. He did not have any good ideas about how I should cope with my love life, and I did not provide him with any profound insights, either. But it was comforting and soothing to share our stories. In some instances in our lives— one thinks especially of major traumas, such as the death of loved ones—we do not want people to give us advice or provide insights. We simply want them to listen, to give us the emotional support we need to carry on.

But sometimes we do seek specific advice in our relationships. We want to know precisely what we should do, how we should cope. Therapists, counselors, ministers, and rabbis get paid for providing this kind of assistance. Through informational support, we receive suggestions, directives, and specific advice offered to help us resolve particular problems, problems ranging from how to fix a leaky faucet to how to mend a relationship with one's daughter. Whereas we seek emotional support from people who, we know, care for us, we look to "experts" for information and advice. (Of course, caring experts are the best. We probably learn the most from those who love us, but it also helps if they know what they are talking about.)

A third kind of social support is appraisal support. Friends, lovers, family members, teachers, ministers, and supervisors give us feedback on how well we are doing in particular areas of our lives. We need reassurance that we are not the worst sinner that the rabbi has ever met, that our four-year-old daughter is more popular among her classmates in nursery school than we were at that age, that our dining room is suitably elegant, our wardrobe sufficient for the job, that we are good, smart, strong, friendly, popular, normal. We provide each other with appraisal support to the extent that we convey the generally affirmative message, "You're okay; so don't worry."

Finally, there is instrumental support—money, labor, time, and other tangible forms of support that help us cope with tangible stresses. When my wife and I moved from St. Paul, Minnesota, to Chicago, we rented a truck to transport our books and furniture. In macho, newly married style, I spurned the offers of help from my in-laws, who lived a few miles away and wanted to assist me in loading the truck. I wanted to do it myself, though inside I feared I would botch the entire enterprise. My fears were right on target: after hours of labor, I was able to fit everything into the truck in such a way that, if we confronted the first turn in the road, the truck would tip over, destroy our belongings, and kill the two of us. I was completely distraught.

Then, out of the blue—it seemed a miracle—my father-in-law and my wife's Uncle Henry, a huge strapping man whom I hardly knew, pulled up in the driveway, saying that they just wanted to stop by, see how the packing was going, and see us off. I think that they had surveyed the disaster even a few blocks away, for they immediately sprang into action to reload the truck. Henry unloaded and loaded like a man possessed. Emptying the truck and starting from scratch, he and my father-in-law successfully finished the job in less than two hours, as I tagged along, picking up odds and ends and holding open the doors. I was overwhelmed with gratitude, to the point of tears. Some forms of instrumental support can have an extraordinary emotional impact.

Many psychologists argue that social support functions to buffer stress, softening its pain, muffling the impact of negative life events. Empirical studies have shown, for instance, that the presence of close, confiding relations with a husband or boyfriend significantly reduces the likelihood that women will become severely depressed in the wake of major life disappointments and losses.[18] Women who have closer relations with their husbands are less likely than other women to experience postpartum depression.[19] In both men and women, support from coworkers at the workplace appears to buffer the stress of jobs.[20]

People who report adequate levels of emotional, appraisal, informational, and instrumental support in their lives are less likely to experience severe depression, anxiety, insecurity, disorders in thinking, and other signs of neurosis and mental illness. A low level of social support is a greater risk factor for psychiatric problems than are stressful events themselves.[21] This means that people who experience considerable stress in their lives but who benefit from considerable social support are less likely to experience depression and anxiety than are people who have little stress in their lives but who also have little in the way of social support.

A number of studies have also documented a positive relation between supportive social relationships and physical health. Sampling almost seven thousand adults in Alameda County, California, researchers discovered that those men and women with extensive social ties—marriage, friendship, community involvement—had a significantly lower mortality rate than those who were isolated and alone. Taking into consideration age, socioeconomic status, and health habits, those men and women with the fewest social ties had a mortality rate twice as high as those with the most ties.[22] Another study investigated the small, close-knit Italian-American community of Roseto, Pennsylvania, during the 1960s.[23] Family and interfamily relationships in this community were extremely close

112

and supportive. The people of Roseto were relatively obese compared to the people of two neighboring communities, while they did not differ essentially in levels of animal fat in their diets, serum cholesterol, hypertension, or smoking and exercise habits. Yet their mortality rate from heart attacks was substantially lower than that of their neighbors, and well below the national average. There were also lower rates of senility and peptic ulcers in Roseto.[24]

Despite the wealth of research documenting the benefits of social support, some studies suggest that in certain stressful situations close and warm relationships can exact a cost, and support can sometimes fail. In an interesting study of Israeli women whose husbands were mobilized for war, the researchers found that strong networks of social support produced higher levels of anxiety. In this case, tight and supportive social groups among the women functioned as rumor mills. News of possible disasters at war spread like wildfire in these groups. Instead of finding comfort and reinforcement with their friends and neighbors, the Israeli women who were well integrated in supportive social networks found their fears heightened and their problems exacerbated. By contrast, those women who were more isolated were less anxious, for they did not have to endure the daily bombardment of news and rumor about their men.[25]

In another study suggesting that social support does not always exert a general positive influence, researchers found that middle- and upper-level executives who experienced high levels of stress in their work reported lower levels of physical illness when they perceived high levels of support from their bosses but higher levels of illness when they perceived high levels of support from their families. In other words, support from the boss helps executives deal with job stress and lowers the likelihood that they will get sick and develop stress-related symptoms. But support from spouse and children may not help. Instead, it can make things worse, increasing the likelihood that the executives will succumb to stress-related disorders. This negative effect of family support proved to be especially strong for those executives who showed lower levels of a personality disposition called "hardiness," which is defined by psychologist Suzanne Kobasa as a tendency to seek challenges and to welcome commitments in life. The highly stressed executives who were less hardy to begin with may have found that social support from their families reinforced their tendencies to avoid challenge and commitment in their work life, which may have ultimately increased stress and exacerbated their problems at work.[26]

Psychologist Karen Rook has recently argued that we need to view the positive, and sometimes negative, effects of warm and close relationships in a more differentiated way. All kinds of social support are not equally good for all kinds of stressful situations, she points out. Furthermore, some benefits from social relationships seem to exist outside the realm of social support. Rook distinguishes between social support and companionship. Echoing the distinction that I made at the beginning of this section, Rook views social support as a means and companionship as an end. Social support exists for the explicit purpose of providing aid or help. Companionship exists as an end in itself, as in "shared leisure and other activities that are undertaken primarily for the intrinsic goal of enjoyment."[27]

In her research with college students and older adults, Rook obtained separate measures of social support and companionship. To assess social support, she asked the participants in her study to report the number of people in their lives with whom they could regularly discuss personal matters, consult for advice in making important decisions, and discuss work problems; from whom they might borrow money in an emergency; and who might take care of their home when they were away and help with household tasks. To assess companionship, Rook asked them to report the number of instances during the previous three months in which they had had someone over for a meal, visited someone's home for a meal, entertained visitors, visited other people at their homes, gone out with people (to movies, restaurants, etc.), or met someone familiar in a public place (like a park).

The results of Rook's study indicate that both social support and companionship help people deal with stress, buffering the negative effects of painful life experiences. Nonetheless, only high levels of companionship, not social support as she defined it, increased overall happiness and satisfaction in life. One implication of Rook's findings is that the most helpful relationships in a person's life may be the ones that are not viewed as primarily help-oriented. Those intimate relationships which are best justified as ends in themselves may also serve as the most powerful means to other ends.

Fantasies That Heal

In his book *Love's Body,* Norman O. Brown writes, "To heal is to make whole, as in wholesome; to make one again; to unify or reunify: this is Eros in action."[28] From Brown's Freudian perspective, eros is the overarching urge to come together with others in loving unity. Love heals, proclaims Brown, let us make ourselves whole with the magical medical elixir of love, let us keep ourselves whole—immune from sickness and separation—with potent inoculations of love.

In our hearts, we may be intrigued by the idea that love can heal and keep us healthy, but in our heads we are probably more than a little bit skeptical. What can love really do in the face of biological realities such as invading germs and viruses, faltering organs, and weakened immune systems? In recent years, some scientists have gone beyond the skepticism and begun to take seriously the possibilities that some manifestations of love and intimacy may actually cure illness and prevent disease and that these effects may be observed and measured in basic biological processes. A focus of their investigations is the human immune system.

The immune system protects the body by mounting responses to foreign tissue, cancer cells, and invading pathogens, including bacteria and viruses. The system is incredibly complex, involving many different and overlapping mechanisms, which work to protect the body from disease in many different ways. One important process in the immune system is called the "humoral response." This involves the production and release of antibodies, also called immunoglobulins, which combine with and neutralize foreign substances. When the mucous membranes of the body are invaded by infectious agents, the body fights back with various types of immunoglobulins found in body fluids, such as saliva. Immunoglobulins are a first line of defense against infections, particularly those of the respiratory, intestinal, and urino-genital tracts.[29]

In his doctoral dissertation, psychologist James McKay investigated the relations between immunoglobulin levels detectable in human saliva and a person's overall approach to loving relationships.[30] Working with David McClelland at Harvard University, McKay hypothesized that a trusting and loving orientation to relationships should be related to higher levels of immunoglobulins in the body's secretions and ultimately to better health. This trusting and loving orientation, McKay maintained, should reveal itself in people's private fantasies, sampled as imaginative narrative responses to pictures. Adopting the method of the TAT that I described in Chapter 2, McKay and McClelland obtained imaginative stories composed by college students under various conditions and then related certain themes in these stories to immunoglobulin levels in saliva and to reports of sicknesses and disease.

To derive a system for interpreting imaginative stories, McKay first showed a film designed to arouse feelings of selfless caring and love for humanity. The film was a documentary about Mother Teresa and her work with the poor and the dying in India. The students provided saliva for the researchers immediately before and shortly after viewing the film, by spitting into test tubes. Immediately after the film, the students wrote imaginative fantasy stories in response to pictures. McKay found that some of the students wrote trustful, positive stories while certain other students wrote cynical, negative stories. Laboratory analyses of the saliva samples revealed that those students who wrote the trustful stories also showed a significant increase in saliva immunities from before the film to afterward, while those students who wrote cynical stories showed a significant decrease. In other words, McKay observed a relation (1) between trustful and loving fantasies and increased immunities after watching a film about selfless love and (2) between cynical fantasies and decreased immunities after watching the same film.

In a later study, McKay asked students to write stories in response to pictures under neutral, nonarousing conditions. In order to test a second dimension of the human immune system, McKay obtained blood samples from all of the students. The blood was analyzed for the presence of "T-cells," a specialized form of disease-fighting lymphocyte. The students in the study also listed the number and types of illnesses they had contracted over the previous year. McKay found that students who wrote stories about positive and trusting relations between people tended to have healthier proportions of T-cells in their blood. The positive relation between trusting fantasies and blood immunities was especially strong among the women in the sample. McKay found a slight tendency for better T-cell proportions to be associated with fewer reported illnesses. And he found that writing trusting stories on the TAT was associated with fewer illnesses, especially for women.

The results of McKay's research are by no means definitive. The samples of participants in the studies are relatively small, some of the measures used are controversial, and the actual correlations obtained are statistically significant in most cases but still relatively small in magnitude. The results do not suggest that the minute you feel a sore throat coming on you should begin kissing people in the street and sharing intimacies with all whom you meet. More likely such a strategy will only spread the germ. Nonetheless, McKay's research is provocative. The findings support a mild, but potentially important, association between a loving, caring perspective in life and immunity to sickness. While love is no penicillin, a trusting and loving viewpoint on the world may give us a slight edge in our fight to stay healthy and whole.

Adaptation to Life

There are many different theories of mental health. Psychiatrists, psychologists, counselors, and a host of other experts have offered a wide range of formulas telling us what it means to be "well adjusted," to be "normal." Virtually all of these formulations underscore the capacity for loving and intimate relationships as a key to mental health. Legend has it that when asked for a sophisticated explication of what it means to be a psychologically healthy adult, Freud once stated simply, "Lieben und arbeiten," which translates from the German as "to love and to work." Therapists of virtually all ilks—from the most mystical Jungians to the most hard-headed behaviorists— tend to agree that people need to love and be intimate with others if they are to adapt to life well.

Despite all of the theorizing, there are only a few scientific studies documenting a strong link between intimacy and overall psychological adjustment, for psychologists have found it difficult to test the linkage in ways that are scientifically sound and convincing. One study that does succeed in testing the relation between intimacy and adjustment, however, was conducted by psychiatrist George Vaillant and myself.[31] Drawing information from an archive dating back to the early 1940s, Vaillant and I examined the relation between intimacy motivation assessed at age thirty and overall psychological and social adjustment at midlife.

One of the big challenges in doing research of this sort is choosing an appropriate way to evaluate a person's overall "adjustment" or "adaptation." Judging another person's mental health and adaptation is risky business, even under the best of clinical conditions. In research it is even more dangerous because the scientist is usually not personally acquainted with the people whom he or she is studying and must rely instead on case summaries, test scores, transcripts of diagnostic interviews, and other second- and thirdhand reports. The written reports may seem objective and reliable, but they generally do not enable the investigator to get "the feel for the person" that many clinicians indicate is so essential in determining the nature of a person's adaptation to life. Whenever you make judgments on mental health and adaptation, furthermore, you run the risk of imposing cultural values on people's lives in inappropriate ways. In order to minimize this problem, therefore, it is very important that the psychologist understand the nature of the population from which the person is sampled and to which he or she is being compared. A person's relative adaptation to life must be seen in the context of the values, standards, mores, and norms of the cultural group of which he or she is a member.

In our particular study, the cultural group concerned was white, upper-middle-class, American men, extremely well educated and generally successful, entering college in the early 1940s and establishing careers in the 1950s and 1960s. The men we studied were all graduates of Harvard College from the classes of 1942–44. With the goal of following over many years the development of a select group of psychologically healthy men, a team of researchers chose about two hundred Harvard men in 1942–44 who were doing extremely well in their academic studies and who seemed to show good overall adjustment to life. The men were interviewed in college and given an extensive battery of medical and psychological tests. After graduation, they received annual questionnaires through 1955 and questionnaires every two years thereafter. In 1950–52, when the men were about thirty years of age, a social anthropologist interviewed most of them in their homes and administered the TAT. The imaginative stories that the men told in response to the TAT pictures were tape recorded and later transcribed. A number of the men were interviewed again in 1967, when they were in their late forties.

In 1977, George Vaillant published an important and popular book describing patterns of life adjustment from college through midlife among these men, entitled *Adaptation to Life: How the Best and the Brightest Came of Age.*[32] The title of the book makes it clear that this is no ordinary group of adults. Described as "the best and the brightest," these men were blessed with many of the attributes and benefits most highly valued by the American middle and upper-middle classes during the forties, fifties, and sixties. They were selected to exemplify the highest standards of achievement and adaptation among elite professional men. Generally firstborns, these Harvard students had exhibited mastery and independence in college, substantial academic achievement, and few signs of pathology or mental illness. One-quarter of the men eventually became lawyers or physicians; 15 percent became teachers, mostly at the college level; and 20 percent went into business. Vaillant adds:

> At age 47, the average man in the study had the income and social standing of a successful businessman, but he had the political outlook, intellectual tastes, and the life-style of a college professor. Twenty five years after college, the subjects remained healthier and occupationally more successful than their classmates. Their mortality rate was 50% less. Four times as many held class offices as would have been expected by chance.[33]

Still, life was not smooth sailing for all of the men deemed to be "the best and the brightest." Vaillant's account of the rich diversity in the lives of these men indicates that there were important individual differences in the ways in which the Harvard graduates adapted to life challenges. While virtually all of the men mastered their college studies, not all of them mastered life.

In searching for a method of differentiating between the men who had adapted well and those who had adapted less well, Vaillant eventually settled on a highly objective procedure that seemed to embody standards of success and adaptation appropriate for this privileged group of American men. According to Vaillant's method, overall "psychosocial adjustment" in these men at midlife—in 1967 when they were interviewed for the last time—could be graded on nine different dimensions:

1. *Income.* Men who were making more than $20,000 a year in 1967 received higher adjustment scores than those who were making less than $20,000 a year.

2. *Steady promotion.* Men who received regular promotions or increasing responsibility in their jobs every five years since graduation received higher adjustment scores than those who did not.

3. *Games.* Men who engaged in regular pastimes or athletic activities with friends received higher adjustment scores.

4. *Vacations.* Men who used their allotted vacation time to take trips received higher adjustment scores than those men who did not use their allotted vacation time or used it to stay home.

5. *Enjoyment of job.* Men who expressed satisfaction with their jobs received higher scores than men who did not express satisfaction or who expressed explicit dissatisfaction with their jobs.

6. *Psychiatric visits.* Men who had visited a psychiatrist on fewer than ten occasions since college received higher adjustment scores than men who had had more than ten psychiatric visits.

7. *Drug and alcohol misuse.* Men with no alcohol or drug problems received higher adjustment scores than men who reported detrimental effects of alcohol or drug use, as in cases in which substance abuse interfered with health, work, or personal relationships.

8. *Days sick leave.* Men with fewer than five days of sick leave per year received higher adjustment scores than men who missed more than five days of work per year due to illness.

9. *Marital enjoyment.* Men who reported a stable and happy marriage for at least fifteen years received the highest adjustment scores. Some of these men had been divorced and had remarried. Only the current marriage was evaluated. Men who reported that they had been married for at least fifteen years but indicated dissatisfaction with the marriage received intermediate scores. Men who reported chronic dissatisfaction with the marriage, had seriously considered di-

121

vorce, or who reported major sexual problems in the marriage received the lowest adjustment scores.

The ratings of psychosocial adjustment were all made in the late 1960s, based on information gathered on the men through the 1967 interview. The nine ratings were added together to arrive at a total score of adjustment. To measure intimacy motivation, I dug up the old TAT stories in 1979 and scored them according to the standard procedure described in Chapter 2. The stories were also scored for other personality variables, such as the power motive. The goal of our investigation was to see the extent to which a desire for close relationships, indicated in the intimacy motive scores obtained at age thirty, predicted overall psychosocial adjustment years later. We hypothesized that high intimacy motivation at age thirty should be positively associated with overall psychosocial adjustment in these men in their late forties.

The results of the study strongly supported our hypothesis. High intimacy motivation at age thirty was positively and significantly associated with better overall psychosocial adjustment at midlife. It also predicted significantly the single adjustment items of income, vacations, enjoyment of job, and marital enjoyment. The last two were the strongest relationships, which indicates a striking tendency for men who were high in intimacy motivation at age thirty to report, seventeen years later, that they were happily married and well satisfied with their professional work. Power motivation at age thirty, by contrast, had no influence on psychosocial adjustment. Men who were high on power motivation were no better adjusted than those who had scored lower on the power motive.[34]

Our study strongly supports the idea that, among highly educated and successful American men attending college in the early 1940s, high intimacy motivation at age thirty led to better life adjustment—measured as a composite of income, occupational success and enjoyment, leisure time use, psychiatric visits, substance abuse, health, and marital enjoyment—at age forty-seven. The results support the various clinical formulations that place the capacity for warm and close relations with others at the center of mental health and adjustment in adulthood. As compelling as these results are, however, we do not know at this point if they apply in the same way to other groups of American men and to women.

One other study has directly examined the relation between intimacy motivation and adjustment. Psychologists Peter Zeldow, Steven Daugherty, and I administered the TAT to a group of students in medical school and then collected a number of measures of psychological health.[35] Most of the students in the study were in their mid twenties. Intimacy motivation was positively associated with "hedonic capacity," which is the capacity to experience pleasure in life. Contrary to what one might expect, intimacy motivation was not directly related to measures of depression and self-esteem. Instead, we obtained an interesting and peculiar finding involving power motivation. Medical students who scored high on both intimacy and power motivation reported higher levels of depression and anxiety and lower self-esteem, compared to the other students. Instead of leading to better adjustment, high intimacy motivation when combined with high power led to poorer adjustment in these students!

The meaning of these results may hinge on the problem of motivational *conflict* in the busy lives of young medical students. Bombarded with a highly demanding curriculum, difficult examinations, and the uncertainties of a new professional identity, these students in medical school may have found that strong internal needs both to feel close to others and to have impact on others were almost too much to handle and virtually impossible to fulfill in their present situation. In view of the rigor and regimen of daily life among medical students, it seems likely that neither intimacy nor power motivation would have much opportunity to find expression and fulfillment.

Strong intimacy motivation and strong power motivation need not come into conflict in every life, but it seems likely that they may do so during times of rapid change, especially when people are in their twenties and early thirties. Psychologists such as Carl Jung[36] and Daniel Levinson[37] have suggested that it is not until midlife that men and women are able to integrate successfully conflicting needs to be strong and to be close. Some younger adults, consequently, may not be ready to negotiate a life story in which both intimacy and power are central and dominant themes. As intriguing as this notion is, however, we have not done enough research yet to know if it holds any truth.

Intimacy and Well-Being

Some psychologists distinguish between psychological adjustment and adaptation on the one hand and subjective well-being on the other. The distinction is roughly equivalent to that between "objective" mental health, as determined (usually) by a psychologist or some other outside "expert," and "subjective" happiness, as judged by the person him- or herself. It is generally believed that the two go together in most lives: people who are mentally healthy are generally happy as well. Indeed, one criterion for mental health may be happiness. The two are not the same thing, however, and we can imagine—perhaps we even know—people who are paragons of mental health but who are deeply anguished in their private lives and other people who are supremely neurotic but who say that life, for them, is wonderfully fun. The study of Harvard men dealt almost exclusively with objective mental health and adaptation, as determined from the outside by experts. A second study that I conducted with social psychologist Fred Bryant, by contrast, deals exclusively with subjective well-being.[38]

Bryant believes that there is a lot more to happiness and well-being than meets the eye. When a friend asks you how you have been and you say, "Oh, not too bad," you may be responding to this seemingly simple question with disarming complexity. If you take the question seriously, as more than a polite salutation, something requiring an honest and thoughtful answer, you are faced with many different ways to respond. You can evaluate your overall mood from the last few days. You can assess how well things are going at work. You can judge yourself with respect to your failure in a recent tennis match or your success in helping out a friend who phoned you this morning. You can survey your marriage, friendships, fantasies, and dreams. You can look at your physical health. A man just released from the hospital after successful surgery may feel on top of the world. Another suffering from a touch of the flu may decide that life is not going well at the time.

Based on a statistical analysis of large surveys in which people are asked to evaluate how happy and satisfied they are with life, Bryant has determined that subjective well-being has at least six different dimensions.[39]

The first is *happiness*. This dimension refers mainly to emotions. How good or bad do you generally feel? Overall, how happy are you at present? How happy have you been in the past?

The second is *gratification*. This dimension concerns evaluations of how well life is going in various areas, such as work, marriage, parenting, and leisure time. Whereas happiness involves emotion, gratification concerns itself more with thought —what a person thinks about his or her present roles in life. How satisfied are you with your role as parent, as wife or husband, as a professional? How satisfied are you with the ways in which you have been able to use your leisure time?

Bryant's third dimension of well-being is called *strain*. Strain includes symptoms such as physical ill health, psychological anxiety, and drug and alcohol abuse.

The fourth dimension is *vulnerability*, which involves how overwhelmed a person feels, how likely the person believes it to be that he or she might have a "nervous breakdown," and how concerned he or she is about bad things happening in the future.

The fifth dimension of well-being is *self-confidence*. People who have low self-confidence report low self-esteem, depression, alienation, and the feeling that problems in life cannot be controlled.

Finally, there is *uncertainty*. This sixth dimension of subjective well-being involves excessive worries and self-doubt, dissatisfaction with the way in which a person is using his or her time, and admitting personal shortcomings. People who have high uncertainty report that they have a difficult time predicting what is going to happen in the future.

According to Bryant, subjective well-being can be broken down into these six separate dimensions. Although the six dimensions are typically related, persons can evaluate themselves in very different ways on the different scales. For instance, an elderly man may report overall high happiness and satisfaction with his roles as grandfather and "retired senior citizen," but he may complain strongly about occasional poor health and thus show considerable strain. A healthy housewife and mother of three may express high levels of general happiness and little strain and vulnerability, but she may also report low self-confidence because she feels that other women and men, of equal intelligence and ability, are "passing her by" in the workplace. Thus, while the various dimensions of well-being may shade into one another, they each retain a certain degree of independence and conceptual integrity.

Bryant and I analyzed data collected in 1976 from a nationwide survey of American men and women. I discussed this particular survey briefly in Chapter 1. Recall that in 1976 the University of Michigan's Survey Research Center interviewed more than two thousand adults living in the forty-eight contiguous states of the United States. The researchers interviewed adults from virtually all occupational categories, socioeconomic positions, and educational levels, from large cities, small towns, and rural areas. The result was about as close to a perfectly representative sample of American adults living at a particular time that a social science project will ever be able to obtain.

More than twelve hundred of the men and women in the survey were administered the TAT. My graduate assistant Carol Kirshnit scored the thousands of TAT stories obtained for intimacy motivation. Fred Bryant and his colleagues at Michigan performed the herculean statistical analyses. The final results of the study provide evidence for a positive relationship between subjective well-being and intimacy motivation. The relationship is not altogether straightforward, however, and it differs markedly for women and men.

Among the more than six hundred women studied in the

nationwide sample, high intimacy motivation on the TAT was positively associated with happiness and gratification. In other words, women who scored high on intimacy motivation reported slightly greater levels of overall happiness in their lives and slightly more satisfaction with their various roles than did women scoring low in intimacy motivation. In women, therefore, a strong desire for close relationships brings with it the benefit of greater overall happiness and gratification. High intimacy motivation in women, however, does not appear to relate to strain, vulnerability, self-confidence, or uncertainty.

Among men, high intimacy motivation was associated with lower levels of strain and uncertainty. Men who showed a strong desire for warm and close relations with others tended to have fewer physical symptoms of illness and psychological symptoms of anxiety, and they tended to report that they were less worried about the future, compared with men who were low in intimacy motivation. At the same time, intimacy motivation among men was not related to their happiness, gratification, self-confidence, or vulnerability.

There are three important points to keep in mind in interpreting these findings. First, we are talking here about connections between a general *desire* to have intimate relationships and different dimensions of well-being. The results do not suggest that having intimate relationships is directly associated with well-being. The study suggests something a bit more radical, I think: that the mere desire to have intimate relationships is directly associated with certain, but not all, dimensions of well-being.

Intimacy motivation is just one aspect of life and relationships. A general desire for intimacy, as assessed on the TAT, may or may not be reflected in intimate relationships in real life. As we saw in Chapter 3, people high in intimacy motivation tend to display certain intimate behaviors and show certain themes of intimacy in their daily lives and in their life stories. But the relation between intimacy motivation and actual intimacy is not perfect. The extent to which we are able to engage other people in intimate relationships is due to many factors—skills, traits, values, beliefs, situations, luck—and many of these are beyond our control. What is particularly impressive in this study, though, is the finding that the mere desire for intimacy brings with it certain benefits in subjective well-being.

A second point is that men and women differ markedly in the way in which the intimacy motive relates to well-being. It is important to note that men and women do not necessarily differ with respect to *how much* intimacy motivation they show. Because men and women in this nationwide study wrote stories to different TAT pictures (men's cards contained male characters; women's cards contained female characters), we cannot compare their stories to each other. Therefore, we cannot draw any conclusions from this study about the overall levels of intimacy motivation in men versus women from this study. (Nonetheless, we can make some conclusions on this subject from other studies, as we will see in Chapter 6.)

Instead, what we learn from this study is that men and women derive different benefits from intimacy motivation. For women, a strong desire for intimacy tends to bring higher levels of happiness and satisfaction with various life roles. For men, a strong desire for intimacy tends to reduce strain and uncertainty. But why doesn't high intimacy motivation make men happier? And why doesn't high intimacy motivation reduce strain and uncertainty for women? We will discuss these puzzling questions in Chapter 6, when we consider the possibility that intimacy means very different things to men and women.

Finally, I would be remiss if I did not offer the appropriate cautions and caveats with regard to this study. As social scientists who read the study in the original form should be able to note, the empirical relationships we did obtain between intimacy motivation and subjective well-being are statistically significant but relatively modest in nature. The findings show an important but only *slight* tendency for women who are high in intimacy motivation to report higher levels of happiness and gratification and for men high in intimacy motivation to report less strain and uncertainty. While even a modest correlation of this kind is worth celebrating if you are a scientist who believes in the power of intimacy to improve human life, one should not get carried away with enthusiasm. For the most part, psychologists do not know a whole lot about why some people are happy and others sad, why some report high levels of life satisfaction and others say they are always miserable. While a small number of psychological variables and some nonpsychological variables (such as income) appear to account for some of the variability in reports of well-being, the source of much of the variability remains a mystery.

There is another interesting wrinkle in the study. Bryant and I wondered if high intimacy motivation might exact a certain price for people who are unable to fulfill their strong desire for close and warm relationships. In order to test this idea, we broke the sample down into two very general groups: those adults living alone versus those living with somebody else. We assumed that, all other things being equal, people high in intimacy motivation would probably prefer to live with somebody else than to live alone. Those people high in intimacy motivation who were living alone, therefore, might report lower levels of subjective well-being, in that their desires and their current living situation would be out of kilter.

The results of our analysis provided some support for our hunch, but only with women. Women who were high in intimacy motivation and who were living alone tended to report greater levels of uncertainty and lower gratification than did other women overall. Again the findings were statistically significant but somewhat modest. Apparently, for a certain number of women who are high in intimacy motivation the frustration or disappointment experienced because they are living alone overwhelms the general positive benefits of a strong desire for warm and close relationships. Consequently, they report that they are less satisfied with their roles in life and more uncertain about the future. Indeed, they are less satisfied and more uncertain than women who are low in intimacy motivation but who are also living alone. It is the combination of the motive and the living situation that produces the effect. When a strong desire for warm and close relationships is met with stiff opposition in one's daily life, one's subjective evaluation of how well life is going is bound to suffer.

In conclusion, recent studies support a positive link between psychological health and happiness on the one hand and intimacy motivation on the other. While the results are not always overwhelming, they are consistent and compelling. People who are high in intimacy motivation tend to show higher levels of life adjustment and mental health. In the study of Harvard men, intimacy motivation was positively associated with various signs of psychological and social adjustment that were chosen to be especially important for a group of adults considered by some to be "the best and the brightest." In the study of medical students, intimacy motivation was positively associated with the capacity for pleasure. Yet, as we also saw in the medical-student study, high intimacy motivation combined with high power motivation can lead to motivational conflict in life, especially among young adults who are experiencing major life transitions.

In the nationwide survey, intimacy motivation is positively associated with subjective well-being, but in different ways for men and women. Men high in intimacy motivation report fewer symptoms of strain and less uncertainty about the future. Women high in intimacy motivation are relatively happy and satisfied with their life roles. Yet, high intimacy motivation may bring frustration and disappointment for women who find that they cannot express their strong desire for closeness and warmth in daily life. Women who live alone but who are high in intimacy motivation report higher levels of uncertainty about the future and lack of gratification in their current life roles.

CHAPTER 5

Intimacy and Human Development

All of you who have children are sure that your children love you; when you say that, you are expressing a pleasant illusion. But if you look very closely at one of your children when he finally finds a chum —somewhere between eight-and-a-half and ten—you will discover something very different in the relationship—namely, that your child begins to develop a real sensitivity to what matters to another person. And this is not in the sense of "what should I do to get what I want," but instead "what should I do to contribute to the happiness or to support the prestige and feeling of worth-whileness of my chum." So far as I have ever been able to discover, nothing remotely like this appears before the age of, say, eight-and-a-half, and sometimes it appears decidedly later.

Thus, the developmental epoch of preadolescence is marked by the coming of the integrating tendencies which, when they are completely developed, we call love, or to say it another way, by the manifestation of the need for interpersonal intimacy.

—Harry Stack Sullivan, *The Interpersonal Theory of Psychiatry*

Anxiety, loneliness, lust—these are the three specters that haunt human life, the dark fates that pursue us relentlessly, stalking us as their hapless prey even in our moments of singular triumph, devouring us when we slip or falter, when we are weak and pitiful and so vulnerably human. Across the human life-span, we flee a three-headed monster, said Harry Stack Sullivan, the enigmatic and influential American psychiatrist who wrote knowingly of the need for interpersonal intimacy.[1] In the first eight years of life, we fight off anxiety, developing a set of defensive strategies that enable us to survive infancy and early childhood without too many battle scars. In late childhood, however, loneliness rises to the fore, and we begin to confront a

131

visage even more frightful than its ugly predecessor. We will risk anxiety—we may even welcome it—in order to stave off the insidious power of loneliness. In adolescence, we face our third enemy. Sexual lust erupts onto the scene, raging like a volcano. For the rest of our lives, we must find ways of dealing with this, the youngest and most impetuous tyrant in the triumvirate, while continuing to do battle with the other two.

Sullivan was not optimistic about the human condition.[2]

In Sullivan's view, all of life, from the moment of birth onward, is negotiated within an "interpersonal field." According to him, it makes no sense to speak of the individual developing on his or her own; *personal*ity is always *inter*personal. In the first few months of life, the interpersonal field is a rather limited one, consisting, for the most part, of the infant and his or her primary caregiver, usually the mother. While there is much that is good and wonderful in this earliest of human relationships, Sullivan emphasized instead the ways in which the infant feels tensions within the field. An especially diffuse form of tension is anxiety, which Sullivan believed to be empathically transmitted from the mother to the baby. When she feels anxious, the baby feels anxious. Regardless of its ultimate origins, the baby feels the mother's anxiety as a palpable, free-floating tension. In that all adults feel some form of anxiety, Sullivan maintained, there is no way to shield the baby from this ubiquitous interpersonal condition. Rather, the baby learns to shield itself.

In the first few years of life, the infant-toddler develops what Sullivan termed a "self-system." The self-system is a set of strategies that the child may use in order to stave off the unpleasant experience of anxiety. These strategies vary widely, from turning back the taunts of schoolchildren with a smile to escaping into a fantasy world when parents fight. We may envision the self-system as a custom-made suit of armor that the child dons in order to traverse the interpersonal field. In the best of scenarios, the armor protects well, at least until about age eight or nine. During this critical period of preadolescence, however, the boy or girl finds that the defensive self-system cannot secure a chum. In order to stave off new feelings of loneliness and isolation, the preadolescent develops new ways of relating to others—ways that may contradict the strategies of the self-system—to find a person whom he or she can call "my best friend," and to cultivate that friendship.

Loneliness arises because of the maturation of a new psychological need, the need for interpersonal intimacy. According to Sullivan, we do not desire to engage others in the reciprocal, I–Thou manner described by Buber until we have reached preadolescence. Before this time, we are unable to relate to people in the mutual give and take of intimacy, for we cannot yet communicate with each other in what Sullivan termed the "syntactic mode." In syntactic communication, I seek to understand you on your own terms and to convey accurately the terms of my own existence to you, so that you will understand me equally well. More than cooperative partners, chums collaborate in the making of a shared reality: they make themselves in the image of each other. Chums devote themselves to each other to the point that the boundaries between them seem to be blurred. It is important that my chum be as much like me as possible. He and I should feel the same things, think the same way. We should see the world and our place in it in similar terms. In preadolescence, chumships affirm our sameness with another, providing a foundation for the development of identity in later years.

The collaborative and syntactic chumship is as close to paradise as we ever get, Sullivan claimed. The emergence of mature sexuality at puberty—what Sullivan termed "the eruption of the *lust* dynamism"—adds new tensions and problems to the interpersonal field, providing a third complicating perspective from which we may view relations with others. To the anxiety–security and the loneliness–intimacy dimensions we must add the problem of satisfying our lust, and doing so in a way that keeps us whole, secure, and connected to others. During the adult years, we strive to satisfy our needs for security, intimacy, and sexual expression. The most satisfying interpersonal relationship is that within which we can integrate the expression of all three needs.

In summary, Sullivan argued that a general intimacy motive builds on a sense of security cultivated in the years of infancy and childhood. Yet the I–Thou experience of intimacy itself is not something that the infant or the young child is capable of feeling or knowing. Rather, intimacy awaits the maturation of preadolescence. Later, in adolescence and adulthood, intimacy becomes part of a more complicated scenario in which various psychological concerns and issues cry out to be addressed and fulfilled. Psychological maturity involves integrating intimacy into a life framework that encompasses all parts of the self.

This is a rough sketch of intimacy's place in human development as viewed by one influential clinician. Sullivan's perspective is both intriguing and wise. Later in this chapter, we will explore in further detail a few of his central concepts. But there are significant aspects to the birth, life, and career of intimacy that go well beyond this sketch. The story of intimacy's development is much richer, more positive, and open to a wider variety of readings and interpretations.

The Role of Temperament: Social Style

It all begins before the beginning, that is, before birth. Each of us comes into the world bearing a particular biological design, sketching out guidelines concerning what we are and what we are to become. There are elements to the design that all of us share by virtue of our status as human beings. Indeed, Sullivan built his interpersonal theory around what he termed the "one-genus postulate": that "everyone is much more simply human than otherwise."[3] Because of a common genetic reality, virtually every human being is endowed with certain fundamental traits that define his or her humanness. All intact humans have two eyes and opposable thumbs; all are blessed with relatively large brains and extremely complex nervous systems; all tend to be quite helpless at birth but are able to walk upright as children, to express themselves in language, to play with their peers, and so on.

Beyond the fundamentals of human nature, however, the genes also account for a tremendous amount of variability.

Some human beings are extremely tall while others are short; some have blue eyes and some have brown. As we know, such physical differences are strongly influenced by heredity. Likewise, certain psychological differences may have a genetic base, though here our knowledge is sketchier. Studies of human infants and analyses of the behavior of twins suggest that some variability in human behavior and experience may result directly or indirectly from genetic differences among humans. Developmental psychologists term these broad, biologically based differences "dimensions of temperament." With respect to a person's approach to interpersonal relationships, temperament appears to provide a basic and pervasive social style.

Dimensions of temperament are not set in concrete. Genetic designs are extraordinarily flexible in some cases, and traits that have a substantial biological base can also be dramatically transformed by changes in the environment. Human development is a product of a complex interplay of forces and factors that reside within the individual human being and in the environment in which he or she lives, factors arrayed on a multitude of levels —chemical, biological, experiential, interpersonal, social. Each of us is biologically predisposed to approach the physical and the social world with a particular kind of personal style, a slight and general tendency to react in one way as opposed to others. While some of us dive headfirst into new challenges and new relationships, others back off timidly to ponder even the slightest change. While some of us revel in the gaiety of a boisterous party, others prefer time alone where things are quieter and more serious. Of course, a generally timid person can act boldly in certain situations. The most introverted person we know may occasionally be the "life of the party." Temperament is not expressed the same way in every instance. It manifests itself instead as a general tendency over time and across many different situations.

Certain dimensions of temperament can be observed shortly after birth. In a landmark study of individual differences in babies during the first months of life, three psychiatrists identified a number of behavioral dimensions in which infants consis-

135

tently and markedly varied, yielding three different tempera- ment types.[4] One group of babies showed an "easy" tempera- ment. Easy babies showed consistently positive moods, low to moderate intensity of emotional reactions, and regular eating and sleeping cycles. Although some parents may say they have never seen one of these, easy babies made up about 40 percent of the infants in this original study. A second group of babies, classified as showing a "difficult" temperament, exhibited con- sistently negative moods, intense emotional reactions, and irreg- ular sleeping and eating cycles. They tended to withdraw from novel events; they laughed loudly, and they cried loudly. Diffi- cult babies made up about 10 percent of the original sample. Finally, "slow-to-warm-up" babies showed a combination of the other two types, with relatively negative moods, low intensity of emotional reactions, and tendency to withdraw from new events followed by eventual approach. They comprised about 15 percent of the sample, leaving some babies unclassified.

While viewing temperament in terms of these three infant types has a certain appeal, a number of psychologists have pointed to the limitations of this approach. First of all, the three types are not as clearly distinguished as one would hope, and over time they tend to blur together, with easy babies, for in- stance, sometimes growing up to be relatively "difficult" tod- dlers. Second, the three types do not tell us much about possible inborn differences in the ways in which people relate to each other over the entire life-span. Psychologists Arnold Buss and Robert Plomin have addressed this second problem in their "temperament theory of personality."[5] Based on careful re- search into personality traits manifested by fraternal and identi- cal twins, Buss and Plomin conclude that there is strong evi- dence for the existence of at least four basic temperament dimensions:

1. *emotionality*—the tendency to express negative emotions such as anger and fear frequently and vigorously;

2. *activity*—the degree of physical movement a person char- acteristically shows;

3. *impulsivity*—the degree to which a person acts quickly without deliberation, moves from one activity to the next, and finds it difficult to practice self-control;

4. *sociability*—the tendency to be outgoing and friendly and to enjoy the company of others.

According to Buss and Plomin, all four of these temperament dimensions are (a) inherited; (b) stable during development; (c) present in infancy, childhood, and adulthood; (d) instrumental in determining how human beings adapt to their social environments; and (e) present as meaningful behavioral dimensions in animals that are biologically similar to humans, such as monkeys and chimps. Persons are born with predispositions to develop these four temperaments to different levels. The social environment reacts to these dispositions, modifying and shaping them in certain ways but only within the limits established by heredity.

Of the four temperament dimensions identified by Buss and Plomin, the one that probably has the most significance for the development of intimacy across the life-span is sociability. Highly sociable infants tend to approach new events with delight and aplomb; sociable children make friends easily and enjoy being with other children; sociable adults are outgoing, friendly, talkative, and warm. Laboratory studies conducted by developmental psychologist Jerome Kagan suggest that young children who are relatively low in sociability—consistently behaving in a shy and inhibited way in the presence of others and when confronted with novel events—respond to social situations with relatively intense biological reactions, such as more dilated pupils and higher heart rates.[6] The extensive research of the British psychologist Hans Eysenck suggests a similar pattern in adults. According to Eysenck, socially inhibited or "introverted" persons show higher levels of general "arousal," as mediated by the reticular activating system, a bundle of nerve fibers ascending from the spinal chord to the thalamus of the brain that is thought to regulate patterns of wakefulness and attention. Highly extraverted, sociable people, by contrast, generally function under much lower levels of internal arousal.[7]

The implication of Kagan's and Eysenck's research is that highly sociable people who are especially friendly and eager to involve themselves with others function in a relatively "relaxed" physiological manner. Because certain features of the central nervous system are tuned at a particularly low level for these people, they are perhaps able to tolerate, even enjoy, higher levels of social stimulation. Introverted, nonsociable people instead find extensive social stimulation too arousing, considering that they are naturally more aroused to begin with. This different tuning of the central nervous system is largely determined by heredity. By virtue of a particular hereditary design, therefore, each of us emerges from the womb already biased to develop a unique interpersonal style. The general style ranges from extremely outgoing and friendly on the one end of the scale to extremely withdrawn and timid on the other.[8]

Yet, style is not motivation. People who are introverted may desire warm and close relationships as much as people who are extraverted. Nonetheless, the way in which they go about forming their intimate relationships is likely to differ markedly as a function of temperament. The highly sociable person is likely to cast a wide net, sampling many different kinds of relationships in order to fulfill his or her intimacy needs. The less sociable person may be more cautious and selective, moving slowly and haltingly through the interpersonal field, evaluating opportunities for the I–Thou with greater care and scrutiny.

The Attachment Bond

For Freud, intimacy begins in sucking:

> Sucking at the mother's breast is the starting-point of the whole of sexual life, the unmatched prototype of every later sexual satisfaction, to which phantasy often enough returns in times of need. This sucking involves making

the mother's breast the first object of the sexual instinct. I can give you no idea of the important bearing of this first object upon the choice of every later object, of the profound effects it has in its transformations and substitutions in even the remotest regions of our sexual lives.[9]

The most primitive manner of knowing the innermost self of another is to suck the other into one's own innermost. I know you and I love you by eating you. You become part of me as I, quite literally, take you in. In the first year of life, the baby obtains both nourishment and pleasure from sucking at the breast (or bottle). Sucking reduces the tension experienced as the hunger drive mounts, and the reduction of tension feels good. The mother is generally the source of these good feelings, the provider of food and pleasure. So she eventually becomes the infant's first love object. From this oral expression of the sexual instinct develops a lasting image of an ideal sensual experience, a legacy of fusion and pleasure that, Freud believed, we may reexperience in later life, usually in fantasy but sometimes in real moments of bodily communion.

While Freud viewed sucking not only as the source of love between baby and mother but also as a paragon for all later sensual experiences, other psychologists have argued that sucking is only part of the story, and a minor part at that. Child psychiatrist John Bowlby has proposed that infants fall in love with their mothers not because of sucking per se but because of a complexly calibrated system of mother–infant attachment, of which sucking is one of many interdependent parts.[10] According to Bowlby's influential view, the infant's love for the mother develops out of early patterns of sucking, touching, eye contact, smiling, vocalizing, and following. These behavioral patterns of relating to others become organized within an attachment system during the second half of the first year of life. The organization is guided by an instinctual blueprint that is ultimately coded in our genes. The behavioral patterns are organized to assure the "predictable outcome" of attachment, which is physical closeness of caregiver and infant. Virtually all human infants in all known societies become "attached" to their caregivers during the first year of life. Throughout evolution, attachment has served to protect the helpless infant from predators by assuring that the caregiver will be in close physical proximity when danger arises.[11]

Attachment develops slowly in the first year of life. Babies do not emerge from the womb ready to "bond" to mother in the first few minutes or hours of their existence on earth, despite what some popular books have claimed.[12] In fact, newborns do not seem to be very interested in people, spending most of their time nursing, crying, or sleeping. It is as if they are in a cocoon, yet to be "born" in any social sense. Psychoanalyst Margaret Mahler suggests that babies do not "hatch" from this psychological shell until the third or fourth month of life.[13]

Yet early signs of an incipient interest in people can be detected, most intriguingly in scientific experiments testing perception and attention. According to some of these studies, newborns come into the world with built-in preferences concerning what they prefer to look at. All other things being equal, a newborn prefers to look at a curved object over a straight one, a moving object over a stationary one, and an object that is moderately complex over one that is extremely simple or extremely detailed.[14] In the natural environment of a human infant, the most prominent stimuli that are curved, moving, and moderately complex are faces, and especially eyes. Inborn perceptual preferences seem to foreshadow what will later become a fascination.

By the time they are two or three months of age, babies are fascinated by faces and eyes, and they are ready to relate to people in more active, sociable ways. During this time, infants begin to make direct eye contact with other people, and they begin to express what psychologists call the "social smile." Eye contact and smiling are key components of the developing attachment system. These two behaviors warm up relationships, signaling that the infant is ready and willing to interact with others in ways that bring excitement, joy, and delight.[15] At first, babies will make eye contact and smile at others in an extraordinarily promiscuous manner. It may not matter if you are little Billy's devoted grandparents or a stranger off the street.

Chances are, if he is feeling cheery enough, Billy will smile at you and look you right in the eye. A few months later, he will be much choosier. But for now, he will seem to love equally almost anybody who happens to venture into his egalitarian world.

Early social play between babies and their caregivers typically involves intricate patterns of smiling, eye contact, and vocalization. Babies and their caregivers engage in a kind of "dance," writes infant psychiatrist Daniel Stern.[16] When the mother, father, and other caregivers feed the baby or change the baby's diaper, they are likely to evoke and respond to complex patterns of smiling, cooing, looking, laughing, approaching, withdrawing, and so on—both partners responding in a mutual and rhythmic way, gliding together across a dance floor of emotional experiences, back and forth, up and down, over and under, to the exquisite delight of both. The baby and the caregiver "tune" the interaction with subtle verbal and nonverbal behaviors, turning up the excitement with a glance or a smile, turning it down when things get a bit too intense by looking away or backing off. Stern believes that such "affective attunement" is at the heart of human sociality. Through the dance, babies learn how to take turns, how to lead and to follow, how to express and receive, how to modulate their own internal states and monitor the innermost of the other. If Stern is right, the fundamentals of the I–Thou may be laid down in the choreographed play of caregivers and their four-month-old babies.

When about six or seven months of age, babies begin to show clear preferences for certain people in their lives. They will not dance with any old partner anymore. Mother, father, and/or one or two other central people in their interpersonal field become their first choices. When they are frightened or hurt, it is from these "attachment objects" that they first seek comfort. When they confront new situations, it is to these attachment objects that they look for security, for a signal saying, "It's okay; don't worry; go for it." At about eight or nine months of age, babies begin to show fear and wariness in the presence of strangers and when separated from their prime attachment objects. Itinerant Uncle Bob who last visited Billy when he was all of three months old and was lavished at that time with smiles and eye contact, may be deeply hurt to see that when he returns six months later Billy shrieks in horror at the sight of his face. Billy is not angry because his uncle skipped town. As far as he can remember, Billy has never seen this big, unshaven man before. And he wants to have nothing to do with him.

The emergence of stranger anxiety and separation anxiety and the consolidation of a selective attachment bond with one or a few special people help close out the end of the first year of human life. Almost all babies are "attached" by this time. Yet different babies are attached in different ways. Some show a secure attachment with their primary caregivers, finding comfort and confidence in the presence of this most important and most-loved person in their lives. In the presence of the caregiver, these infants will explore their environments in a vigorous and independent manner, checking back with the caregiver every once in a while to "refuel" with security. When they are separated from their caregivers, they may cry and show great distress. But when reunited, they seem to forgive and forget, reveling in the return of the loved one, enjoying the moment for the blessing of security it invariably offers.

Other babies show patterns of insecure attachment. In one such pattern, the infant may avoid the caregiver when they are reunited, as if to say, "Because you left me, I'll leave you." The infant may seem relatively passive and uninterested in exploring the environment, even when the caregiver is right there. In another pattern of insecure attachment, the infant may express strong ambivalence, especially when reunited with the caregiver after separation. The baby may approach the caregiver with loving eagerness one moment and then angrily reject the caregiver the next. In general, the insecure attachment bond signifies a lack of what Erik Erikson calls "basic trust."[17] Unlike the securely attached one-year-old, the infant whose attachment follows an avoidant or ambivalent pattern seems to lack the trust that his or her caregiver will make things right, that the world is okay as long as the caregiver is there.

Developmental psychologist Mary Ainsworth pioneered the

scientific study of individual differences in attachment by developing a sensitive laboratory procedure through which secure and insecure patterns between infant and caregiver could be reliably observed.[18] Her own research along with studies conducted by such prominent infant psychologists as Alan Sroufe[19] and Bryan Egeland[20] suggest that mothers of babies who are securely attached show consistently higher levels of sensitivity when interacting with their infants in the first few months of life. A mother who is especially sensitive to her baby is "alert to perceive her baby's signals, interprets them accurately, and responds appropriately and promptly."[21] Observations of mothers and babies at home and in the laboratory during the infant's first three months of life suggest that mothers of infants who are later classified as securely attached respond more frequently to crying, show more affection when holding the baby, acknowledge the baby with a smile or conversation when entering the baby's room, and are better at feeding the baby because of their attention to the baby's signals, compared to mothers of babies later deemed insecurely attached.[22]

Do different patterns of attachment have long-term significance for human development? Some research points to generally positive effects of secure attachment through at least age five. For instance, children who are securely attached at age one tend to show somewhat more pretend play and exploratory behavior at age two than do their peers who were insecurely attached.[23] In nursery school and kindergarten, children securely attached at age one are rated by their teachers as more socially competent, by their peers as more popular, and by observers as showing more dominance and initiative.[24] Infants who experience their first love relationship as a highly trusting and secure one, therefore, show greater levels of autonomy at age two and initiative at age five. But what about the development of intimacy? What is the relation between attachment and intimacy?

It seems likely that the attachment bond provides the earliest unconscious pattern or model for warm and close relationships.[25] As Freud suggested, the bond of love between mother and infant may serve as a "prototype" of later intimate involvements, both those which include a sexual component and those

143

which do not. The person who emerges from the first year of life engaged with another human being in a trusting and secure relationship is likely to carry within him or her a legacy of trust, hope, and optimism about matters of the heart. The person who experiences insecure attachment, by contrast, incorporates a model of relationship that emphasizes anxiety and frustration, unconsciously coloring his or her expectations about intimacy in muted, shadowy hues. If temperament provides us with social *style,* the earliest attachment bond may leave us with a deep and pervasive social *attitude.* If temperament partly determines the behavioral ways in which I confront the Thou in interpersonal relationships, attachment may partly determine the extent to which I dare to hope that the Thou can indeed be confronted. Dare I trust the Thou to appear? Dare I expect that I can share my innermost self with another in mutual, affectively tuned delight? Trust and hope may stem from many sources—sources that go well beyond the earliest bond of love. Yet no single source is likely to be consistently more important in shaping hope and faith than is the nature of the first attachment bond.

Love Triangles

When it comes to intimacy, three is almost always a crowd. Buber did not call it the "I–Thou–Thou." Although we may be intimate with many different people in our lives, it is difficult to experience intimacy with more than one person at the same moment in time. In the ideal I–Thou encounter, two persons meet to focus unswervingly on each other, so that each, in Buber's words, "fills the firmament." The firmament is not large enough for more than this, Buber implies. Yet triangular relationships involving intimacy are common phenomena in human lives, from childhood onward. The intimacy I feel with one person may be threatened, challenged, undermined, or occasionally even augmented by the intimacy I feel with another.

Freud taught us that the prototype for these love triangles is the Oedipus Complex.

The ancient story of Oedipus is the tragedy of a brave and brilliant young man who solves a riddle and becomes king but who eventually falls from his throne because of two unspeakable crimes. Unknowingly, he has killed his father and made love to his mother. When he realizes the truth, he blinds himself and leaves the kingdom, only to appear again in later dramas as a wise and generative sage. It is difficult to blame Oedipus for his fate, for he never knew the truth until it was too late. His only sin seems to have been an inflated sense of his own power, an egocentrism that places him, for a short time, in the center of an orbiting galaxy of admirers. Banished to the periphery in the end, he becomes just another planet like everybody else. Yet there is dignity in the defeat of Oedipus, and the attainment of a worldly wisdom that is deeper and more caring than the brilliance of his youth.

Between the ages of about four and six, Freud said, the child unconsciously lives a tragic drama that closely parallels the Oedipus myth. Unwittingly and unknowingly, on an unconscious stage where actors play but no audience is there to see them, little boys and girls become kings and queens. In their consummate egocentrism, they seek to love and to possess all that they desire and to kill what stands in their way. The drama is projected onto family life. Mothers and fathers, friends and relatives are incorporated into the tragedy, fleshing out the plot and characters involved and lending an interpersonal significance to what is essentially a private battle in the mind. With the eventual resolution of the Oedipus complex, the child attains a kind of maturity that parallels the worldly wisdom given to the ancient king.

In a vague, unspeakable, and mysterious way, claimed Freud, young boys seek to possess—to conquer in a powerful and erotic manner—a primal feminine love object that exists in their fantasies and may correspond in reality to their mothers or to other women in their lives. Equally vague and unspeakable is an unconsciously perceived threat—that from a powerful masculine force that stands in the way of the boy's conquests.

This internal enemy, which may be projected onto the young boy's actual father, threatens to castrate the boy. What Freud termed "castration anxiety" literally means the fear that one's penis will be cut off, but more profoundly it symbolizes the child's fear that he will, like Oedipus, lose his power (and his love object as well). Thus, the boy harbors an unconscious wish to kill the father, as Freud indeed discovered in the analysis of his own unconscious life.

The normal resolution of the Oedipus complex follows the ancient myth. The young boy eventually comes to identify with the aggressor of his fantasies. He cannot *have* mother, so instead he seeks to *be* like father (and thereby have mother in a vicarious way). The unconscious shift from having to being marks a major defeat for the boy. Like Oedipus, he can no longer have his kingdom. On an unconscious level, the young boy at the close of the Oedipal period understands that he is weaker, smaller, and more mortal than he (unconsciously) ever imagined. The loss of power is a kind of castration, symbolized in the Greek myth when Oedipus blinds himself. Omnipotence is replaced by a definite but painful sense of limitations. Yet, from the standpoint of healthy personality development, the Oedipal defeat is ultimately a good thing. Like the blind Oedipus who knows the truth, the young boy who suffers the Oedipal defeat eventually attains the rudiments of a *moral attitude* about life. Identification with the father (and to a lesser extent with the mother) at the end of the Oedipus complex leaves the boy with what Freud called a superego, which forever more serves as an internalized moral vanguard, a private censor that works to keep sexual and aggressive impulses in check.

But what about the girl? Freud attempted to adapt his Oedipal theorizing to the unconscious lives of girls and women, but even he was forced to admit that his efforts were far from satisfactory. According to his view, the young girl's unconscious dilemma begins with a positive attraction to the mother. But the fantasized mother figure disappoints the girl when she realizes that both she and the mother lack a penis, which symbolizes a lack of power. The little girl may blame the mother for the perceived deficiency, resulting in what Freud called "penis envy"—a jealous craving for power. As a result, the girl shifts some of her unconscious affections to a "stronger" father figure. For reasons that are not altogether clear, the girl eventually resolves the Oedipus complex by repressing her second attraction to the father and completing an identification with the mother. She, therefore, ends up seeking *to be* like mother in order *to have* father.

The great unconscious lesson of the Oedipus complex is that we cannot be kings and queens. The human need to be the center of the universe—what philosophers like Nietzsche and Sartre have viewed as the need to be God—is so great that it takes an unconscious Armageddon like the Oedipus complex to convince us of our mortality, if not our impotence. With the resolution of the Oedipus complex, unmitigated egocentrism receives a crushing blow.

Developmental psychologists who study how children think and consciously understand their worlds have documented a parallel decrease in egocentrism in thought between the ages of about five and seven, roughly corresponding to the period within which Freud believed the Oedipus complex to be resolved. It is during this time, argued the eminent Swiss developmentalist Jean Piaget, that children make the transition from the magical and intuitive thought of the preschool years to a more systematic and logical form of thinking, what Piaget called "concrete operations." Before the advent of concrete operations, young children reason about the world in a highly egocentric manner. Asked why the grass is green, a four-year-old may answer "because green is my favorite color." The young child finds it very difficult to view reality from perspectives other than his or her own. Adopting an objective and rational approach to a problem requires that a person take the self out of the center of that which is to be understood. Young children find this to be an extremely arduous, if not impossible, chore; their cognitive self-centeredness prevents them from adopting an objective third-person perspective. Cognitively speaking, they are too much at the center of things. Until they attain the "distance" of the banished Oedipus, they will not be able to understand how the world really works.

Therefore, whether you prefer to interpret the shift in terms of the resolution of an unconscious Oedipus complex or in terms of the emergence of a new stage in conscious cognitive thinking, egocentrism in children appears to decline markedly between the late preschool years and second or third grade. Developmental psychologist Robert Selman has documented the shift in the realm of children's friendships.[26] Selman's intensive interviews of children suggest that to a three- or four-year-old a friend is a "momentary physical playmate." At this time, children cannot conceive of friendship as something independent of specific activities. My three-year-old daughter, Ruth, is good friends with four-year-old William because the two of them, in her words, "tell good kid secrets" together. As they giggle and scream during the ride to preschool, Ruth and William whisper "kid secrets" in each other's ears—fantastical plans about how they will poison the Wicked Queen and rescue Snow White, how Ruth and the Seven Dwarfs will find diamonds in the mines, how William will soar around the world in his flying car. Somewhat later on, suggests Selman, children begin to view friendship in terms of "one-way assistance." For a five-year-old, a friend is somebody who does things that are pleasing and helpful. Friends must become aware of each other's likes and dislikes and respond accordingly. Nonetheless, there is still no awareness of the reciprocal nature of friendship: friendship is still based on that egocentric notion of "what's in it for me."

With the advent of concrete operational thinking in later childhood, children come to understand friendship in more mutual and less egocentric ways. About the age of six or seven they begin to view friendships in terms of "fairweather cooperation." Friendship is now a two-way street, and each friend must adapt to the needs and perspectives of the other. At about nine or ten, argues Selman, friendships come to be seen in terms of "intimate and mutual sharing." Children commit themselves to the common interests of the friendship itself, realizing that such interests may go beyond their own personal, egocentric concerns. A good friend is someone who is loyal and genuine, who will stick with the relationship over the long haul, even when fair weather turns to storms.

But triangles remain a problem. Selman writes that throughout childhood and into adolescence friendships are often viewed as exclusive and possessive relationships. The loyal best friends in fourth grade do not eagerly welcome a third party into their intimate nexus. When a best friend takes on a second friendship, the first one may be seriously jeopardized. Jealousy and betrayal among friends can be as common as it is among lovers later on. In late adolescence and adulthood, Selman argues, people finally come to understand friendships in terms of "autonomous interdependence." We are likely to understand now that a particular friend cannot fulfill all of our emotional needs, and we cannot hope to fulfill all of his or her needs either. Friendships become more inclusive and fluid. Friends grant each other more autonomy, realizing that each person functions in a somewhat different system of interdependent relationships.

We generally do not reach a stage like this, however, with our romantic love affairs. As we saw in Chapter 2, eros is by nature a jealous god. Love triangles smack of infidelity, not "autonomous interdependence." Psychoanalyst Ethel Person suggests that the Oedipal complex is reactivated in our romantic relationships of adolescence and adulthood. We appear to be naturally inclined to recognize the exclusive pairing of two lovers in the context of a third, rival lover, an ever-present outside force who may influence the pair in a wide variety of ways. This tendency to apprehend triangularity in love relations is more common in men than in women, suggests Person, but can be observed frequently in both sexes. She writes:

Romantic love has been described as a religion of two, but love pairs can be infected by triangles and may even be wholly contaminated by them. Or, more positively, triangles may sometimes help love along: Some pairings first crystallize in the context of a triangle. Others, especially those of older, more established couples, may be reenergized by a triangle. And, as we know, many of the most celebrated lovers were adulterous: Tristan and

Iseult, Lancelot and Guinevere, Paolo and Francesca. Moreover, some triangles are not mere way stations into or out of love, nor are they intended to protect against intimacy or revive intensity, but they are themselves the main event: the lover is fixated on triangles and can achieve some of the gratification of love only within a triangular configuration.[27]

We first encounter the triangular nature of interpersonal relationships as young children, sowing the wild oats of egocentrism, if only in unconscious fantasy. Even though egocentrism wanes and we begin to approach the interpersonal world in a more objective and realistic manner as we grow older, the problem of triangularity does not go away. As Ethel Person suggests, love triangles are an ancient obsession, and each of us is likely to grapple at one time or another with the complications that third parties bring to romantic love. When it comes to the sharing of one's innermost self with another—be the other a lover or a friend—triangularity persists as a complicated and complicating factor. The intimacy we experience with one person is colored by the intimacy we feel with another. We first apprehend this fact in childhood. But exactly what this influence is and how it is likely to play itself out in our various relationships are questions that each of us struggles with throughout our lives.

The Chumship

As we saw at the beginning of this chapter, Sullivan believed that the need for interpersonal intimacy does not emerge as an important force in the human life cycle until a child is about nine or ten years of age, during the period he termed "preadolescence." From a Freudian perspective, therefore, Sullivan suggests that the intimacy of the chumship must await resolution of the Oedipus complex. From a cognitive point of view, he suggests that the child must reach concrete operational thinking before he or she can know the experience of the I–Thou. From the perspective of Selman's work on friendship, the person cannot experience intimacy until his or her conception of a friend matures beyond the stage of "one-way assistance." Intimacy requires a loss of egocentrism, for the Thou cannot "fill the firmament," as Buber puts it, if the I is always at the center.

The preadolescent clearly understands that he or she is not the center of the universe. The preadolescent knows that other people have other points of view, that they see themselves and their worlds in their own terms, terms that are foreign to one's own. As a result, one striking fact finally hits home: everybody is different; nobody is like me; *I am alone.* Sullivan argued that the need for interpersonal intimacy emerges in the context of a devastating loneliness that we first experience in preadolescence. In part, the loneliness stems from the loss of egocentrism. The child now craves the warmth and closeness of friendships to ward off that post-Oedipal sense of being a lone and cold planet in a distant galaxy. The most satisfying friendship is the exclusive, collaborative, and syntactic chumship.

In the chumship of preadolescence, two friends devote themselves to each other, as interested in the well-being of each other as they are in their own, Sullivan claimed. Chums are almost always of the same sex during these years, partly, Sullivan maintained, because of the preadolescent's concern that he or she find somebody who is as much like him or her as possible. As a ten-year-old, I know that I am alone in the world and that nobody is exactly like me. So I strive to find somebody who is as much like me as possible, to soften the sharp reality of aloneness. If I am a boy, then I want a boy for a chum. Beyond that, the boy should like to do what I like to do, should like the same kinds of people that I like, should have the same kinds of fears and hopes that I have, and so on. In my relentless quest to affirm my sameness with another, I will exaggerate the extent to which my chum and I are alike. If I am a star shortstop on my little league team, I may play up my chum's rather meager skills in catching, throwing, and hitting a baseball. If I am a Christian who attends Sunday school every week, I may try to convert

151

him to my beliefs, or at least drag him along on Sunday mornings. If his favorite food is hamburgers, I may start spending my allowance at McDonald's.

The chumship draws me out of old habits and defensive strategies that used to keep me secure, loosening the strings of what Sullivan called the self-system. In the intimacy of the chumship, I take big risks. I dare to be like another. I dare to find myself in another and to let another find himself in me. Long ago I learned that I cannot have it all. Since then I have sought to be like others. And now in the chumship somebody else seeks to be like me, too. We seek to be like each other, to create a shared reality that defines the two of us. The chumship is a soothing balm for the battle scars of the Oedipal fiasco. Dethroned and banished to a distant shore, I now inch back to the center. But it is a different sort of center. It is a meeting place where I and a single other person—someone who has also been banished—come together and, as Forster put it, "only connect."

Sullivan's description of the chumship is an ideal, and it is not clear how many of us actually experience this kind of intensive relationship when we are nine or ten years of age. In a thorough review of the scientific literature on friendships in late childhood and early adolescence, developmental psychologist Thomas Berndt concludes that "the intimacy of friendships increases dramatically between middle childhood and early adolescence."[28] He goes on, however, to discuss significant individual differences among children during this time in the patterns of their friendships. For example, girls seem to have somewhat more intimate and exclusive friendships in preadolescence than do boys, a sex difference to which we will return in Chapter 6. Furthermore, preadolescence may be a time when significant individual differences appear in children's overall desire to engage in warm and close relations with their peers. If Sullivan's perspective on intimacy is correct, then we would expect that individual differences in the strength of intimacy motivation should begin to appear in children at this time and that such differences should be meaningfully related to differences in friendship patterns.

Michael Losoff, my wife, and I examined such individual differences among students attending a private elementary school in St. Paul, Minnesota.[29] We studied children in the fourth and sixth grades, ranging in age from about nine to twelve. At the beginning of the school year, my wife interviewed each of the girls and I interviewed each of the boys, asking various questions about their friendships. We also administered an imaginative storytelling exercise similar to the TAT. The following spring, we returned to the classrooms and reinterviewed all of the children. We also obtained teacher ratings and intelligence test scores from the school.

Imaginative stories that children tell in response to pictures are much less sophisticated than those told by adults. In order to assess individual differences in intimacy motivation among the children, therefore, we modified the standard scoring system for the intimacy motive to make it more appropriate for these simpler stories. We analyzed them in terms of four thematic categories bearing on the quality of the relationships manifested by the characters in the story:

1. relationship produces happiness or good feelings;

2. relationship leads to friendship or romantic love;

3. characters talk to each other in a mutual way; and

4. characters help each other.

Therefore, stories that scored high on intimacy motivation included themes of happy relationships, friendship and love, mutual talking, and cooperative helping. The children's stories showed marked individual differences in this regard, ranging from some children who scored very high on intimacy motivation to some others who scored extremely low.

The results of the study showed that fourth graders did not differ significantly from sixth graders on overall levels of intimacy motivation. Girls, however, scored slightly higher on the average than boys. Intimacy motivation was not significantly related to intelligence test scores, and we found no evidence to suggest that high intimacy motivation was either positively or negatively associated with academic performance. Teacher ratings, though, were strongly related to intimacy motivation scores. Those children who scored high on intimacy motivation, based on their imaginative stories, were evaluated by their teachers as significantly more "friendly," "happy," "affectionate," "cooperative," "sincere," and "popular" than children scoring low on intimacy motivation. In the teachers' eyes, at least, children whose imaginative stories indicate a strong concern for warm and close relationships tend to behave in warmer and more loving ways in the classroom.

In both the autumn and the spring interviews, we asked each child to identify his or her "best friend" in class and to describe that friend in detail. We also asked each child if there was anybody in class whom he or she did not like very much. Contrary to what we expected, we did not find that children high in intimacy motivation were nominated more often by their peers as a best friend. But we did find that they were rarely nominated as a disliked person.

In the spring interview, we asked each child to answer ten factual questions about his or her best friend, such as "What is your best friend's favorite TV show?" and "What are the names of your best friend's sisters and brothers?" We found that children who were high in intimacy motivation were able to report many more facts about their best friends. Not only did these children know more about their friends, but furthermore, they tended to remain close to the same best friends for a longer period of time. Comparing the autumn and spring interviews, we found that children high in intimacy motivation tended to identify the same best friend on both occasions, while those scoring low in intimacy motivation tended to shift from one best friend to another over the course of the school year.

A final analysis examined the relation between intimacy motivation and the *depth* of a child's best friendship. We conceived of deeper friendships as those approximating Sullivan's description of the collaborative chumship and Selman's description of higher and more reciprocal stages of friendship. We concentrated on the children's responses to the questions "Why is this person your best friend?" and "What does it mean to say that the two of you are best friends?" We found that children who scored high on intimacy motivation tended to describe their best friends in terms closely paralleling Sullivan's description of the chumship and Selman's higher stages. For these children, a best friend was someone with whom they could talk and share things, someone who would listen and be there during times of need, someone who was loyal and true. Children high in intimacy motivation emphasized that best friends must make a commitment to each other: "We never lie to each other"; "You have to trust your friends like they trust you"; "You have to be loyal to each other." Children low on intimacy motivation, by contrast, tended to describe their friendships in physical-behavioral terms or as examples of what Selman terms "one-way assistance." When asked why a person was their "best friend," these children respond in ways like these: "She's the prettiest girl in the class"; "She and I play Barbie dolls"; "He helps me with my homework"; "She sticks up for me when the teacher gets mad."

In summary, preadolescent children appear to differ markedly in the manner in which they engage others as friends and conceive of friendship. Those children who seem to have developed close friendships approximating Sullivan's description of the ideal preadolescent chumship score higher on intimacy motivation, based on a storytelling exercise, than those children whose friendships seem more primitive and superficial. In addition, preadolescent children high in intimacy motivation report greater stability in their best friendships and more personal knowledge about their best friends. Although children high in intimacy motivation may not have a greater number of friendships than those scoring lower, they are rarely disliked strongly by their classmates. Finally, their teachers report that children high in intimacy motivation behave in consistently warm and friendly ways in the classroom.

Intimacy and Identity

In Sullivan's story of human development, lust seems to wipe out the chumship at the beginning of Act Three. What follows is a depressing denouement in which the protagonist continually seeks but rarely finds a grand reconciliation with lust, loneliness, and primitive anxiety. Sullivan seems to be saying that if it were not for sexuality, the glowing intimacy of preadolescence might sustain us for the rest of our days. But sexuality is not the only "villain," and as the famous psychoanalyst Erik Erikson has pointed out, it may not even be the primary one. The bigger problem is *identity*.[30] In late adolescence and young adulthood, we seek to discover who we are. We seek to define ourselves in such a way that we experience what Erikson terms a sense of inner "sameness" and "continuity." This is not the kind of "sameness," however, that we feel with the chum at age ten. The ten-year-old does not care about identity; indeed, he or she generally cannot even understand what identity is. Similarly, the intimate chumship is generally not structured in such a way as to address the identity of the chums. When it comes to identity, chumships do not do a whole lot of good.

I am not saying that friendship is irrelevant in the development of identity in adolescence and adulthood. Neither am I saying that the need for interpersonal intimacy—the intimacy motive itself—plays only a tiny role in helping us figure out who we are. Sullivan's model of the chumship works well when it comes to the human problem of loneliness, first encountered in preadolescence. Chums find themselves in each other, affirming that they are as much like each other as they can be, that they are no longer alone but together, connected and defined by the connection. But the problem of identity urges us to separate ourselves from others, in many different ways, so that we can ultimately reconnect as beings who are fundamentally both the same and different. If we find it difficult, therefore, to carry the chumship with us into adolescence and young adulthood, it is not primarily because our sexual needs demand atten-

tion, though of course they do. It is instead because the chumship cannot tell us who we are.

How do we discover who we are? We do it by consciously
and unconsciously crafting a self-defining "life story," a mythological narrative of the self that provides our life with a sense of
inner sameness and continuity.[31] In late adolescence and young
adulthood, we first confront the problem of multiple selves. We
notice for the first time in our lives that we seem to be one
person in one situation and another person in another, one person yesterday and another one today. What is the essential "me"
that I carry along in my various daily travels—as I walk
through the supermarket, study for an examination, talk to my
mother, dance at a party, raise my hand in a lecture, make love
to another, when I am with others and when I am completely
alone? And what was the essential "me" last year? What will it
be next year? How am I different than and the same as I was
when I was six years old? How will I be different and the same
when I am sixty? In late adolescence and young adulthood, we
primarily seek to discover how we are the same person from
one situation to the next—not necessarily how we are the same
as other people. And we seek to discover threads of continuity
linking our personal past, present, and expected future. We seek
sameness and continuity of the self, and we find it through a
long and creative process of discovering and making a story for
ourselves, a story by which and through which we live.

In order to discover the self through story, we must see our
lives in historical and biographical terms. The ten-year-old has
virtually no sense of history or biography. In his mind, the past
is a series of things that happened, a chronicle of discrete
events; the future is the things that will happen. History and
biography are issues of *facts*. Beginning in late adolescence,
however, we become curious about the meaning of facts while
questioning the validity of facts themselves. We look for the
meaning in the past and the future; we demand that history
make sense, that it show a certain kind of narrative continuity.
People's lives, too, should make sense. Events do not follow
events in random sequence. Rather, we discern cause-and-effect
relationships in people's lives, and we look for narrative coher-

157

ence. "I am this way now *because* of what happened to me then." "I will be like this when I am sixty *because* I was like that when I was six." "If I do this now, I will live happily ever after."

Biological, cognitive, and social changes during the teenage years transform us from the concrete ten-year-old to the self-making and story-seeking adult. The biological changes of puberty jolt us into the realization that we are no longer kids. Our bodies tell us that we are now truly different from what we used to be. In that I am now different, what was I before? And what am I now? The growth of facial hair, the enlargement of the testes and penis, the emergence of breasts and pubic hair, the changing body contours, the adolescent growth spurt, the new and overt sexual longings—all of these changes and more suggest a turning point in the way the adolescent sees him- or herself. Childhood becomes a bygone era, a matter of personal history.

With respect to cognitive development, the adolescent attains the last stage of thinking in Piaget's scheme, called "formal operations."[32] According to Piaget, we are generally not able to reason in highly abstract terms until adolescence. The ten-year-old, embedded in concrete operations, understands the world in very literal, concrete ways. The ten-year-old is great with facts, but meanings prove elusive. In formal operations, however, we can reason about the concrete world of what is and the abstract, hypothetical world of what might be. For the first time, we are able to reason about our own lives in terms of hypotheticals. What might have happened if I had been born rich instead of poor? How might I be different if my parents had not divorced? What might happen if I change my college major? Change my religion? What might the perfect religion be? How might I lead a perfect life? With the power of formal operations, we can question the past, the present, and the future. We can imagine viable alternative realities, different meanings for different sets of biographical facts. Through such questioning we are likely to separate ourselves from our own pasts and, to a certain extent, from other people. Alas, the chumship cannot directly address our abstract and personal concerns. We finally come to understand something that Buber suggests is at the heart of mature intimacy: that the I does not define itself in the Thou.

Social changes also play a major role in ushering in the developmental issue of identity. Society expects us to begin putting our own stories together in late adolescence and young adulthood. Compulsory schooling ends at age sixteen. Parents, teachers, counselors, and friends urge us to think about what we are going to do as adults, whether we are going to continue our education, what occupation we wish to pursue, who we will marry, and so on. We address the identity questions of "Who am I?" and "How do I fit into the adult world?" in a complex interpersonal environment. Society helps us write our own story by providing occupational and ideological resources, presenting us with choices about what we should do and what we should believe, issuing standard scripts for identity from which we may draw. Ideally, our social world should encourage us to explore a wide variety of occupational, ideological, and interpersonal possibilities before we finally commit ourselves to a self-defining life story. Erikson describes the ideal arrangement for identity formation, an exploring individual acting within an affirming society:

> The period can be viewed as a psychosocial moratorium during which the individual through free role experimentation may find a niche in some section of his society, a niche which is firmly defined and yet seems to be uniquely made for him. In finding it the young adult gains an assured sense of inner continuity and social sameness which will bridge what he was as a child and what he is about to become, and will reconcile his conception of himself and his community's recognition of him.[33]

Identity and intimacy enhance each other in the adult years. A person with a coherent sense of who he or she is—a well-articulated life story that guides his or her action—is often better able to open up and share that which is innermost with another, compared to a person whose identity is more diffuse or confused. If I know who I am, I do not search desperately for myself in the other. I can confront the other as a separate Thou with whom I long to connect. A person who is more open and intimate with others, furthermore, may find that intimacy reaps rewards in the search for identity. Although others can never ultimately tell us exactly who we are—they cannot write our stories for us—they can assist us in our questioning and in our formulations. They can even travel with us on our identity quest, as supportive compatriots in the search for meaning and truth. A small but growing body of scientific research supports the mutually enhancing relationship of identity and intimacy.[34] Adults who have established a firm sense of self tend to report richer and more supportive networks of intimate relationships, assessed as relatively stable and happy marriages and deep, satisfying friendships.

Generative Gifts

In our adult years, we seek intimacy in many different kinds of relationships. In a great variety of ways and to substantially varying degrees, we share our innermost selves with lovers, friends, family members, acquaintances, and other people in our lives with whom we relate, if for only fleeting moments, as I and Thou. Intimacy can enrich our lives on many different levels, and intimate relationships may serve as the greatest sources of satisfaction and happiness in our lives. Furthermore, the intimacy motive may express itself in a number of ways, in what we do and how we think about what we do. People who have a high level of intimacy motivation fashion life stories that center on interpersonal relationships, emphasizing themes of communion and care. As we have seen in the cases of Sara, Dean, Richard, and Sandy in previous chapters of this book, adults who are high in intimacy motivation may understand their own lives as tales of love and friendship, caring and peace-making. The personal answers that they give in response to the questions "Who am I?" and "How do I fit into the adult world?"

are couched in the language of intimacy. In these lives, identity is steeped in intimacy; the adult self is articulated through intimate relations.

One of the greatest challenges of adulthood, writes Erik Erikson, is *generativity*. Generativity is the concern for guiding and promoting the next generation through such creative behaviors as parenting, teaching, leading, and making and doing things that benefit a community as a whole. Once we have established an identity and committed ourselves to long-term intimate relationships such as marriage, writes Erikson, we are ready to commit ourselves to the larger sphere of society as a whole and to its continuation, even improvement, through the next generation. In generativity, we nurture, support, guide, teach, lead, and promote the next *generation* while simultaneously *generating* life products and producing outcomes that aim to benefit the social system and promote its continuity from one generation to the next. Generativity draws on our desire to be close to others, to share that which is innermost. But it also draws on our desire to feel strong vis-à-vis others, our agentic need to assert and expand ourselves in forceful, powerful ways. Generativity entails, therefore, a highly creative integration of intimacy and power motivation.

The prototype for generativity is bearing and raising children. As parents, we assume the responsibility of directly nurturing and supporting the next generation, as personified in our very own daughters and sons. In so doing, Erikson suggests, we act on a basic human instinct that reaches maturity in the adult years—the need to be needed by others. Erikson suggests that in mature adulthood we are dependent on the presence of other persons and things that are dependent on us. We need to be in the presence of beings and entities that need us. We generate children who need us to survive, fulfilling our own reciprocal need to be needed. An essential component of generativity is the realization that other people and things are worthy of our care and that our care is worthy of them. In the best scenario for generativity, we see our children as eminently worthy of our own care, and we strive to make our care worthy of them.

In this case, we act on faith—we implicitly behave according to what Erikson calls a "belief in the species," an assumption that our children in particular, and the next generation in general, are ultimately worth generating, promoting, nurturing, guiding, supporting, helping, teaching, loving, and even saving.

But raising children is not the only way in which adults can be generative.[35] Generativity may be expressed in the realms of work, service, and even play. Writing a book, playing the piano, teaching a class, contributing to charity, building a business, giving a piece of advice—these activities and many others with which we are involved as adults may be expressions of generativity. What determines the extent to which they are generative is largely our attitude about them.

The attitude of generativity is a curious blend of narcissism and nurturance, self-expansion and self-surrender. In generativity, we generate, produce, or create someone (for example, a child) or something (for example, a piece of art) of lasting significance, a legacy of the self that lives on. The legacy is created in our own image. The child we bear, the reputation we build, and the piece of advice we offer are more or less extensions of ourselves. As much as our arms and our legs, these things we make are who we are, for in the making, we make ourselves. But if these creations are to be expressions of generativity, we must do more than simply create. We must also give them up, in a caring and loving manner. Ultimately, we grant our children autonomy to live their own lives. The business we build must be passed down to others. The advice we formulate must be offered in the spirit of selfless giving. The generative attitude is the attitude of *creating and then presenting a gift.* Without this attitude, adult life degenerates into hopeless narcissism or stagnation.

In generativity, the creation of a product requires that we powerfully expand the self, while giving the creation up requires that we intimately share that which we have created—a part of the self, an expression of what is innermost—with others. In generativity, the I creates a Thou, taking care to grant the Thou all the autonomy and freedom it is due. Our creations are narcissistic, however, when we fail to grant them autonomy, when we regard them as achievements rather than gifts. Generativity, therefore, challenges us to be both powerful and intimate, expansive and surrendering at the same time. In motivational terms, generativity draws on our desire to be strong and our desire to be close to others, mandating that we integrate and reconcile power and intimacy motivation.

Jeanne Foley, Karin Ruetzel, and I examined the relation between power and intimacy motivation on the one hand and generativity on the other in a study of fifty men and women in their late thirties and forties.[36] All of the adults wrote TAT stories that were later scored for intimacy and power motivation. In our life-story interview, we asked the adults to describe in detail their hopes and dreams for the future. We analyzed the responses for the degree to which the adults expressed concerns about and commitments to generativity. The highest generativity scores were given to those adults who saw themselves making lasting contributions to particular other people or to society at large, through their work, family life, friendships, leisure activities, or any other realms in which generativity might be expressed. The lowest scores were given to adults whose future goals centered exclusively on their own well-being, suggesting that they did not see themselves as making important contributions in the future to the continuity of human generations.

The results of our study showed that those men and women who scored relatively high on both power and intimacy motivation expressed the strongest commitments to generativity in the future. Those adults who were low on both power and intimacy motivation were the least concerned with generativity. The findings of the study support the idea that generativity, like the phenomenon of peacemaking that we discussed in Chapter 3, challenges us to be both powerful and intimate in our daily lives. Adults who seek both to have impact on others and to engage others in warm and communicative ways seem best able to meet the complex challenge of adult generativity.

As far as generativity in adulthood is concerned, therefore, power motivation is expressed in the agentic creation of a product that lives on, a legacy of the self as humble as making up a story to tell one's grandson or taking the neighborhood kids to the zoo, as momentous as a scientific discovery, a masterpiece of art, a tenure as President. The intimacy motive is expressed in the communal giving of the product, the offering, the sharing. Our generative gifts are expressions of our innermost being. They are parts of ourselves that we ultimately surrender to the world at large, pieces of the self to be shared with others. Ideally, our children, our advice, our artistic endeavors, our legacies live on in some way, surviving us as expressions of our own power and intimacy, gifts of the self that ultimately generate gifts of their own.

CHAPTER 6

Intimate Women, Intimate Men

The images of hierarchy and web, drawn from the texts of men's and women's fantasies and thoughts, convey different ways of structuring relationships and are associated with different views of morality and the self. But these images create a problem in understanding because each distorts the other's representation. As the top of the hierarchy becomes the edge of the web and as the center of a network of connection becomes the middle of a hierarchical progression, each image marks as dangerous the place which the other defines as safe. Thus the images of hierarchy and web inform different modes of assertion and response: the wish to be alone at the top and the consequent fear that others will get too close; the wish to be at the center of connection and the consequent fear of being too far out on the edge. These disparate fears of being stranded and being caught give rise to different portrayals of achievement and affiliation, leading to different modes of action and different ways of assessing the consequences of choice.

—Carol Gilligan, *In a Different Voice*

While men build towers, women spin webs.

The proud bearer of the phallus, *he* seeks to create a world that soars straight and powerful into the sky. He strives to reach the top of that world, to attain the pinnacle of the hierarchy, to relate to the other from above as he gazes down on the layers below. But he cannot be heard from the lofty perch, and he cannot hear what happens below. There is no Thou with whom to share at the top, except God, and he (or is it *she?*) proves forever inscrutable. In Genesis, men tried to reach heaven by building a great Tower of Babel. But they ultimately failed because they could not communicate with each other. In punishment for their temerity, God tangled their native tongues, and their words became meaningless in the ears of their neighbors.

Her womb is her essence; *she* bears children, and they cleave to her for a time, for a long time in fact, a very long time while he watches, perplexed, maybe charmed, maybe envious, but al-

165

ways from afar, even when he is right next to her. She is by nature connected, it seems, and even when he penetrates her with his body, inside her, warm and surrounded, he cannot become part of that connectedness. He must always withdraw. She is part of a *web*; she seeks to make a world of webs, and she is made by it. Of course, she may get lost in the web; she may become so much a part of the web that you cannot find her, while you can always find him. He is in the hierarchy, if not at the very top, on top of something and underneath something else. He stands out; she may fade away. But she is always connected.

E. M. Forster implores us: "Only connect!" But is it only women who can connect? Are men so transfixed by the vertical power of hierarchy that they cannot be caught within the intimate webs of relationship? Psychologist Carol Gilligan suggests that men view the world as hierarchy and women see it as web. Each sex fears the other's vision. Men fear being trapped in webs; women fear being isolated in hierarchies. Our stereotyped images of the "typical" man and woman in contemporary Western society fit Gilligan's characterization. We tend to see men as relatively strong, assertive, aggressive, and analytical. We see women as gentle, compassionate, submissive, and contextual. In the terms of David Bakan, men are agentic; women are communal. Bakan writes, "agency manifests itself in isolation, alienation, and aloneness; communion in contact, openness, and union."[1]

As the women's movement reached a crescendo in the late 1960s and 1970s, Americans seemed to be growing more and more comfortable with the idea that sex-role stereotypes were social myths that should ultimately be transcended. Women could be powerful, too, and men should cultivate their sensitivity and gentleness. Each man or woman should learn to be psychologically androgynous, behaving in both highly agentic and highly communal ways, deftly alternating between strength and gentleness as the demands of situations change. As women were to exercise their newfound agency in the workplace, men were to explore the possibilities of communion in family life. As we close out the 1980s, it does seem that middle-class American men and women under the age of about forty-five have moved appreciably toward a more androgynous vision of what it means to be a mature man or woman, though it is difficult to measure this precisely. Women have made significant inroads into many traditionally masculine professions, proving that they can flourish in agentic settings from which they have been excluded in years past. And there is a lot of talk about the "new man," who is more open to the possibilities of communion and less willing to sacrifice family and friendships on the altar of "success" in the world of works.

Amid the realities and the rhetoric, however, a countervoice can be heard, both in the popular press and among psychologists and other social scientists who study this sort of thing. The countervoice suggests that, especially when it comes to intimate interpersonal relationships, sex differences may be more deeply ingrained than we initially thought. And in light of our rising middle-class expectations that men and women should behave in more flexible and androgynous ways than we think they have in the past, these nagging differences may be more troubling today than they used to be. The trouble may be greatest in love relations between men and women. In her most recent and widely hailed report on the state of love and sex in men and women, Shere Hite claims that an overwhelming majority of American women are extremely dissatisfied with their male husbands and lovers. Although their complaints run the gamut, the most significant cry among American women, according to Hite, is that men do not know how to be intimate.[2]

The same conclusion is hammered home in *The McGill Report on Male Intimacy,* published in 1985.[3] Analyzing questionnaire responses from more than thirteen hundred American men and women, McGill concludes that men approach virtually all meaningful human relationships in extraordinarily nonintimate ways. Men are generally unable to share private thoughts and feelings with their wives and lovers. Instead, they gauge the quality of intimacy in their love lives by the quality of sex. When it comes to "being there" for children, many so-called "family men" are, in McGill's words, "phantom men": they just are not there. Even when physically present, they are emotionally miles away.

McGill's most telling observations, however, may come from the realm of friendships. Friendships between women seem to grow and deepen over time as women come to share more of themselves with each other. Writes McGill, "the intimacy that comes from knowing a great deal about another person, from sharing all aspects of each other in the relationship, is an important source of closeness for women."[4] Women disclose much more of themselves with many of their female friends than do men with their very best buddies. It is not uncommon, concludes McGill, for a woman to remark of her best friend, "She knows everything there is to know about me" or "She knows me better than I know myself." Men rarely speak of their friendships in this way. Male friendships rarely grow beyond common interests, and conversations between men who are close friends are dominated by the topics of sports, business, politics, sex, and tales of "the good old days." Consider, for example, Tom Davidson, manager of a local hamburger joint called "Tommy's." Tom has been taking his morning coffee at another local diner for as long as he can remember:

> My first day at Tommy's, my boss brought me down here to Bill's for coffee. That was seventeen years ago, and I've been coming for coffee every morning ever since. Most everybody else has, too. Shit, outside of my family, I'm closer to these guys than to anybody else I know. Nowadays I'm closer to these guys than I am to my family! We've been through it all down here. The town has grown up and fallen down around us, the Rams have come and gone, the country's been to war and back, we even had one of the guys die. We've seen it all to where it seems like there ain't nothing new—same guys, same stories, same shitty coffee. Still, I wouldn't trade these guys for anything. When I retire, I'll still be coming down here for coffee. Where else are you going to find friends like these?
>
> Funny thing is, away from Bill's, I hardly know these

168

guys at all. I know what they do for a living, of course, but that's about it. I couldn't tell you where more than two or three of them live. I don't know their wives or their kids or even if they have any. It's like we're really close here at Bill's, but when we're not here, we're just *not*. I'll tell you, one time I saw Charlie, the banker, at a wedding. I had to go right up to him before he knew who I was. He said he didn't recognize me without my apron and away from Bill's. It was kind of awkward. We couldn't very well talk to each other the way we do at Bill's, where he's "Charlie the Cock," since he got divorced, and they call me "Burger Butt." Without all the other guys there, we didn't have much to say to each other, and yet we've been getting together every morning forever. I guess you can know somebody really well one place and then you put them someplace else and it's just not the same. When you look at it that way, I guess if it weren't for coffee at Bill's, I might not have any friends at all.[5]

Are Women More Intimate Than Men?

In the early and mid 1970s, it was fashionable among empirical psychologists to believe that men and women are really not very different from each other. In 1974, psychologists Eleanor Maccoby and Carol Jacklin published an exhaustive synthesis of the research literature on sex differences in human behavior, which exploded many of the so-called "myths" of gender. One of these myths was that girls (and women) are more "social" than boys (and men). Reviewing many different scientific studies from the sixties and seventies, Maccoby and Jacklin concluded that (1) the two sexes are equally interested in "social stimuli," (2) girls are no more "dependent" on others than are boys, (3) girls do not spend more time with their playmates than do boys, and (4) the two sexes appear to be equally "empathic,"

169

in the sense of understanding the emotional reactions of others. In conclusion, they wrote:

> Any differences that exist in the "sociability" of the two sexes are more of kind than of degree. Boys are highly oriented toward a peer group and congregate in larger groups; girls associate in pairs or small groups of age-mates, and may be somewhat more oriented toward adults, although the evidence for this is weak.[6]

But the difference in "kind" to which Maccoby and Jacklin point may be much more important than differences in "degree," when it comes to intimacy. From an early age onward, boys play and talk together in large groups while girls prefer to interact with each other one-on-one or in smaller groupings.[7] It is generally in one-on-one interaction that people experience the I–Thou of intimacy. Boys may be missing out on this experience by virtue of their early preference for the large group. In their intensive relations with their young peers, girls may develop skills and motives that prepare them well for spinning webs of intimacy when they grow older. Boys may have fewer opportunities to learn the art of web-making, or even to develop a taste or preference for webs.

In our study of fourth- and sixth-graders described in Chapter 5, we found that young girls scored higher in intimacy motivation, assessed through imaginative stories, than did young boys. In addition, girls knew more about their best friends than did boys, reporting more factual information about their best friends. Beyond differences in observable social organization, therefore, girls and boys between the ages of eight and eleven appear to show significant differences in their creative fantasies about relationships and in their knowledge about one of the most important relationships in their lives. More than boys, girls tend to emphasize themes of positive interpersonal feelings, love and friendship, communication, and helping in the imaginative stories they tell in response to pictures. And they have at their disposal a larger repository of factual information about their best friends.

In Chapter 3, I reviewed studies of intimate behavior and intimate lives. Most of these studies involved college students. A few interesting sex differences emerged. In our study of non-verbal behavior expressed in a friendly interview, we found that women tended to smile and laugh more and to make more eye contact with the same-sex interviewer than did men. Psychologists have suggested that smiling, laughter, and eye contact are important nonverbal signals of openness and warmth in interpersonal relations. By showing greater levels of these behaviors, the women in this study were sending a clearer message to the interviewer that they were ready to share some of themselves with the other and to enjoy the sharing. Overall, the nonverbal message of intimacy was muted for the men. Of course, there were exceptions: Men who were high in intimacy motivation on the TAT showed relatively high levels of smiling, laughter, and eye contact. But overall, the gender difference was strong.

In our beeper study of Chapter 3, we found that intimacy motivation was strongly related to the amount of time college students spent during a normal week thinking about people and relationships. Intimacy motivation was also positively related to the frequency of conversations and of writing personal letters. Women tended to engage in much higher levels of interpersonal thinking than did men, even when they did not differ in intimacy motivation. Women spent about 25 percent of their time thinking about people and relationships; men averaged about 13.5 percent. In other words, when we monitored the spontaneous thought processes of college students over the course of a normal week, we found that women spent almost twice as much time thinking about people and relationships as did men. In addition, women tended to engage in more conversations and to write more personal letters over the course of the week than did men, though this difference was not quite statistically significant.

Echoing the sex differences we obtained, a growing body of recent research suggests that women are generally more oriented to intimate relationships than are men. A sensitive barometer of this is self-disclosure, or the extent to which men and women will reveal personal information about themselves with friends, family, and acquaintances. In general, women show higher levels of self-disclosure than men.[8] They express more feelings for longer periods of time than do men.[9] In psychotherapy, they are more open with their therapists and more likely to reveal their inadequacies and their conflicts.[10] In their friendships, women place greater emphasis on emotional sharing and talking, while men tend to emphasize shared activity.[11] In adolescence and young adulthood, women show stronger bonds of intimacy with their female friends than do men with their male friends.[12] In their forties and fifties, women report richer networks of friendships and greater emotional fulfillment with their friends than do men. Older women are more apt to have close confidantes with whom they can share personal information than are older men.[13]

Overall, men's friendships appear to be less intimate than women's. One social scientist lists four possible reasons for the paucity of intimacy in male friendships.[14] First, men may compete with each other so much that they are generally unable to regard each other as equals with whom it is appropriate to share. From the perspective of a vertical and hierarchical world, other men are seen as rivals with whom one must compete for the limited resources of money, prestige, power, and women. Second, men may fear seeming vulnerable in the eyes of their peers. Intimacy mandates that a person risk being vulnerable in order to share that which is innermost with another. But males learn from a very early age that they are to be tough and invulnerable. Third, men may fear that being intimate with others will be viewed as a sign of homosexuality. Men appear to be much more homophobic than women, perhaps because the incidence of homosexuality among men is higher than among women. Fourth, men are exposed to very few intimate role models. Their male heroes are more likely to be strong and independent than warm and compassionate. The behaviors young boys emulate as they first observe them in fathers, older brothers, coaches, and other men and older boys are likely to be colored in agentic rather than communal hues.

When it comes to love affairs, men may be more romantic

while women are both more pragmatic and more intimate.[15] Men tend to fall in love more quickly than do women.[16] Interestingly, women are more likely than men to say that they might marry somebody with whom they were not "in love" if that person had a number of other positive attributes. Whereas men tend to place a premium on passion and sexual fulfillment in love, women are more inclined to assess the quality of a love relationship in terms of the couple's compatibility and the extent to which the two are able to communicate with each other. When women complain about their love relationships, they are likely to cite the absence of intimacy in the relationship. Men are more likely to complain about the loss of romance or passion.

In Tom Wolfe's novel *The Bonfire of the Vanities*, thirty-eight-year-old Sherman McCoy, a rich Wall Street bonds trader, finds that the excitement in his marriage is gone.[17] His wife is a high-society socialite, mother of his beloved child and part-time interior designer. Their two-million-dollar apartment on Park Avenue has been featured in *Architectural Digest*. But Sherman wants more. He rekindles his sexuality in an affair with the younger and more voluptuous Maria Ruskin, who herself is nominally married to a rich old aristocrat. Sherman and Maria meet regularly in a modest but funky Manhattan flat, subsidized by her husband. Driving Maria home in his Mercedes one night, Sherman misses the turn to Manhattan and ends up deep in the South Bronx. In a nightmarish and ambiguous mishap, his car strikes a young black man. Sherman and Maria panic. They speed away, and she convinces him not to call the police.

A few days later, the boy lapses into a coma. The press picks up and sensationalizes the story as an allegory of race relations in the big city. As the police zero in on his Mercedes, Sherman realizes that he will soon be arrested. Two weeks after the incident and the night before he is to be picked up, he finally confesses the story to Judy, his wife. She had guessed he was having an affair, but the news of the accident leaves her devastated. She is livid about the affair and concerned about the well-being of her husband and her family. But what Sherman truly cannot fathom is the depth of her disappointment, along with her utter

173

astonishment, that he had kept this information *inside of him* for two entire weeks. Side by side, they had watched the television reports of the police investigation into the hit-and-run accident. Yet he had never said a word. More than his sexual infidelity, this failure in intimacy was the unforgivable betrayal. Sherman apologizes and makes excuses for his affair with Maria. But his wife does not hear a word of it. She is overwhelmed by the vacuum, the light-years of distance that have separated them. Her husband is an utterly isolated planet from a galaxy she has never heard of. And all he can do is make excuses about a sexual fling.

Sex and Fantasy

The intimacy motive is assessed through imaginative fantasy. As we saw in Chapter 2, the creative stories that people tell in response to ambiguous picture cues are analyzed for various themes of intimacy in order to assess the relative strength of intimacy motivation in the storyteller's life. Individual differences in intimacy motivation have proved to be significant predictors of many important aspects of human behavior and experience, ranging from the amount of eye contact a person makes to the degree of health and happiness he or she experiences. In general, intimacy motivation plays an important role in the lives of both men and women.

Nevertheless, *women score higher in intimacy motivation than men.* The sex difference is not overwhelming, but it is relatively consistent and statistically quite significant. The difference refers to average levels of intimacy motivation as manifested in the fantasy stories told on the TAT. Women tend, on the average, to obtain slightly higher scores on intimacy motivation than men. The distributions of scores for the two sexes do overlap considerably, however. In absolute terms, there are many men who score extremely high in intimacy motivation, higher than most women. And there are many women who score extremely low, lower than most men. Furthermore, certain populations

174

are less likely to show the sex difference than are others. For instance, a couple of our early studies employing small samples of relatively nontraditional college undergraduates from Harvard University tended to show that men and women were about equal on intimacy motivation, while larger samples of college students from other universities have tended to reveal a consistent difference in favor of women. And to the extent that we can determine it, older adults tend to show a similarly slight but consistent sex difference in intimacy motivation.

In the largest study of TAT stories ever conducted outside the nationwide survey I discussed in Chapter 4, my students and I analyzed imaginative stories written by more than 1,500 college students between 1979 and 1986.[18] A little more than half of the students were women; a little less than half were men. A total of 153 students making up sample 1 wrote ten TAT stories, using picture cues that are commonly employed by clinical psychologists in the assessment of the personality functioning of their patients. More than 1,300 students in sample 2 wrote six TAT stories to a set of standard pictures commonly used in research. The thousands of TAT stories were individually scored by experts who were not acquainted with the gender of the story writers.

The main finding of the study was a consistent and highly significant sex difference. College women tended to score higher than college men in intimacy motivation as assessed in the imaginative fantasies. In these two very large samples employing a wide variety of TAT pictures as test stimuli, women wrote imaginative stories that were significantly higher in intimacy imagery than did men. Although the mean differences were not huge, they were consistent: higher scores for women than for men were obtained on total intimacy motivation scores in both samples, on five of the ten individual scoring themes for intimacy motivation in sample 1, and on nine of the ten independent scoring themes in sample 2. The most discriminating scoring themes in both samples appeared to be "positive affect," "time–space," "surrender," and "connection to outside world." Significantly more often than college men, therefore, college women composed imaginative fantasies in which characters who have loved or liked each other for a long time interact in gentle and noncontrolling ways, while opening themselves up to the world around them.[19]

We should be careful, however, in interpreting this sex difference. While the findings do support the general belief that women are in fact more intimate than men, we must remember that (1) the difference is not huge, though it is consistent, and (2) the difference refers to the intimacy *motive*, not to all manifestations of intimacy overall. Women score higher than men in a motivational disposition to prefer intimacy—a recurrent desire for or preoccupation with warm, close, and communicative relationships—but not necessarily higher in intimacy "beliefs," "attitudes," "values," or self-ascribed "traits." We may presume that women spend more time thinking about intimacy than do men, that intimacy is a more salient concern in conscious thought for women than men, and that women, therefore, have a stronger recurrent preference or readiness for the particular quality of interpersonal experience that lies at the core of the intimacy motivation system.

Are there other sex differences in imaginative fantasy that have a bearing on intimacy? Psychologist Robert May suggests that there are. Undertaking his own investigations of TAT stories written by men and women, May concludes that the sexes differ with respect to the ways in which they structure imaginative narrative accounts.[20] Men seem to begin their stories in a positive way but end them with a negative consequent. Women seem to organize fantasies in the reverse, starting out negative but ending up positive. May relates the sex difference to the ancient Greek legends of Icarus and Persephone.

In the story of Icarus, a young boy desires to fly in the heavens. He fashions wings and flies toward the sun. As he soars higher and higher, the heat from the sun melts the wax in his wings, sending him plummeting to the sea below. The Icarus legend is a story about the hot sun and the cold sea, about fiery ambition that is ultimately quenched by watery defeat, about rising and then falling. In the Icarus, legend as in the stories of

Adam and Eve and the Tower of Babel, pride comes before the fall.

In another legend, beautiful and innocent Persephone, the beloved daughter of Demeter (goddess of fruit and fertility), is gathering flowers when she is swallowed up by the earth and seized by Hades, lord of the underworld. Stricken with grief and rage, Demeter lashes out against the earth and causes a most dreadful famine. Zeus, king of Olympos, eventually intervenes and forces Hades to return the lost daughter to her mother. Demeter and Persephone embrace in a joyful reunion. But Demeter soon learns that her daughter has made the mistake of tasting forbidden food while she was in captivity. As a result, Persephone must return every year to the underworld, where she must live with Hades for about four months. These months, therefore, become the season of winter, during which Demeter mourns her lost daughter and the earth is barren and cold. But at the end of winter, Persephone rises up from the underworld, and the earth is blessed with the springtime abundance.

The stories of Icarus and Persephone are opposites in one fundamental way: in Icarus, one goes up and then comes (crashing) down; in Persephone, one goes down (to the underworld) and then comes back up. The Icarus myth is a story of enhancement followed by deprivation; the Persephone myth portrays deprivation followed by enhancement. May argues that this mythic distinction is reflected in the different fantasies of men and women. In general, men construct imaginative narratives in which one first rises and is thus enriched, enhanced, or victorious and then falls and is finally impoverished, deprived, or defeated. By contrast, women construct narratives of deprivation, sacrifice, and pain followed by enhancement, reward, and pleasure. Like Icarus, man burns out early; like Persephone and Demeter the woman's initial sacrifice is ultimately rewarded.

May suggests that the male fantasy symbolizes the pride of the ever-climbing but isolated man. The female pattern emphasizes care, the sacrifice of caring for and committing oneself to another, as we see in Demeter's intense love for and endless devotion to her daughter Persephone. The sacrifice eventually

177

brings fulfillment. Care yields the reward of springtime, as the cold deprivation gives way to gentle warmth. But the warmth of pride is not gentle warmth. The scorching sun strikes down the man, who ends up alone and cold at sea.

May's notion is intriguing and thought-provoking. One can imagine a number of different explanations for such a sex difference, if in fact it exists. For example, there may be something about the generally expected life course of males and females that engenders these different stories. Being a mother may be viewed in part as a self-sacrifice, a "going-down-under" that is eventually rewarded with freedom from child-rearing responsibilities when children grow up, and as the fulfillment of having given life and nurtured it along. The initial pain of labor and delivery is followed by the joy of a baby's birth. The prototypical life course for the man, by contrast, may be seen as dominated by instrumental striving to "make it to the top," in many different senses, in the first half of life, followed by the realization, perhaps at midlife, that one is not going to make it. While these possibilities have been suggested by a number of observers of contemporary Western society, psychologist David Gutmann has suggested that such a sex difference might be even more striking in more traditional non-Western societies.[21] Gutmann claims that in many nonindustrial societies men rise to prominence in the first half of life but settle down into less active roles after midlife, while women rise to powerful positions in society only after midlife, once children have been raised.

The actual research evidence for May's distinction between Icarus and Persephone in imaginative fantasies is not abundant, though there is some. May has developed a system for scoring TAT stories for these two thematic patterns. Essentially, the researcher compares the first half of the story to the second half, with the expectation that men will show a generally positive first half followed by a negative second half and that women will show the opposite sequence. Research in support of May's claims has been reported with college students and with older (age eleven) but not younger (age five) children.[22] But some other studies have failed to find the same difference.[23]

178

Do Men Fear Intimacy?

One of May's favorite TAT pictures for eliciting stories that portray themes of Icarus and Persephone shows a man and a woman on a trapeze in midair. Both trapeze artists are young and attractive. He is muscular, and she is shapely. They are suspended in space, both stretched out almost parallel to the ground, arms clasped tightly. His knees are wrapped around the swing. She is flying free through the air as he catches her in a secure grip. According to May, men are more likely to tell a story in response to this picture that begins in glory but ends in catastrophe: the acrobats are the greatest show on earth, but he drops her and she is killed. Women tell stories in which things start out badly but end up well: the acrobats are a minor, trifling act, but through hard work they become the greatest of them all.

Psychologists Susan Pollack and Carol Gilligan, however, have underscored a different distinction in the fantasies men and women tell in response to this picture.[24] Underneath the flying trapeze artists, women tend to place nets! If the acrobat falls, she (or he) is caught in the net and saved. There is, however, no actual net in the TAT picture. In one particular study, Pollack and Gilligan found that 22 percent of the women added nets in the stories they wrote. Only 6 percent of the men imagined the presence of a net, and 40 percent either explicitly mentioned that there was no net or implied its absence, as one or both of the acrobats fell to death. Pollack and Gilligan suggest that the absence of a net signals a larger theme in the stories that men write. According to these researchers, men tend to attribute an excessive amount of violence in TAT stories to the results of potentially intimate relationships. The proliferation of violence in TAT stories that hold potentially intimate themes signals a perception among men that intimacy is dangerous. In the view of Pollack and Gilligan, these stories indicate that men fear intimacy to a greater extent than do women.

It is one thing to say that women have a stronger intimacy motive than men, that they show a consistently greater preference for warm, close, and communicative interaction with others. Studies of TAT stories suggest that this is true. It is quite another thing, however, to say that men are not as strongly drawn to intimacy as are women because they fear it. Is it fair to say that Sherman McCoy in Tom Wolfe's *Bonfire of the Vanities* really fears intimacy? He does not seem frightened by the possibilities of warm, close, and communicative relationships. True, he is not very intimate with anybody except, perhaps, his daughter. He rarely, if ever, shares his innermost feelings with another. Even his mistress and partner in crime is a stranger to him, and he to her. But Sherman's lack of intimacy seems more tied to ability and motivation than to fear. He does not seem to know *how* to be intimate. And he does not really want to be extremely intimate, anyway. He does not have to run away in the face of intimate threats. He simply has better things to do—that is, things that he considers better, like trading bonds, making money, being seen, seducing Maria, having influence, feeling strong. In his private fantasies, he imagines that he is a "Master of the Universe." His is a classic story of immense pride followed by the fall. Sherman McCoy is the Icarus of Park Avenue. But what frightens him? Falling.

Pollack and Gilligan present evidence for their assertion that men have a greater fear of intimacy than do women in a study of imaginative stories written to four TAT pictures by eighty-eight males and fifty females attending Harvard University. The findings showed that men included more overall violence in their fantasies than did women. More importantly, though, the sex difference in violent imagery was especially pronounced for stories written in response to two particular pictures that appeared to suggest warm and friendly relations. One of them portrayed a man and a woman sitting on a bench near a river. The other was the trapeze picture. Men's stories in response to these two pictures tended to show markedly greater levels of violence than women's stories written to the same pictures. Pollack and Gilligan concluded that the violence in these stories signals an underlying fear of the intimacy implied in the friendly scenes. As a way of dealing with their fear of being

180

close to others, men tended to write stories about death, homicide, suicide, rape, and fatal disease when confronted with scenes of potential intimacy. When confronted with these same scenes, women were much less likely to create fantasies of violence.

Efforts to confirm these findings in other research projects, however, have not met with success. And a number of critics of the study have taken issue with Pollack's and Gilligan's interpretation of their own results.[25] In an effort to resolve the controversy, my students and I analyzed the TAT data from sample 1 in our large study of sex differences described above. As I have mentioned, a total of 153 students wrote imaginative fantasies to ten TAT pictures, including the original ones used by Pollack and Gilligan. Following carefully the scoring procedures used in the original study of fear of intimacy, we found no evidence that men show more violence in potentially intimate scenes than do women. For none of the ten different pictures used did we find a sex difference in fear of intimacy that even approached statistical significance.

Except for the results of the original study conducted by Pollack and Gilligan, psychologists have yet to provide evidence from adults' imaginative fantasies that men fear intimacy to a greater extent than women do. Of course, this does not mean that such a sex difference in fear does not exist. We have simply been unable to document it using our current measures of analyzing TAT stories. More sensitive procedures might prove the original hunch correct. In any case, it is not warranted to make more of the general sex difference in intimacy than we know to be true. Women do appear to be more intimate than men in the overall, when you examine such indicators as self-disclosure and friendly behavior. They also score slightly higher on intimacy motivation, based on analysis of their fantasies in response to the TAT. But women's slight advantage over men in the realm of intimacy does not seem to stem from any higher fear of intimacy in men, for they do not seem to fear intimacy more than women do. From what, then, does women's advantage stem?

Development and Sex Differences

When it comes to the matter of sex differences in human intimacy, many psychologists believe that both biology and culture are deeply implicated very early on. Psychologist Helen Block Lewis argues that baby girls may have a slight edge over baby boys in what she terms "innate sociability."[26] Lewis uses the term "sociability" in a somewhat broader sense than I did in Chapter 5 when I discussed a temperament "style" of outgoing behavior and general friendliness. Lewis suggests that from birth onward human females may be slightly and generally more responsive to people than are males. It is a subtle biological edge, remarks Lewis, but it is enhanced from the beginning by social events and social practice that reflect cultural norms.

Newborns will respond with primitive distress when they hear the cry of another baby. Newborn girls, however, show a slightly greater responsiveness in this regard than do newborn boys.[27] In the first month of life, babies exhibit what has been called a "reflex smile"—a spontaneous half-smile that appears to be a result of internal neural activity. Some psychologists suggest that the reflex smile is a forerunner to the full social smile that appears about two months of age. Newborn girls show slightly higher levels of reflex smiling than do newborn boys, a difference that may reflect a potential advantage in sociability, suggests Lewis. When babies begin to make eye contact with people in the second and third months of life, infant girls show slightly higher levels of eye contact, while infant boys are somewhat more likely to look away when others look at them.[28] In the first months of life, boys cry and fuss more than girls; girls sleep more. Overall, boys appear somewhat more irritable and difficult to console. Girls seem to respond more favorably to the caregiver's attempts to soothe and comfort them when they are upset.[29] By the age of six months, girls show slightly more interest than do boys in pictures of the human face.[30]

While these differences may suggest a slight biological edge, subtle cultural norms produce differences in parents' reactions to babies that can be observed in the first few days of life. In general, adults judge female babies to be "softer" than male babies, though no literal physical difference of this sort exists. Mothers and fathers treat their newborns differently as a function of gender. Mothers tend to hold their baby boys farther away from their own bodies than they hold baby girls. Mothers stimulate and arouse their infant boys more often than their girls, and they attend more often to their boys. They are more likely to hold a baby boy in a sitting or standing posture, exercising the boy's musculature. At the same time, mothers tend to imitate their baby girls more often.[31] By mimicking the behavior of their baby girls, mothers are displaying a primitive form of face-to-face communication with them. These subtle differences in parental behavior mirror our culture's norms for masculinity and femininity, agency and communion. Boys must be stimulated and aroused, their bodies must be exercised, so that they can grow up to be autonomous individuals, separate and strong. Girls must be held closer, and we must communicate with them, face to face, I to Thou.

When it comes to interpersonal communication, females appear to have a consistent advantage over males. The most obvious example of this is language. One of the most solidly established findings in the literature on sex differences is that adolescent girls and women perform better than adolescent boys and men in verbal tasks. On the average, females show a consistent superiority in language skills. Males show a consistent superiority in mathematical and spatial ability. These differences do not appear in a consistent fashion, however, until the age of twelve or thirteen. Until puberty, girls and boys perform at approximately equivalent levels. Therefore, most explanations for these differences cite the divergent expectations that society holds for male and female performance. Females are supposed to be better communicators, to express themselves through the social medium of language. By contrast, males are encouraged to master the relatively nonsocial world of things and abstractions, the objective world of the I–It.

Another form of communication reveals consistent sex differences at an even earlier age. By the time they are four years old, girls are more adept than boys in decoding nonverbal mes-

183

sages. They more accurately interpret the smiles, frowns, and other facial expressions that people communicate as signals of their emotional states. Girls and women are consistently more sensitive than boys and men to subtle cues such as body posture and tone of voice. They are more likely to detect slight irregularities in nonverbal expression, as when, for instance, the tone of a voice and the expression on a face do not match.[32] Psychologist Judith Hall proposes both biological and cultural explanations for this sex difference. Hall suggests that females may be biologically "wired" from birth to show an advantage in nonverbal decoding. At the same time, society expects girls and women to be better communicators, implicitly reinforcing the female's cultivation of both verbal and nonverbal skills of dialogue. Hall also proposes that the oppressed status of women in Western societies may create a greater need for them to assess accurately the wishes of powerful others.[33]

In most societies, boys and girls spend the first few years of their lives in an environment in which the central actors are, for the most part, women. In even the most egalitarian echelons of modern Western societies, women tend to do most of the caregiving for very young children. Most babysitters, nannies, daycare workers, and nursery school teachers are women. Mothers and the "mother role" are familiar to virtually all children. In their daily life, very young boys and girls see what mothers and other female caregivers do. In relative terms, men are strangers in this world. Even when the father enthusiastically shares in the caregiving, children will still tend to know less about what men in general do. They spend much less time with men than with women. They cannot acquire the intimate familiarity with the father's major roles—as the man who brings home the money and supports the family—that they naturally develop with their world of women.

According to psychologists Dorothy Dinnerstein[34] and Nancy Chodorow,[35] men and their roles remain mysteries for the very young. In Dinnerstein's view, children have a deeper knowledge of women and, consequently, a more complicated emotional reaction to them. Because so much of our early experience is mediated by women, we are likely to feel greater ambivalence to women than to men. Throughout our lives, Dinnerstein suggests, we find that women elicit more feelings from us—both positive and negative feelings—than do men. If the expression of emotions is one way in which we can share our innermost selves, then Dinnerstein's view implies that women stimulate greater levels of intimacy in us than do men. One intriguing research finding to support this idea comes from a study of loneliness. The researchers found that loneliness in both men and women was associated with spending *less time with women.*[36] Whether we are male or female, interacting with women may be more effective in staving off our loneliness than interacting with men. Women may be better providers and elicitors of intimacy.

Chodorow focuses on the different experiences of little girls and boys as they grow up in a world dominated by women. She argues that by the age of three or four, children have developed a basic sense of themselves as either female or male. Because mother and mother figures are central components of their daily lives, little girls learn directly what it means to be female. They emulate the women they observe. Thus, the little girl's basic gender identity is developed in the context of ongoing relations with women. The self is defined *in relation.* For little boys, however, gender identity is a greater puzzle, a mysterious problem to be solved. Because there are few salient men within his everyday world, the boy must figure out how to be a man on his own and *through opposition.* According to Chodorow, the little boy experiences his own masculinity in opposition to the world of women. He knows that men are different from women, but he does not know exactly how. The little boy identifies with a disembodied "position" in the world—he renders a guess about what the position of men might be, and then he patterns himself after the guess. Therefore, the little boy must resolve the puzzle of gender identity in a way that forces him to separate himself from others. The masculine self is defined through separation and guesswork. By contrast, the feminine self develops from the connectedness of human relations.

What are the results of these two different pathways to gender identity? Chodorow suggests that girls emerge from early childhood "with a stronger basis for experiencing another's needs or feelings as one's own." Girls come to experience themselves as "less differentiated than boys, as more continuous with and related to the external object-world, and as differently oriented to their inner object-world as well."[37] The girl's early advantage in innate sociability, therefore, may be magnified and reinforced in the dynamics of family experience during the first three years of life. If little girls enter their second year slightly more responsive to people than are their little male counterparts, they appear to emerge at the end of their third year with an even more clearly established edge. In the child's world of women, the girl comes to develop the rudiments of a sense of self in relation to other women. Consciously and unconsciously, she experiences herself as continuous with her environment, connected in a web. The boy, instead, must work to separate himself from the web, to identify the essential nature of maleness through separation, opposition, and individuation.

As children move from nursery school through the juvenile years and into adolescence, their understanding of interpersonal relationships, including those which involve intimacy, becomes more firmly situated within a personal framework of morality. Interpersonal conflicts and dilemmas come to be regarded from the standpoints of right and wrong, good and bad, individual rights and responsibilities to others. Carol Gilligan argues that differences in the ways the two sexes see themselves in relation to the world are reflected in two different perspectives on morality.[38] According to Gilligan, boys and men tend to view moral issues from the standpoint of autonomy, rights, and fairness. They tend to evaluate the moral dimensions of a situation by considering what the individual person's rights are and how a conflict in rights may be resolved fairly. Girls and women, by contrast, perceive moral issues in more contextual and concretely interpersonal terms. They judge what is right and what is wrong in a particular situation in terms of the various responsibilities that people have to one another.

Females are more likely than males to consider the concrete relations between actors in a moral dilemma and to couch their final judgments in terms of care and compassion. Males are more likely to invoke abstract rights and principles of justice in resolving moral dilemmas. For many men, Gilligan argues, morality is a matter of assuring that people do not infringe on one another's individuality. The world is made up of autonomous agents, hierarchically arranged. And abstract principles may be formulated to assure each agent's autonomy and freedom from coercion. For many women, morality is premised on the assumption that people are interdependent, linked in a web. A woman must determine what her duties are to specific other people within a particular community that defines her very self, and then act accordingly.[39]

Even in areas that have nothing to do with intimacy and relationships, women appear to emphasize connection, men separation. From late childhood on, females tend to exhibit a "field-dependent" style of thinking; they perceive and conceptualize reality in terms of the relations of parts within a whole. Males tend to show more "field-independence," analyzing separate parts as distinct from the whole.[40] In their characteristic ways of thinking—whether thinking about things or people—females tend to be slightly more contextual; men, slightly more analytic.

The tendency for women to express greater levels of intimacy than men seems to hold up at least through early adulthood. Again biology and culture conspire to point the way. When they launch their families, many married couples adopt sharply differentiated sex roles, even if both husband and wife are professionals. It is not uncommon to see highly competent professional women—lawyers, physicians, businesswomen, teachers—take an extended leave of absence from their careers with the birth of a first or especially a second child, so that they can devote more of their time to child care. For a few years or maybe even longer, they will reimmerse themselves in that familiar, intimately interconnected world of women and children of which Nancy Chodorow speaks. We virtually never hear of men who do this.

What happens to intimacy after the children grow up? Some psychologists suggest that midlife brings a shift in intimacy for the two sexes. After children have been raised, women may adopt a more agentic approach to life, at the expense, perhaps, of communion. The Swiss psychiatrist Carl Jung insisted that women in their forties and fifties are ready to come to grips with their deeply buried masculinity, or what he called the woman's *animus*. Similarly, men at midlife confront their *anima*, the unconscious core of femininity within them. Men should adopt a gentler approach to life and take a greater interest in warm interpersonal relationships. Women should become more assertive, and presumably less oriented to intimacy. Based on intensive interviews of forty midlife men and forty midlife women, psychologist Daniel Levinson has proposed a similar idea.[41]

As yet, we do not have much scientific evidence to support or refute these claims. One interesting piece of evidence, however, comes from our nationwide study of intimacy motivation, described in Chapter 4. In that large sample of American adults ranging in age from twenty-one to about eighty, intimacy motivation was negatively associated with age for women. In other words, older women had lower scores on intimacy motivation than did younger women. But age was not related to intimacy motivation among men. The result, however, is difficult to interpret because the study assesses different people of various ages at the same time, not the same people over time as they get older. Therefore, we do not know if intimacy motivation actually decreases in women as they get older. Perhaps the older women in the current study had low intimacy motivation when they were young as well. Further, if Jung and Levinson are correct, we would expect a sharp drop in intimacy motivation at about age forty or forty-five as the women enter midlife, rather than a gradual decrease from age twenty-one on (which is what we got). Finally, Jung and Levinson suggest that men bring greater warmth and intimacy to interpersonal relationships at midlife, implying an increase in intimacy motivation for older men. We could detect no such increase.

How do the sexes differ in intimacy in later years? Here we have virtually no clues. Psychologists have just begun to study personality development in middle and later adulthood. As men and women become grandparents and reach retirement, it seems that traditional sex roles mandating that men be independent and women be connected fade considerably. Yet, whether this influences the expression of intimacy and intimacy motivation in the later years remains to be seen. We have yet to explore in any systematic fashion how intimacy is shaped by changing occupational and social roles in middle and later adulthood, by changing patterns of sexuality, and by the loss of friends and loved ones. My hunch, though, is that women retain their more intimate perspective, even as so many of them become widows in their last years. I think it is extremely difficult to undo what the conspiracy of biology and culture has done. Perhaps what gives me my hunch are accounts like this one, excerpted from *The New York Times Magazine* and written by a middle-aged journalist who tells us that the lessons of childhood are never forgotten.[42] At age ten, he was enrolled at the Nyack Boys Boarding School:

The man I became had its beginnings at Nyack. It was there that I learned Kipling when I was barely 10 years old. I wore my first male uniform at Nyack: blue blazer with red piping, gray wool trousers, striped tie—the dress for dinner. Once a week, each boy was summoned to sit at the table of the headmaster and there take part in the conversation; thus we learned how to hold opinions and how to defend them.

I saw for the first time at Nyack how men tend to run in packs. We were roommates and teammates and classmates. When one boy in a room of four broke a rule, his cellmates suffered. Yet the aim of all of this uniformity— from rigid standards of dress and deportment to high expectations in the classroom and on the playing field— was designed to make us self-reliant, to prepare us for the time when we would be alone.

The coaches who preached team spirit must have known this, for they also told us that our games were a kind of conditioning for life, a rehearsal for the real race, which, "in a tough competitive world," was always run alone. Their ambivalence does not surprise me now. They, after all, were men already, well along in loneliness, looking out from the green playing fields of myth at a solitary world.

The lesson of boarding school was the lesson of separation, perhaps the fundamental lesson of manhood: through codes and rituals, men are taught to remove themselves and live a step apart. There is no reaching across that space—no handhold for wives or children, for the other men they want to love, for the mothers who left them behind.

Attachment Versus Chumship: Men Versus Women

Throughout the human life-span, the most mature and most fulfilling manifestation of intimacy is what Buber characterized as the I–Thou encounter. Two completely separate individuals, secure in their own identities, come together to share that which is innermost with each other. They come together to communicate, to engage in a mutual and spontaneous dialogue, to tell their own stories, and to listen to the stories they hear. The I does not look for security in the Thou. He does not look to the Thou to assuage anxiety, to empower him so that he can move on to conquer the world. The I does not look for identity in the Thou. She does not seek to find in the Thou a reflection of herself or to reveal in her words a reflection of the Thou, as mirror facing mirror, reflecting a single reality into infinitude. I and Thou meet for the sake of connection, for closeness, but not to lose themselves in each other, or to use each other for themselves. The true, the mature, the perfect I–Thou does not boost us up in the hierarchy; neither does it ensnare us in a web.

But people are not perfect, and they rarely relate to each other in "perfect" ways. Too often the intimacy of the I–Thou degenerates into something less mutual and dynamic, a paltry manifestation of the I–It. Opportunities for sharing become occasions for the expression of power or the alleviation of fear.

Dreading the vulnerability that intimacy brings, people may settle for friendly chitchat and harmless half-lies, or they may enact grander deceptions as they perform roles and put on masks to conceal that which is innermost. A great many human experiences, some of them quite worthy of acclaim, parade under the banner of intimacy. We say we are intimate with our lovers, our parents, our children, our friends, and occasionally even all of humankind. But we are probably intimate less often than we think.

In our desire to be intimate in personal relationships, we may fall short in characteristically masculine and feminine ways. For the ideal model of intimacy put forth by Buber, we may often find ourselves substituting our own lesser renditions, relating to our friends and loved ones in ways reminiscent of patterns from childhood. From childhood, we assimilate many different models of relating to people. Two of the most significant models have their developmental roots in (1) the bond of love between mother and infant and (2) the same-sex friendships of preadolescence. In other words, we may find that as adults we often relate to each other in the manner of *attachment* and *chumship*. Those critical patterns of relation, which—as we saw in Chapter 5—are so significant in the development of mature intimacy, are resurrected in adulthood to substitute for mature intimacy. It is my belief that men are more likely to resurrect attachment. Women bring back the chumship.

Recall the ideal model of the secure attachment bond. During the first year of life, the infant develops an exclusive relationship with one or a few central caregivers, who are the infant's attachment objects. They provide for him the basic trust that psychologists such as Erik Erikson view as the most fundamental legacy of healthy childhood. In attachment, the mother or other attachment object functions as a secure base for the infant. The infant uses the mother as a base from which to explore the world. From the secure attachment bond, infants obtain the psychological sustenance—indeed, the courage—to move forward in the world, to become autonomous, to explore their environments, to master and manipulate their surroundings in effective and competent ways. According to Erikson, upon the foundation of basic trust the infant builds a psychological edifice of autonomy, initiative, industry, and identity—a tower, of sorts.

We use the same vertical imagery to conceptualize our own closest relationships when we think of them as providing us with "social support," as we saw in Chapter 4. Warm and close relationships are a foundation for the self. They are a secure base from which we can move forward and upward in order to explore and master our world. When things get tough, our relationships support us and keep us strong. They provide us with the background, the context, the foundation of basic trust and security. Upon that foundation, we build a self. In his novel *The Good Soldier*, Ford Madox Ford suggests that it is precisely this quality of human relationship that a man seeks first when he is in love with a woman:

> For, whatever may be said of the relation of the sexes, there is no man who loves a woman that does not desire to come to her for the renewal of his courage, for the cutting asunder of his difficulties. And that will be the mainspring of his desire for her. We are all so afraid, we are all so alone, we all so need from the outside the assurance of our own worthiness to exist.[43]

I believe this to be a characteristically masculine model for many different relationships in adulthood. Men tend to view relations with lovers, family, and friends as providing them with security and support, to renew their courage and cut asunder their difficulties. Upon this supportive foundation, they build a tower of the self. The most important interpersonal relationships in a man's life are generally taken for granted, as we take for granted the secure foundation of the mighty Sears Tower in downtown Chicago. As Chodorow and Gilligan maintain, men do not define themselves in terms of relationships. Rather, they define themselves *on top of relationships*. The man's identity rests on a secure base of interpersonal relations. He consciously understands his life in terms of the various achievements and explorations he has undertaken. He knows that his relations with people have given him the strength to carry on his explorations. He even knows that without the important people in his life he would not be able to explore an inch. But like the securely attached infant in the presence of the beloved attachment object, the man explores on his own. Mom does not get a whole lot of the credit, though we all know that if she left for good the infant would shrink away in terror, immobilized.

It is wrong, therefore, to suggest that men need people and relationships less than women do. Granted, men score slightly lower in intimacy motivation. As we have repeatedly seen, a lower score on intimacy motivation means a weaker desire for warm, close, and communicative relations with others, a weaker desire for intimacy. But people and relationships provide many benefits beyond intimacy, and it is for some of these other benefits of close relationships that men, even those with the lowest intimacy motivation, need people. Satisfying interpersonal relationships of all kinds may provide the man with a secure foundation for the self. When that foundation is shaken, however, the self may crumble to the ground. Men's reactions to divorce, for instance, may be even more negative than the reactions of women, bringing into serious doubt the notion that men are autonomous and do not need people. Some studies show that men experience significantly more stress as a result of divorce than do women, with divorced men showing higher rates of hospitalization, outpatient mental health care, and mortality as a result of suicide, homicide, and disease, than nondivorced men or divorced women.[44]

We can now make sense of the finding from Chapter 4 concerning the relation between intimacy motivation and subjective well-being in the nationwide sample of men. Recall that men high in intimacy motivation reported less strain in their lives and less uncertainty. In other words, men with a stronger need for warm, close, and communicative relations with other people seem to be more secure in the world and less bothered by anxiety, bad health, and immobilization. Willingness to seek the intimacy and security of close relationships in their lives may enable them to share with others while supporting them during times of need.

To the extent that the model of attachment dominates a man's overall pattern of relating to people, however, his life may become a failure in intimacy. Instead of sharing one's innermost self in the experience of the I–Thou, some men settle for security and the knowledge that they are supported and strong. Although they stand tall in a hierarchical world, they do not truly know the inhabitants of that world. Securely attached men may feel safe and protected, but they may still be lonely. While friends and lovers may provide emotional sustenance and support, such men consistently fail to bridge the horizontal void between the I and the Thou. Such men rise from the earth majestic and grand, but their stark veneer is cold to the touch.

When women substitute childhood patterns for the ideal intimacy of I–Thou, they tend to revive a different model from their developmental pasts—the chumship, described by Sullivan as the crown jewel of preadolescence. As we saw in Chapter 5, chumship features many of the qualities of mature intimacy. Chums relate to each other in a reciprocal way. Each friend cares for the other, even to the extent of placing the other's well-being ahead of his or her own. The friends share their innermost selves. But the psychological parameters of chumships are different than those of the I–Thou. The chums seek to affirm their sameness in relation: the I seeks *itself* in the Thou. While the preadolescent needs to affirm his or her sameness with another person, mature adults must understand the ways in which they are similar to and different from their "chums." While the friends of grade school create a shared reality that defines the two of them as one, intimate partners in adulthood must share their independent realities with each other, for only in the sharing of things that are different can we see each other for what we truly are.

Although Chodorow marvels at the webs women create to connect themselves to the whole, she laments women's characteristic failure to escape from the clinging net. Women tend to define themselves through relationships rather than on top of relationships. In the extreme, a woman is the web. So contextualized is her identity that she cannot tell where she begins and her relationships end. As Gilligan suggests, a woman's relationships are woven into the fabric of her identity. The male picture of the tower with its interpersonal foundation does not apply to the woman. She is more like a tapestry, as relationships run through in different colors and textures, making different designs. Whereas relationships provide a secure foundation for the man, they give the woman a characteristic design and stitching. As old threads are ripped out and new fabric is woven together with old, the essential design of the tapestry may change, sometimes in dramatic ways.

To the extent that women relate to their friends and loved ones in ways reminiscent of the childhood chumship, they are missing out on an essential feature of the I–Thou. Like the chums, the woman is prone to look for herself in relationships, to define who she is solely in terms of the Thou. As such, she does not see the Thou for what the Thou is. And she does not see herself for what she potentially might be. This is a characteristically feminine failure in intimacy. Yet we must admit that it seems less a failure than the male pattern of attachment. The chumship appears a closer approximation of the I–Thou, despite its crucial shortcomings. After all, Sullivan held up the chumship as the perfect model for the expression of the need for interpersonal intimacy. In light of the stringent requirements of the I–Thou, I think he was wrong. But he would have been more wrong had he found the paragon of intimacy in the mother–infant bond.

Overall, then, women are more intimate than men. A slight biological edge in innate sociability may combine with a complex pattern of social and cultural factors to render women somewhat more responsive than men to warm, close, and communicative relations. Analyses of imaginative stories written in response to pictures indicate that women score slightly higher than men in intimacy motivation. Both men and women commonly fail to experience intimacy in its truest and richest form, however, even in their closest and warmest relationships. A common pattern of failure in men is the substitution of attachment for intimacy, as men implicitly use their interpersonal relationships as secure bases or foundations upon which to build a self. A common pattern of failure for women is the substitution of the chumship for mature intimacy, as women seek to define themselves in relationships instead of confronting the Thou on its own terms. Yet, despite their failures, most men and women can and sometimes do experience the true sharing of what is innermost that Buber describes as the I–Thou. And they are blessed and enriched as a result.

Epilogue

When we study other people, we implicitly study ourselves. Every behavior I see, every life I record takes meaning in relation to *me* the observer, the recorder. When I tune into a conversation between two people, I hear what they say in the context of every conversation that I have ever had. If I discern that they are arguing, I may dredge up old arguments of my own, comparing and contrasting what I hear to what I have experienced firsthand. In the comparing and the contrasting, I impart meaning to their conversation, viewing their moment together from the perspective of moments in my own past, appropriating their dialogue into the ongoing stream of my own experience. Of course, I should not take this process too far. I should not project my own life in toto into every scene I encounter, lest I suffer the fate of Narcissus who could see nothing but himself. Except for those most afflicted with the grandiosity of self, the world is not a shiny mirror with a true and clear reflection. It is rather more opaque and variegated than that, casting reflections in an uneven and capricious fashion, presenting us with overdetermined images of who we are, cleverly disguised as objective

197

perception. Therefore, I can claim integrity and sincerity in my attempts to observe and understand other people even though I know that in so doing I am *also* observing and understanding myself. My apprehension of things and people is both subjective and objective. I can obtain knowledge in no other way.

My own scientific inquiry into intimacy motivation has been and continues to be carried out on both subjective and objective levels. While I have tried to observe the behavior and the accounts of the people I have studied in an open and conscientiously objective manner, I must recognize that my own life has partially determined what I have seen and how I have interpreted it. Perhaps more importantly, my life has influenced just what I have looked for and what I have chosen to interpret. When I began my studies of intimacy motivation in 1977, I thought I was studying *love*. Indeed, I was "in love" at the time. In a symbolic scene from my own past reminiscent of Sara's Valentine's Day conversion in Chapter 1, I proposed marriage to my fiancée and administered the first round of TATs in my fraternity/sorority arousal study on the same rainy evening. That evening certainly rates an "A+" for intimacy. But just as my marriage has evolved into a richer and more complexly fulfilling relationship than I could have foreseen, so has my research into intimacy motivation changed and grown in unexpected ways over the past twelve years.

I now see that I was never studying love per se. Although I read many of the great sources on love in my first two years of graduate school, I found from the beginning that such writers as Buber and Sullivan—who rarely used the term "love"—were more compelling for me than the classic literature of Western love, from Plato through Freud. I also now think that my soon-to-be-married status had little to do with my choice to study intimacy. More important was the fact that I had just left what was probably the most fertile environment for everyday intimacy I will ever know. For me, college was my golden age for the collaborative and syntactic chumship, not preadolescence as Sullivan would maintain. Sharing one's innermost self with others—with many close friends and teachers—was a central part of my college experience. I think that I knew at some level that the golden age was over when I left that small, midwestern university for good and traveled east for graduate school and adulthood. Since then I have come to value intimacy more and more, but I have experienced it very rarely, outside one intensely intimate relationship. I was, therefore, mourning the loss of widespread intimacy in my life when I began my research into intimacy motivation. For the most part, I am still mourning, though there seems much more to do now and less time to mourn.

Chance—pure and simple—was another factor. I began studying intimacy, though I called it love, partly because it was what one of the professors at Harvard University thought somebody should study. In the fall of 1976, David McClelland sent out a memo to all of the new graduate students in the Department of Psychology and Social Relations advertising five different research areas for which he had recently received funding. He needed students to help him with the research. One of the five topics was "affiliation and love." Upon receipt of the memo, I immediately scaled the fifteen floors of William James Hall—I was worried that if I took the elevator somebody might beat me to the top—and offered my services as an unconditional research assistant, willing to look into this business about love in any way Dr. McClelland deemed fit. I was lucky. Had David not been in his office, I might have gone home and become very nervous about approaching this unknown professor with a research idea.

When I began my work with McClelland, I thought that a basic need for love was at the core of human existence. The need was erotically tinged, but capable of being transformed into all kinds of productive and exciting activities—like Freud's eros. The need was something that everybody could conceivably act upon and benefit from. In general, I saw love as universal and basic, and rather easy to obtain if one merely opened oneself up to its possibilities. By contrast, I now see intimacy as one of a small number of basic human needs, all of which are important for human adaptation. As I argued in Chapter 2, intimacy plays itself out in erotic love relationships, but it is not synonymous with love per se. Intimacy refers to the sharing of

199

one's innermost self with another. While I believe the need for intimacy to be universal and basic, I do not view intimacy as a particularly "easy" experience to have. Instead, I return again and again to Martin Buber, who held up the most stringent standards for the perfectly intimate I–Thou encounter. Intimacy is a much greater challenge than I thought it was twelve years ago. And it may be a greater challenge than love.

Throughout this book I have entertained reasons for intimacy's difficult and challenging nature. We have seen that people vary significantly with respect to how strong their need for intimacy is, an individual difference assessed through imaginative fantasy. We have seen that a number of different factors may play determining roles in the way in which intimacy motivation develops and ultimately expresses itself—factors ranging from innate temperament to the negotiation of identity in young adulthood. We have seen that men and women differ markedly with respect to intimacy motivation, both in degree and in common behavioral and experiential manifestations. Women are generally more intimate than men. But both sexes often approach intimacy in less than ideal ways, falling back on childhood models of relating that stem from early patterns of attachment and chumship. For men, the intricate and egalitarian I–Thou too often degenerates into the I–It world of attachment and "secure bases." For women, I and Thou often fail to distinguish themselves, as mature intimacy degenerates into the undifferentiated merger of chums.

Buber challenges us to transcend attachment and merger in intimacy, to relate to each other as autonomous beings who are dynamically connected as equals—distinct, but as close and as open as two entities can be. Buber challenges us to be ready for intimacy, to be sensitive to opportunities for experiencing the I–Thou in everyday life. Unlike so many challenges that exhort us to *act* quickly and vigorously, to attack forcefully, to persevere and carry on, Buber exhorts us to *wait*. Be *ready*, he says. Be attentive, lest you miss the fleeting moments when intimacy offers itself to you as a gift. For, "The Thou encounters me by grace—it cannot be found by seeking."

Notes

Chapter 1: Connection and Separation

1. This study of fifty men and women between the ages of thirty-five and fifty years is described in my first book: D. P. McAdams, *Power, Intimacy, and the Life Story: Personological Inquiries into Identity* (Chicago: Dorsey Press, 1985; 2d ed., New York: Guilford Press, 1988). The case of Sara N. is featured on pages 199–200 of that book. Like all of the cases used in this book, "Sara N." is a pseudonym, to assure the anonymity of the subjects in our studies.

2. Freud writes most famously of psychological symbolism in everyday life in *The Psychopathology of Everyday Life* (orig. 1901), in vol. 6 of *The Standard Edition of the Complete Psychological Works of Sigmund Freud*, ed. J. Strachey (London: Hogarth, 1960). In this classic work, Freud shows how such seemingly trivial "mistakes" in everyday life as slips of the tongue and forgetting people's names may have deep psychological significance. Such symptomatic acts, when carefully interpreted, may be shown to reveal deep-seated anxieties and conflicts concerning sexuality, aggression, and family relationships. The symbolic meaning of such acts, however, is cleverly disguised, never obvious. By contrast, my rather obvious interpretation of the symbolism in Sara's Valentine's Day baptism might have struck Freud as a bit too superficial. But my interpretation might have found a more sympathetic ear in Alfred Adler's theory of personality. A former disciple turned rival of Freud, Adler argued

201

that particular biographical events—especially one's earliest memories—may symbolize key themes in a person's "style of life." See A. Adler, *The Practice and Theory of Individual Psychology,* trans. P. Radin (New York: Harcourt Brace, 1927).

3. I have taken a few liberties with the Creation story here. Actually, there are *two* Creation stories in Genesis, and I have mixed the two together. In the first (Genesis 1), God creates the Earth and its inhabitants in seven days, with the animals being created before humans and man and woman created together. In the second (Genesis 2), God creates the Earth and its vegetation and then jumps straight ahead to create man (Adam). Then, God decides Adam needs a helpmate, so he then creates animals and brings them to Adam, hoping Adam will find one suitable. None of them meets Adam's approval as a viable companion, so God then creates Eve, the woman. In drawing partly from this second account, I make the assumption that Adam was *lonely,* not just *alone,* though we really never hear anything explicit about Adam's internal feelings and thoughts in this regard. Instead, we hear that God decided that Adam needed a helpmate. I would like to think that what motivated God in this regard was his realization that Adam was indeed lonely. (The quotation from Genesis is taken from *The Jerusalem Bible: Reader's Edition* [Garden City, N.Y.: Doubleday, 1966], p. 6.)

4. E. Fromm, *The Art of Loving* (New York: Harper & Row, 1956).

5. J. Bowlby, *Attachment and Loss* (New York: Basic Books, 1969–80); vol. 1, *Attachment;* vol. 2, *Separation;* vol. 3, *Loss.* I have simplified things a bit here. I will have more to say about attachment, fear, sadness, and loneliness when I consider intimacy in the context of human development in Chapter 5.

6. H. S. Sullivan, *The Interpersonal Theory of Psychiatry* (New York: Norton, 1953).

7. L. F. Buscaglia, *Living, Loving, and Learning* (New York: Fawcett Crest, 1983), p. 157.

8. J. Conrad, *An Outcast of the Islands* (New York: Doubleday, Page, 1920), p. 250.

9. T. Wolfe, *Look Homeward, Angel* (New York: Modern Library, 1929), Preface.

10. N. Bradburn, *The Structure of Psychological Well-Being* (Chicago: Aldine, 1969).

11. It is difficult to keep up with the burgeoning research literature produced by personality, social, developmental, and clinical psychologists on the experience of human loneliness. In the subsequent section of the text, I will review general trends from a number of different scientific sources. Among the more important recent sources for research and theory on loneliness are

these: S. Duck, *Human Relationships: An Introduction to Social Psychology* (London: Sage, 1986); J. Hartog, J. R. Audy, and Y. A. Cohen, eds., *The Anatomy of Loneliness* (New York: International Universities Press, 1980); W. H. Jones, S. A. Hobbs, and D. Hockenberg, "Loneliness and Social Skills Deficits," *Journal of Personality and Social Psychology* 42 (1982): 682–89; I. Levin and J. P. Stokes, "An Examination of the Relation of Individual Difference Variables to Loneliness," *Journal of Personality* 54 (1986): 717–33; L. A. Peplau and D. Perlman, eds., *Loneliness: A Sourcebook of Current Theory, Research, and Therapy* (New York: Wiley, 1982); K. S. Rook, "Research on Social Support, Loneliness, and Social Isolation," *Review of Personality and Social Psychology* 5 (1984): *Emotions, Relationships, and Health,* ed. P. Shaver, pp. 239–64; D. Russell, L. A. Peplau, and C. E. Cutrona, "The Revised UCLA Loneliness Scale: Concurrent and Discriminant Validity Evidence," *Journal of Personality and Social Psychology* 39 (1980): 472–80; P. Shaver and C. Rubenstein, "Childhood Attachment Experience and Adult Loneliness," in *Review of Personality and Social Psychology* 1 (1980), ed. L. Wheeler, pp. 42–73; R. S. Weiss, *Loneliness: The Experience of Emotional and Social Isolation* (Cambridge, Mass.: M. I. T. Press, 1973).

12. Two currently popular books that I find interesting and useful are J. Amodeo and K. Amodeo, *Being Intimate: A Guide to Successful Relationships* (New York: Arkana Paperbacks, 1986); and D. D. Burns, *Intimate Connections* (New York: William Morrow, 1985).

13. W. A. Sadler, Jr., and T. B. Johnson, Jr., "From Loneliness to Anomie," in *The Anatomy of Loneliness,* ed. J. Hartog, J. R. Audy, and Y. A. Cohen (New York: International Universities Press, 1980), pp. 56–57.

14. C. Lasch, *The Culture of Narcissism: American Life in an Age of Diminishing Expectations* (New York: Norton, 1979).

15. Kernberg's explanation of narcissism is only one popular view in psychoanalytic circles. A rival interpretation has been offered by Heinz Kohut, who suggests that narcissism develops when the child fails to integrate in his or her unconscious mind images of a powerful self and an idealized parent. The argument is complicated and requires an understanding of Kohut's rather involved "self" psychology. See H. Kohut, *The Analysis of the Self: A Systematic Approach to the Psychoanalytic Treatment of Narcissistic Personality Disorders* (New York: International Universities Press, 1971); idem, *The Restoration of the Self* (New York: International Universities Press, 1977); and E. S. Wolff, "Comments on Heinz Kohut's Conceptualization of a Bipolar Self," in *Psychosocial Theories of the Self,* ed. B. Lee (New York: Plenum, 1982), pp. 23–42. Other clinical references on narcissism include O. Kernberg, *Borderline Conditions and Pathological Narcissism* (New York: Jason Aronson, 1976); J. H. Kirman, "Modern Psychoanalysis and Intimacy: Treatment of the Narcissistic Personality," in *Intimacy,* ed. M. Fischer and G. Stricker (New York: Plenum, 1982), pp. 99–

114; and T. Millon, *Disorders of Personality. DSM III: Axis II* (New York: Wiley-Interscience, 1981), chap. 6.

16. R. Emmons, "Narcissism: Theory and Measurement," *Journal of Personality and Social Psychology* 52 (1987): 11–17; R. N. Raskin and C. S. Hall, "The Narcissistic Personality Inventory: Alternative Form Reliability and Further Evidence of Construct Validity," *Journal of Personality Assessment* 45 (1981): 159–62; R. N. Raskin and R. Shaw, "Narcissism and the Use of Personal Pronouns," *Journal of Personality* 56 (1988): 393–404.

17. P. Rose, *Parallel Lives: Five Victorian Marriages* (New York: Alfred A. Knopf, 1984).

18. H. Gadlin, "Private Lives and Public Order: A Critical View of the History of Intimate Relations in the United States," in *Close Relationships: Perspectives on the Meaning of Intimacy*, ed. G. Levinger and H. L. Rausch (Amherst, Mass.: University of Massachusetts Press, 1977), pp. 33–72.

19. L. B. Rubin, *Intimate Strangers: Men and Women Together* (New York: Harper & Row, 1983).

20. A. Swidler, "Love and Adulthood in American Culture," in *Themes of Work and Love in Adulthood*, ed. N. J. Smelser and E. H. Erikson (Cambridge, Mass.: Harvard University Press, 1980), pp. 120–47, at p. 133.

21. R. N. Bellah, R. Madsen, W. M. Sullivan, A. Swidler, and S. M. Tipton, *Habits of the Heart: Individualism and Commitment in American Life* (Berkeley: University of California Press, 1985). Bellah et al.'s book is more concerned with group commitment than personal intimacy, though both are addressed. As such, the book is focused more on alienation than on loneliness. The distinction between these two domains is important, though the two are also related. Bellah finds that Americans have difficulty committing themselves to social enterprises such as church, community groups, and social organizations. Though they feel a longing to dedicate themselves to something larger than their own personal lives, they find it extremely difficult to do so, partly because they have lost faith in many traditional institutions. Therefore, they find it difficult to integrate themselves in a meaningful and fulfilling way into society. In his book *Loneliness* (see note 11), Robert Weiss calls this problem "social isolation," and he contrasts it to "emotional isolation," which stems from a failure to be intimate with people in one's personal life. Weiss sees both forms of isolation as aspects of loneliness in general. Most scholars who study this topic, however, use the term "loneliness" to mean emotional isolation only. The term "alienation," by contrast, is often used to refer to Weiss's social isolation.

22. J. Veroff, E. Douvan, and R. A. Kulka, *The Inner American: A Self-Portrait from 1957 to 1976* (New York: Basic Books, 1981).

23. Ibid., p. 19.

24. S. Freud, *Beyond the Pleasure Principle* (1920), in *The Standard Edition of the Complete Psychological Works of Sigmund Freud,* ed. J. Strachey, vol. 18 (London: Hogarth, 1955). Over the course of his career, Freud put forth three successive theories of motivation. In the first, Freud pitted the "ego instincts" against the "sexual instincts." The ego instincts were forces within the individual that assured the preservation of the self and the maintenance of daily life. For example, the hunger drive promotes the survival of the individual by motivating him or her to eat. The sexual instincts assure the preservation of the species by motivating the organism to seek out love objects in the world, ultimately culminating in sexual intercourse and the generation of progeny.

Freud's second theory of motivation viewed these two classes of instincts as derivatives of a common pool of energy, which he termed "primary narcissistic libido." According to this view, a finite quantum of narcissistic libido or sexual energy could be channeled into two different directions: toward the self (ego libido) or toward others (object libido). Ego libido promotes the survival of the individual, while object libido promotes the survival of the species. The narcissist, therefore, invests too much libido in the self and not enough in others.

Freud's third and final theory of motivation appeared in 1920, with the publication of *Beyond the Pleasure Principle.* In this radically transformed view, Freud argued for the existence of two discrete classes of instincts, one promoting life and the other serving death. Grouped together now under one rubric are both the ego libido (self-love) and the object libido (love of others). Ego libido and object libido are the two central components of Eros, or the sexual instincts in general. A second independent source of energy comes from the death instincts, sometimes termed Thanatos. When the death instincts are directed toward the self, we encounter inner aggression or masochism. When the death instincts are directed toward others, we encounter external aggression or sadism.

For people (like myself) who appreciate symmetry in their theories, Freud's final view of motivation is a tour de force. Two perfectly opposed instincts—Eros and Thanatos—work against each other to effect opposite ends: life (union) and death (separation). Within each of the two classes, two opposite tendencies can be seen, as the "energy" of the instincts is directed either inward (self-love, self-hate) or outward (object-love, object-hate). Conflict between opposites exists throughout. Of course, both classes of instincts work behind the scenes, as the forever unconscious and masterfully disguised ultimate forces in human personality. Freud believed, furthermore, that both classes of instincts are ultimately grounded in human biology and evolution. He argued that both instincts are vestiges of an evolutionary past, working to "return" the organism to its past. The death instincts work to return the organism to the inert state of death that preceded the state of life. The sexual (life) instincts work to "return" the organism to an earlier stage in evolution—

a kind of primal bisexuality or unity of male and female, which, Freud speculated, was the characteristic mode of existence of the primitive species who were our evolutionary forerunners, millions of years ago. Both classes of instincts, therefore, are "conservative," in that they seek to "conserve" some basic aspect of the past.

Freud's last theory of motivation has been strongly criticized, especially for its fanciful assertions about biology and evolution. Nonetheless, some still find the general outline of the theory quite compelling. A very fine discussion of Freud's theory of life and death instincts can be found in C. F. Monte, *Beneath the Mask: An Introduction to Theories of Personality,* 3d ed. (New York: Holt, Rinehart and Winston, 1987), chap. 3, pp. 95–105. See also N. O. Brown, *Life Against Death: The Psychoanalytical Meaning of History* (New York: Random House, 1959); and F. J. Sulloway, *Freud, Biologist of the Mind: Beyond the Psychoanalytic Legend* (New York: Basic Books, 1979).

25. These theories include Angyal's distinction between *surrender* and *autonomy,* Rank's *fear of death* (which motivates us to seek union) versus *fear of life* (which motivates us to separate from others), Adler's *social interest* versus *striving for superiority,* Kegan's "psychologics" of *inclusion* versus *independence,* Gilligan's ethics of *interdependence* (and care) versus *individuation* (and pride), Hogan's evolutionarily adaptive tendencies to gaining *acceptance* versus *status* in social groups, Tomkins's "psychological magnification" of *joy/enjoyment* versus *excitement/interest,* and my own distinction between *intimacy* and *power* motivation. Sources: Adler, *Practice and Theory* (n. 2 above); A. Angyal, *Foundations for a Science of Personality* (New York: Commonwealth Fund, 1941); C. Gilligan, *In a Different Voice: Psychological Theory and Women's Development* (Cambridge, Mass.: Harvard University Press, 1982); R. Hogan, "A Socioanalytic Theory of Personality," in *Nebraska Symposium on Motivation,* ed. M. Page (Lincoln: University of Nebraska Press, 1982), pp. 55–89; R. Kegan, *The Evolving Self: Problems and Process in Human Development* (Cambridge, Mass.: Harvard University Press, 1982); McAdams, *Power, Intimacy, and the Life Story* (n. 1 above); O. Rank, *Truth vs. reality* (New York: Norton, 1978; orig. 1936); and S. S. Tomkins, "Script Theory: Differential Magnification of Affects," in *Nebraska Symposium on Motivation,* ed. H. E. Howe and R. A. Dienstbier (Lincoln: University of Nebraska Press, 1979), pp. 201–36.

26. D. Bakan, *The Duality of Human Existence: Isolation and Communion in Western Man* (Boston: Beacon Press, 1966).

27. Roberta K. is the case of "Rebecca K." in my *Power, Intimacy, and the Life Story* (n. 1 above), pp. 193–95.

28. D. P. McAdams, "Experiences of Intimacy and Power: Relationships Between Social Motives and Autobiographical Memory," *Journal of Personality and Social Psychology* 42 (1982): 292–302. See also idem, *Power, Intimacy, and the Life Story* (n. 1 above), chap. 5.

29. Quoted in S. L. Charme, *Meaning and Myth in the Study of Lives: A Sartrean Perspective* (Philadelphia: University of Pennsylvania Press, 1984).

30. I have identified four components of a person's life story. The first is the *ideological setting* of the story, which exists as a backdrop of fundamental beliefs and values about self and world. Like the setting of any story, a person's beliefs and values about what is good (ethics), what is true (epistemology), and indeed what "is" (ontology) locate a person's life story in a particular "time" and "place." The ideological setting is the context or background for the life story. It is generally well established by early adulthood and changes very little thereafter. Like a story's setting, furthermore, it is generally taken for granted once it has been established.

Nuclear episodes constitute the second component of the self-defining life story. Nuclear episodes are the critical scenes that stand out in bold print in the text. These are the high points, low points, and turning points in the story. What we recall as the major incidents in our lives says a lot about who we are, who we were, and who we wish to be. Nuclear episodes typically affirm what we believe to be basic truths about ourselves, providing evidence from our own biographies for our own interpretations of our lives. In the life of Sara N., a key nuclear episode was her baptism on Valentine's Day.

The third component of the life story is *character*, captured in my concept of the "imago." An imago is a personified and idealized image of the self that plays the role of "main character" in a life story. Imagoes are parts of myself—little, personified "mes" within me, which assume prominence in particular parts of my life story. Imagoes are like stock characters in a person's life story, in that they are rather one-dimensional and not fully representative of the person's many-faceted self. In Sara's life story, one dominant imago is "the lover." In many different ways, Sara enacts the role of the consummate lover in her daily life. Yet the lover is not the only role she enacts, and no single imago can define the complex life of a single person. In Roberta's life story, a central imago is what I have called "the swift traveler." A second imago in Roberta's story is "the naïve idealist."

The fourth component of a life story is what I have termed the *generativity script*. The generativity script is an outline for the future plot of the story that specifies precisely what the person is going to do in order to extend his or her story into future generations. In adulthood, most people seek to leave a legacy of some kind, through their children, their work, their relations with others, or a variety of other channels. We seek to do something or make something or act in some way to assure that part of us is left behind for the next generation. Our plans for doing so constitute our generativity script. The generativity script provides a kind of *ending* for our life story, while suggesting that the story itself does not really end but continues into the next generation. I will have more to say about generativity in Chapter 5.

My life-story approach to human identity is described in detail in the following sources: McAdams, *Power, Intimacy, and the Life Story* (n. 1 above);

idem, "A Life-Story Model of Identity," in *Perspectives in Personality*, ed. R. Hogan and W. H. Jones (Greenwich, Conn.: JAI Press, 1987), vol. 2, pp. 15–50; idem, "Self and Story," in *Perspectives in Personality: Approaches to Understanding Lives*, ed. A. J. Stewart, J. M. Healy, and D. J. Ozer (Greenwich, Conn.: JAI Press, 1988); and idem, *The Person: An Introduction to Personality Psychology* (San Diego, Calif.: Harcourt Brace Jovanovich, in press), chap. 10.

31. The main characters in a person's life story are termed "imagoes." Each is a personified and idealized image of the self. The concept of the imago has its roots in traditional clinical writings (especially Carl Jung and the object-relations theorists) and in modern social-cognitive psychology (writings on "schemas," "scripts," and "plans"). Drawing together a number of different theoretical approaches from these two domains, I have enumerated eight basic principles of the imago. (1) The self is composed of personified and idealized internal images, or "imagoes," that are affect-laden. (2) The origins of a particular imago lie in the internalization of loved (and hated) "objects" (significant people) in the person's world. (3) A person's most significant interpersonal relationships are profoundly influenced by imagoes. (4) Imagoes are often arranged in the self as dialectical opposites. (5) The synthesis of opposing imagoes is a hallmark of the mature self. (6) Imagoes are superordinate schemata for organizing and evaluating information about the self. (7) Imagoes specify recurrent behavioral plans. (8) Imagoes give cognitive form to personal goals, fears, and desires. Sources include D. P. McAdams, "Love, Power, and Images of the Self," in *Emotion in Adult Development*, ed. C. Z. Malatesta and C. E. Izard (Beverly Hills, Calif.: Sage, 1984), pp. 159–74; and idem, "The 'Imago': A Key Narrative Component of Identity," in *Review of Personality and Social Psychology* 6 (1985): *Self, situations, and social behavior*, ed. P. Shaver, pp. 115–41.

Chapter 2: The Intimacy Motive

1. J. A. Mohler, *Dimensions of Love: East and West* (Garden City, N. Y.: Doubleday, 1975).

2. R. J. Sternberg and S. Grajek, "The Nature of Love," *Journal of Personality and Social Psychology* 47 (1984): 312–29, at p. 327.

3. C. Hendrick and S. Hendrick, "A Theory and Method of Love," *Journal of Personality and Social Psychology* 50 (1986): 392–402. On the "Attitudes About Love and Sex" questionnaire, each of the six dimensions of love is represented by seven items. The person answers "true" or "false" to each item. There follow two sample items from each of the six scales. For *eros:* "My lover and I were attracted to each other immediately after we first met." "Our lovemaking is very intense and satisfying." For *ludus:* "I believe that what my lover doesn't know about me won't hurt him/her." "I enjoy playing the 'game of

love' with a number of different partners." For *storge:* "Genuine love first requires caring for a while." "Love is really a deep friendship, not a mysterious, mystical emotion." For *pragma:* "It is best to love someone with a similar background." "I try to plan my life carefully before choosing a lover." For *mania:* "I cannot relax if I suspect my lover is with someone else." "When my lover doesn't pay attention to me, I feel sick all over." For *agape:* "I would rather suffer myself than let my lover suffer." "I would endure all things for the sake of my lover."

The relations between Hendrick and Hendrick's model of love and other social-science models—such as those presented by Walster and Walster, Kelley, Blau, Maslow, and Clark and Mills—are detailed in D. P. McAdams, "Personal Needs and Personal Relationships," in *Handbook of Personal Relationships,* ed. S. Duck (New York: Wiley, 1988), pp. 7–22. Sources mentioned above are: P. M. Blau, *Exchange and Power in Social Life* (New York: Wiley, 1964); M. S. Clark and J. Mills, "Interpersonal Attraction in Exchange and Communal Relationships," *Journal of Personality and Social Psychology* 37 (1979): 12–24; H. H. Kelley, *Close Relationships* (San Francisco: Freeman, 1983); A. Maslow, *Toward a Psychology of Being* (New York: Van Nostrand Reinhold, 1968); and E. Walster and G. W. Walster, *A New Look at Love* (Reading, Mass.: Addison-Wesley, 1978).

4. C. S. Lewis, *The Four Loves* (New York: Harcourt Brace, 1960).

5. Ibid., p. 103.

6. It is always risky to speculate about what is "natural" in human evolution. But many scholars agree that humans probably evolved as a moderately gregarious species, traditionally living in small nomadic groups. Group living required a modicum of cooperation and friendliness. Thus, a biologically rooted tendency to relate to known others in a nonthreatening and cooperative manner is likely to have proved adaptive throughout human evolution. The point is expressed well in R. Hogan, "Personality Psychology: Back to Basics," in *The Emergence of Personality,* ed. J. Aronoff, A. I. Rabin, and R. A. Zucker (New York: Springer, 1987), pp. 79–104.

7. C. Rogers, *On Becoming a Person* (Boston: Houghton Mifflin, 1961).

8. R. A. Johnson, *We: Understanding the Psychology of Romantic Love* (San Francisco: Harper & Row, 1983), p. xi.

9. S. Peele and A. Brodsky, *Love and Addiction* (New York: Taplinger, 1975).

10. M. S. Mahler, F. Pine, and A. Bergman, *The Psychological Birth of the Human Infant: Symbiosis and Individuation* (New York: Basic Books, 1975).

11. L. H. Silverman, F. M. Lachmann, and R. H. Milich, *The Search for Oneness* (New York: International Universities Press, 1982).

12. Much has been written on courtly love. One of the more penetrating

analyses is offered by Irving Singer in his monumental study of love from antiquity to the modern age. Singer makes the point that medieval courtly love differs markedly from more modern versions of romantic love, especially those prevalent in the eighteenth and nineteenth centuries. In courtly love, the lovers typically exist as perfect individuals whose perfect love is a natural extension of their own flawless natures. In more modern romantic literature, however, two ordinary and imperfect people find perfection *through* their erotic union. In this latter case, it is love that makes people perfect, not perfect people who make love:

> The perfectionism in courtly love comes ultimately from Plato. But Romantic love often turned to other philosophers for inspiration. Platonism sees love as an intermediary between the aspiring soul and the perfect object it naturally desires. Romanticism focuses upon the inherent creativity of love. Medieval theology had always insisted upon the creative character of agape, God's love, but no one dared suggest that anything comparable originated in human beings. For theorists of Romantic love, however, the erotic underlies everything in man that is creative. Far from uniting persons who are antecedently perfect, the experience of love *makes* their ideality. From merging and the return to wholeness there accrue values that the lovers could not have had previously or in isolation. In addition to the notion of merging, the Romantics introduced organic and genetic metaphors. As a child is an organism that results from the fusing of male and female biology, so too Romantic lovers become in their totality a new and higher form of life.

I. Singer, *The Nature of Love*, vol. 3: *The Modern World* [Chicago: University of Chicago Press, 1987], pp. 15–16.)

13. M. F. Weiner, "Healthy and Pathological Love: Psychodynamic Views," in *On Love and Loving*, ed. K. S. Pope and Associates (San Francisco, Calif.: Jossey-Bass, 1980), pp. 114–32.

14. As a takeoff of these last two sentences, Freud might say, "No wonder that *life* can make us miserable. It asks us to accomplish the impossible!" One of the most compelling ideas in all of Freud is the notion of overdetermination. All of our behavior and experience is determined by a multitude of forces over which we have very little control. They are in constant conflict with one another. And, for the most part, we are not even able to identify these forces in our lives, in that they exist outside of our own awareness as agents of the unconscious. In *Civilization and Its Discontents*, Freud lamented the fate of all civilized persons: that contemporary men and women, driven by their ancient sexual and aggressive inclinations, must find ways of living in modern societies that, ironically, must be designed to squelch the direct and immediate expression of instinctual urges. In other words, persons are driven

by instincts while societies are driven by the suppression of instincts. Beyond the conflict between the individual and society, however, are the related and equally vexing conflicts that rage within the person himself or herself.

The Freudian man or woman is a bundle of contradictions, living according to simultaneous internal dictates that run counter to each other. A man wishes he could be honored as the greatest American president of all time, and at the same time he seeks to be publicly humiliated as a fraud. Another wants to kill his father, and he wants his father to take him to a Cubs game. A woman wants to commit the most egregious sins the world has ever known, and she would love to be a saint. Such are the conflicts by which we live and die, and by which we become miserable. Yet, this is the nature of human life, Freud maintained. And each of our moves in life represents a compromise among a myriad of conflicting, determining, unconscious forces within.

15. G. Marcel, *The Philosophy of Existence* (New York: Books for Libraries, 1949), p. 25.

16. W. Wilner, "Philosophical Approaches to Interpersonal Intimacy," in *Intimacy*, ed. M. Fisher and G. Stricker (New York: Plenum, 1982), pp. 21–38.

17. Quoted ibid., p. 24.

18. Maslow, *Toward a Psychology of Being* (n. 3 above), p. 41.

19. M. Buber, *I and Thou* (New York: Charles Scribner's Sons, 1970), p. 62.

20. The study of human motivation centers on the recurrent wants and needs that energize and direct human behavior and thereby provide human lives with organization and purpose. Western scholars have traditionally viewed human motivation from four different perspectives, suggesting that (1) human beings are motivated by reasons to attain that which is "good" and "rational" in life (e.g., Plato, Carl Rogers, and modern humanistic psychologists); (2) human beings are motivated by "bad," irrational, and/or instinctual internal forces that usually bring pain and misery (e.g., Freud, certain biological approaches); (3) motives are determined solely by environmental learning (e.g., Locke, B. F. Skinner, and most behaviorist approaches to psychology); or (4) there exists an indeterminate number of different motives about which individual views vary widely (William James, numerous twentieth-century psychologists, such as Henry Murray and David McClelland). Among contemporary views of human motivation, those focusing on the biological bases of motives have emphasized generalized drives, the nature of reward, and the instinctual foundations of human behavior in the context of human evolution. Contemporary cognitive approaches, by contrast, have emphasized the energizing and directing influences of such factors as expectancies, cognitive plans, schemata, scripts, conscious strivings, and attributions. See R. Geen, W. W. Beatty, and R. M. Arkin, *Human Motivation: Physiological, Behavioral, and Social Approaches* (Boston: Allyn and Bacon, 1984); and D. P. McAdams, "Per-

sonality and Motives," in *Contemporary Research in Personality*, ed. W. H. Jones, B. A. Winstead, and V. J. Derlega (Chicago: Nelson-Hall, in press).

21. D. C. McClelland, *Personality* (New York: Holt, Rinehart and Winston, 1951); idem, "Is Personality Consistent?" in *Further Explorations in Personality*, ed. A. I. Rabin, J. Aronoff, A. M. Barclay, and R. A. Zucker (New York: Wiley-Interscience, 1981), pp. 87–113.

22. After falling into disrepute in academic circles in the 1960s and 1970s, trait psychology has come back with a vengeance in the past decade. A number of impressive studies conducted since 1980 have shown that certain basic personality traits appear to be fairly stable over time and may be linked to biological predispositions that vary widely across different people. Some psychologists have suggested that individual differences in infant temperament, assumed to be genetically determined, may pave the way for the development of certain traits in the adult years. While traits are surely shaped by learning and experience, therefore, some psychologists are coming around to the view that a significant biological component may also be involved.

Factor analytic studies employing long questionnaires administered to large samples of subjects have recently suggested that the many different traits of human personality can be reduced to a short list. One popular list is called "the Big Five." Psychologists Paul Costa and Robert McCrae have argued forcefully for five basic trait dimensions in human personality: extraversion/introversion, neuroticism, openness to experience, agreeableness, and conscientiousness. With respect to the first dimension, people who score high on extraversion are described as sociable, fun-loving, affectionate, friendly, spontaneous, and talkative; people who score low on extraversion (which is the same as scoring "high" on introversion) are rather shy, sober, reserved, aloof, inhibited, and quiet. For the second dimension of neuroticism, higher scorers are described as nervous, worrying, high-strung, insecure, self-pitying, and vulnerable; low scorers are calm, at ease, relaxed, secure, self-satisfied, and hardy. For the third dimension of openness to experience, high scorers are original, imaginative, creative, complex, and curious; low scorers are conventional, down-to-earth, uncreative, simple, and uncurious. For the fourth dimension of agreeableness, high scorers are good-natured, softhearted, courteous, forgiving, and sympathetic; low scorers are irritable, ruthless, rude, vengeful, and callous. Finally, for the last dimension of conscientiousness, high scorers are careful, reliable, well organized, self-disciplined, and persevering; low scorers are careless, undependable, disorganized, weak willed, and negligent.

Each of these five trait dimensions, therefore, is a bipolar, linear continuum upon which various persons can be arrayed. Most people fall in the general middle of most trait dimensions, though it would not be unusual to score extremely high or low on one or two of the dimensions. Therefore, you may be mildly introverted, not very neurotic, moderately open to experience, and moderately agreeable, but extremely conscientious. Trait approaches to personality assume that the person can be well described as the sum of his or her various trait standings. For further discussion, see D. P. McAdams, *The Person: An Introduction to Personality Psychology* (San Diego, Calif.: Harcourt Brace Jovanovich, in press), chap. 6; and R. R. McCrae and P. T. Costa, Jr., "Validation of the Five-Factor Model of Personality Across Instruments and Observers," *Journal of Personality and Social Psychology* 52 (1987): 81–90.

23. From G. Wilson, "Introversion-extraversion," in *Dimensions of Personality,* ed. H. London and J. E. Exner, Jr. (New York: Wiley-Interscience, 1978), pp. 217–61 at p. 219.

24. "Schema" is one of the most popular terms used in psychology today. In its most general sense, a schema is an abstract knowledge structure. Schemata contain information, but they are not necessarily the information per se. Rather, a schema is like a "package" for information, a characteristic form that information can take. For instance, I may organize information about American political candidates according to the schema of "liberal–conservative." When one candidate argues that he or she favors high defense spending, cutbacks in social programs, and overall fiscal constraint, I may lump this information together to conclude, tentatively at least, that the candidate espouses rather conservative political views. The schema of conservative–liberal, therefore, helps me reduce, digest, and organize political information in an efficient manner. In processing the plethora of information we encounter in daily life, we make extensive use of a great variety of schemata, most of which have been built up over years of learning and experience. Some of these schemata are rather common cultural categories, like my example of conservative–liberal, while others are private and idiosyncratic. Over time and experience, our schemata change and develop, often becoming more articulated and differentiated as we learn more about the world.

25. S. Freud, *The Interpretation of Dreams* (1900), in *The Standard Edition of the Complete Psychological Works of Sigmund Freud,* ed. J. Strachey, vols. 4 and 5 (London: Hogarth, 1953).

26. Dr. M. is the eminent Dr. Josef Breuer, with whom Freud collaborated in his first major book on psychoanalysis, entitled *Studies in Hysteria* (1895). A prominent physician in Vienna, the elder Breuer had taken young Freud under his wing in the 1880s and helped him get started as a physician. He also loaned Freud money and gave him personal advice. Their close personal and professional relationship ended in bitter feud, however, sometime in the early 1890s (shortly before Freud's dream of Irma) for reasons that have never been made completely clear. Freud's official biographer, Ernest Jones, underscores disagreements between Freud and Breuer about the proper role of sexuality in the etiology of hysteria and other mental disturbances (Freud claiming that all neuroses have a sexual component and Breuer disagreeing). Some have argued

that Breuer functioned as Freud's last father figure and was therefore destined to be "killed" (that is, overcome), in line with Freud's strong Oedipal inclinations.

For whatever reasons, Freud came to feel that Breuer had betrayed him, and once they parted as enemies the two were never again to meet as friends. During the time of the dream, therefore, Freud felt alone in the world of medicine and science, betrayed by his early mentor and either scorned or neglected for his emerging theoretical formulations. His only confidant was Wilhelm Fliess, a younger colleague with whom Freud exchanged a voluminous correspondence.

Volumes have been written on the relations between Freud and Breuer and between Freud and Fliess. Especially illuminating are these sources: E. L. Freud, ed., *The Letters of Sigmund Freud* (New York: Basic Books, 1960); E. Jones, *The Life and Work of Sigmund Freud*, 3 vols. (New York: Basic Books, 1953–57); R. S. Steele, *Freud and Jung: Conflicts of Interpretation* (London: Routledge and Kegan Paul, 1982); and F. Sulloway, *Freud, Biologist of the Mind* (New York: Basic Books, 1979).

27. C. D. Morgan and H. A. Murray, "A Method of Investigating Fantasies," *Archives of Neurological Psychiatry* 34 (1935): 289–306; H. A. Murray, *Explorations in Personality* (New York: Oxford University Press, 1938).

28. Paul Ricoeur distinguishes between two different ways to approach a text that is to be interpreted, a text such as a dream or narrative fantasy. The first way is to view the text as a *cunning distortion*. In this case, the text is seen as disguising the meanings it contains. Interpretation of the text involves delving below the surface, moving beyond appearances, in order to reveal that which has been buried, hidden, and disguised. The text is structured in such a way as to make this kind of discovery very difficult. Freud viewed dreams as cunning distortions, containing a deceptively simple manifest content that concealed deeper latent meanings. The second approach is to view the text as an *innocent analogy*. In this case, interpretation may proceed in a much more straightforward manner. The interpreter is to trust the manifest content of the text to reveal important information itself. Texts are not necessarily tricky, though interpretation must still be careful and conscientious. Murray's approach to the fantasy stories produced by the Thematic Apperception Test (TAT) and the approach followed in this book rest on the assumption that texts are, at least partly, innocent analogies. Interpreting TAT stories for motivational themes involves careful scrutiny of the manifest content of the text to discern recurrent narrative motifs that reveal important information about the person. See P. Ricoeur, *Freud and Philosophy: An Essay on Interpretation*, trans. Denis Savage (New Haven, Conn.: Yale University Press, 1970).

29. Psychologists David McClelland and John Atkinson pioneered the use of the TAT to assess individual differences in motives, focusing first on the "achievement motive." McClelland and Atkinson conceived of the achieve-

ment motive as a recurrent desire for "doing well" or "performing better" in various tasks. In their original derivation studies, McClelland and Atkinson asked college students to write short TAT stories under various laboratory conditions. In one condition, the students were first administered a series of cognitive tasks (such as unscrambling words) and told that their performance on the tasks would be an indication of their general intelligence and leadership ability. It was assumed that such instructions would temporarily arouse achievement thoughts and feelings in these subjects, and that these thoughts and feelings would be projected into the stories written on the TAT, administered immediately after the task. In another (neutral) condition, students were administered the same tasks but were told that the tasks were newly developed and not likely to be valid measures of much of anything. It was assumed that these subjects would be less "aroused" with respect to achievement strivings than the subjects in the first group.

McClelland and Atkinson examined carefully the stories written in response to the TAT by students in both conditions. They detected a number of consistent content differences between the groups, with students in the arousal group tending to write more stories involving characters striving to do better, compared to students in the neutral group. Further comparisons from different studies and various refinements produced a content scoring system for the TAT. The system is made up of the particular content themes that *consistently differentiated between stories written under achievement arousal and under neutral conditions.* Most of the themes concern characters' strivings to perform better in various situations, their feelings and anticipations about performing better, and obstacles in the path of better performance.

Although the achievement motive scoring system was derived by examining group differences in narrative content, the system has proved extremely sensitive and valuable as an index of individual differences within groups. In a typical individual-differences study, a large number of persons are administered the TAT under standardized neutral conditions. The subjects' TAT stories are then scored by trained coders according to the system derived in the original arousal studies. The results typically reveal a normal distribution in the sample, with scores ranging from high to low achievement motivation. It is assumed that the person's "natural" level of achievement motivation will be expressed in TAT stories written under such neutral conditions.

A substantial empirical literature suggests that people who score high on TAT achievement motivation behave in different ways from people who score low, supporting what psychologists call the "construct validity" of the TAT measure. For instance, people high in achievement motivation tend to prefer and show high performance in tasks of moderate challenge that provide immediate feedback concerning success and failure; they tend to be persistent and highly efficient in many kinds of performance, sometimes cutting corners or even cheating in order to maximize productivity; they tend to exhibit high self-control and a future time perspective; and they tend to be restless, innovative, and drawn toward change and movement. For further discussion, see J. W. Atkinson, ed., *Motives in Fantasy, Action, and Society* (Princeton, N.J.: Van Nostrand, 1958); D. C. McClelland, *Human motivation* (Glenview, Ill.: Scott, Foresman, 1985); and D. C. McClelland, J. W. Atkinson, R. A. Clark, and E. L. Lowell, *The Achievement Motive* (New York: Appleton-Century-Crofts, 1953).

30. A total of forty-two students wrote TAT stories under the fraternity/ sorority arousal conditions, half men in the fraternity and half women in the sorority. These were compared to stories written by forty-two students (half fraternity members and half sorority members) under neutral, classroom conditions. The TAT was administered in the standard group format, in which a series of pictures is shown on a screen and each person is given five minutes to write a story in response to each of the pictures. In this study, six pictures were used, so the entire procedure required a little more than half an hour to complete.

For the fraternity, the ritual ceremony was conducted on a weekend evening, and it lasted about one hour. The ceremony was chosen as an arousal condition because of the intense feelings of brotherhood and good cheer traditionally engendered at this celebration. On these occasions, the fraternity members reported, a general atmosphere of warmth, closeness, and conviviality ordinarily prevails. I administered the TAT directly after the formal festivities, and because I am a former member of the fraternity, the administration was not viewed as intrusive. All of the members of the fraternity participated in the ceremony, of course, but twenty-one had been asked beforehand to take the TATS at the end of the ceremony. During the testing, the other members and initiates of the fraternity (about fifty in number) continued the celebration in a less formal way in another room of the fraternity house. After the testing period, the subjects returned to the larger group.

The sorority ceremony, held on a Sunday afternoon, was comparable, though it lasted almost two hours and included the performance of skits by various members and initiates. Approximately the same number of women attended the ceremony as did men for the fraternity event. The twenty-one sorority participants in the arousal study were chosen ahead of time and informed that they would be completing the TAT after the ceremony. Because I was also personally acquainted with a number of the sorority members and because the administration of the TAT was conducted by a sorority sister herself, the testing procedure was not viewed as intrusive. As the sorority does not own its own house, the celebration was conducted in a lounge rented by the university to the group for special occasions. During the testing, the other members of the sorority waited for the subjects in various adjoining rooms and in the hallway.

For the neutral condition, the forty-two subjects were administered the TAT together in a large classroom in which they were assigned seats spread out around the room, so as to minimize intimacy cues. These TATS were administered on a weekday evening, approximately two weeks after the arousal conditions. See D. P. McAdams, "A Thematic Coding System for the Intimacy Motive," *Journal of Research in Personality* 14 (1980): 413–32.

31. For the second arousal study, TATS were administered to thirty-eight undergraduates (nineteen women, nineteen men) attending a dancing party sponsored by a college organization. Approximately two hundred people attended the party. The dance was not a "dating party" per se, though some heterosexual couples did attend. Most of the guests, however, came in various groups numbering between three and ten individuals in each. About an equal number of men and women attended the party. Over the course of the evening, I administered the TAT in five groups, four containing eight participants each and one containing six. All of the participants were volunteers who reported that (1) they were having a "good time" and (2) they had had no more than two alcoholic drinks in the course of the evening and were not "feeling the effects" of the alcohol. The participants completed the TAT at a special table that I set up in one of the rooms for the party, on top of which sat a sign advertising my study of "imagination in story writing." The TAT stories written under the party arousal condition were compared with those written in the neutral classroom condition described in note 30.

Data from ninety-two subjects (forty-six female and forty-six male) were used for the third arousal study. Twenty-three dating couples were selected from a sample of 101 dating couples studied by L. A. Peplau, Z. Rubin, and C. Hill ("The Sexual Balance of Power," *Psychology Today* [November 1976]: 142–51). The 101 couples had been administered the TAT and a self-report questionnaire assessing the intensity of their love for each other. The twenty-three couples used in this arousal study reported extremely high levels of love on the questionnaire. The state of being in love, therefore, was considered the arousal condition. Their TAT stories were compared to those written by forty-six other undergraduates chosen randomly from a large sample. These latter forty-six constituted the "neutral" control group for the study.

For the fourth arousal study, students wrote TAT stories before and after an intensive laboratory experience designed to promote feelings of warmth, friendliness, and communication. Their stories written before the experience were considered to be the "neutral" stories, and the stories written after the experience were considered to be the "arousal" stories. A total of forty-three students (twenty-three male and twenty female) participated in this fourth arousal study.

32. A person's score on intimacy motivation is strongly influenced by the types of TAT pictures to which he or she writes stories. Therefore, in a particular research project the subjects always write stories to the same pictures, so that comparisons across subjects can be made. No standard set of pictures, however, has ever been developed for research employing the TAT. In studies of intimacy and power motivation, I usually employ a set of six pictures commonly used by other researchers: (1) two people sitting on a bench; (2) a man

sitting at a desk upon which sits a photograph of a family; (3) a ship captain talking to another man; (4) a man and woman flying through the air on a trapeze; (5) two women in a laboratory; and (6) a younger woman and an older man walking through a field with horses and a dog. Because different TAT pictures pull for different kinds of story imagery, there exists no consensually validated set of "cut-off scores" to determine what is "high" and what is "low" for intimacy motivation. Rather, scores are compared to one another within the same study. Therefore, a "high" or a "low" score is always relative to the other scores in that particular study.

Despite impressive construct validity, TAT scoring systems for the intimacy, power, and achievement motives are not without their detractors (e.g., D. E. Entwisle, "To Dispel Fantasies about Fantasy-Based Measures of Achievement Motivation," *Psychological Bulletin* 77 [1972]: 377–91; E. Klinger, "Fantasy Need Achievement as a Motivational Construct," *Psychological Bulletin* 66 [1966]: 291–308). Most criticisms of the method are based on psychometric grounds. The most damning have asserted that the general method of measuring motives through content analysis of fantasy is not psychometrically reliable or consistent. A person's score on achievement motivation, for instance, can vary significantly from one testing session to the next—a situation that should not occur if the measure is tapping a relatively stable personality disposition. Defenders of the TAT have argued that low test–retest reliability coefficients are partially due to the fact that when a subject takes the TAT a second time, it is phenomenologically no longer the same test. Further, subjects who remember the pictures to which they wrote stories in a previous TAT session will most likely write different stories the second time, not wishing to repeat themselves. Indeed, D. G. Winter and A. J. Stewart ("Power Motive Reliability as a Function of Retest Instructions," *Journal of Consulting and Clinical Psychology* 45 [1977]: 436–40) and A. Lundy ("The Reliability of the Thematic Apperception Test," *Journal of Personality Assessment* 49 [1985]: 141–45) have shown that when subjects are told they may, if they wish, write stories similar or identical to ones they have written in previous TAT sessions, test–retest coefficients rise to psychometrically respectable levels.

The controversy over the psychometric reliability of the TAT as a measure of human motives is extremely complex and beyond the scope of this book. Although there is little doubt that the TAT is more subject to the vagaries of random, extraneous effects (e.g., mood, level of fatigue) than are highly structured questionnaires in which subjects choose listed responses instead of generating their own, the impressive array of findings supporting the construct validity of TAT measures of achievement, power, and intimacy motivation suggests that content analysis of narrative fantasy can be an extremely sensitive and valuable method of personality assessment. McClelland provides a thoughtful analysis of the merits and limitations of the TAT in "Motive Dispositions: The Merits of Operant and Respondent Measures," in *Review of Personality and Social Psychology* 1 (1980), ed. L. Wheeler, pp. 10–41. Atkinson has also considered in detail the controversy and has proposed a sophisticated theoretical model, termed the "dynamics of action," to explain why traditional psychometric indexes of test–retest reliability cannot be logically applied to open-ended assessment devices such as the TAT; see "Studying Personality in the Context of an Advanced Motivational Psychology," *American Psychologist* 36 (1981): 117–28.

33. The discussion of the scoring system for the intimacy motive is excerpted from the full-length scoring manual, complete with 210 practice stories and instructions for attaining high scoring reliability: D. P. McAdams, *Scoring Manual for the Intimacy Motive*, Psychological Documents 14, abstract 2614 (San Rafael, Calif.: Select Press, 1984), The manual may be obtained from Select Press at P.O. Box 9838, San Rafael, CA 94912. An abbreviated version appears as Appendix C of my *Power, Intimacy, and the Life Story* (Chicago: Dorsey Press, 1985), pp. 291–99.

34. See McAdams, "Thematic Coding System" (n. 30 above); and idem and J. Powers, "Themes of Intimacy in Behavior and Thought," *Journal of Personality and Social Psychology* 40 (1981): 573–87.

Chapter 3: Intimate Behavior, Intimate Lives

1. D. Ignatow, *David Ignatow: Selected Poems,* ed. Robert Bly (Middletown, Conn.: Wesleyan University Press, 1975), p. 82. Reprinted by permission.

2. J. L. Moreno, *Psychodrama*, vol. 1 (Beacon, N.Y.: Beacon House, 1946).

3. The methodological details of this study are reported in D. P. McAdams and J. Powers, "Themes of Intimacy in Behavior and Thought," *Journal of Personality and Social Psychology* 40 (1981): 573–87. In order to minimize the problem of participants' choosing their psychodramas on the basis of those created by other participants, we asked all of the students in the study to jot down the central ideas of their intended psychodrama *before* any of the psychodramas were performed.

4. The forty-three videotaped psychodramas were coded by independent raters who had no knowledge of the subjects' motive scores as assessed via the TAT. Behavioral coding was conducted at two levels of analysis: discrete behaviors and behavioral themes. We delineated seven simple coding systems for discrete behaviors hypothesized to be associated with the protagonists' intimacy motive scores: (1) physical proximity to other group members, (2) amount of time giving instructions to others relative to amount of time acting out the scenario, (3) number of commands delivered to others, (4) number of references to self, (5) number of references to "we" or "us," designating the group, (6) number of outbursts of laughter by group members (assumed to

indicate joy or some kind of positive affect in the scenario), and (7) order of volunteering to be the protagonist (from first to last). Subjects scoring high in intimacy motivation were found to spend less time introducing their scenarios to the group and more time acting out the psychodrama, to make more references to "we" or "us" when referring to themselves and the group, to issue fewer commands to their peers, to stimulate more frequent outbursts of laughter from the group, and to position themselves in closer proximity to other group members, than subjects scoring lower on the motive.

When the psychodrama tapes were coded for behavioral themes in a fashion analogous to coding TAT stories for themes manifested in narrative, very high correlations between intimacy motivation on the TAT and intimacy behavior in scenarios were obtained. With the help of David McClelland and Richard Boyatzis, we devised a set of behavioral themes applicable to the psychodrama scenarios that (1) could be reliably coded by independent judges viewing the tapes and (2) would reflect patterns in the protagonists' behavior theoretically related to the superordinate theme of the intimacy motive—experiencing warm, close, and communicative exchange with others. Blind to the motive scores of the subjects, we initially viewed nine of the forty-three taped scenarios and rated them in terms of intimacy value. By contrasting scenarios rated as high and low in intimacy, we tried to codify the major differences in terms of a few well-defined themes. We came up with five such themes.

1. Positive affect. Score +1 if the scenario manifests consistent expression of happiness, mirth, surprise, joy, or tenderness. Score 0 if the scenario manifests only sporadic positive affect, mixed affect, or no affect. Score −1 if the scenario manifests consistent negative affect such as anger, boredom, grief, anxiety, shame, or disgust.

2. Reciprocal dialogue. Score +1 if the scenario manifests mutual dialogue and/or exchange (not necessarily verbal) that is not argumentative, competitive, or hostile. Score 0 if no such dialogue is present.

3. Surrender of control. Score +1 if the protagonist surrenders control of the scenario by giving participants considerable leeway to structure their own roles and behaviors in the context of the protagonist's drama. Score 0 if the protagonist controls the scenario.

4. Personal meaning. Score +1 if the protagonist remarks that the scenario is personally meaningful to him or her. Score 0 if no such remark is made.

5. Nature. Score +1 if the scenario manifests heightened sensory imagery with reference to the natural world, fantasies of interaction between participants and nature. Score 0 if no such nature theme is present. (This theme is related to the cow category in the intimacy motive scoring system described in Chapter 2. It designates a relationship established between a person and the external world in which there is openness, receptivity, union.)

The total intimacy behavior index was simply the sum of the scores of the five behavioral themes. When the two independent coders did not agree exactly on a particular subject's total score, then the mean of the two scores was used in the data analysis. The scores ranged hypothetically from -1 to 5. In this sample, they ranged from -1 to 4, with a mean of 1.5.

A sixth behavioral theme of nonthreatening touching was also coded, but because of technical difficulties in two of the five tapes this theme could be reliably coded for only twenty-eight of the forty-three scenarios. Scores for this theme were either $+1$ or 0. It was not included in the intimacy behavior index.

The results of the behavioral theme analysis showed that subjects who scored high in intimacy motivation tended to structure behavioral scenarios in which themes of positive affect, mutual dialogue, and surrender of control in an interpersonal encounter were central. To a lesser extent, these scenarios manifested behavioral themes of nonthreatening touching, interaction with nature, and personal meaningfulness (indicating a willingness to share personal experiences with the group). When the five behavioral themes (excluding nonthreatening touching) were combined to form the total intimacy behavior index, the correlation between the two summary indexes of intimacy, in thought and behavior—that is, the intimacy motive score on the TAT and the intimacy behavior index—was quite striking, r (41) $= +.70$, p { .001. See D. P. McAdams, "Intimacy motivation," in *Motivation and Society: A Volume in Honor of David C. McClelland*, (San Francisco, Calif.: Jossey-Bass, 1982), pp. 133–71; and McAdams and Powers, "Themes of Intimacy" (n. 3 above).

5. S. E. Hormuth, "The Sampling of Experiences *in situ*," *Journal of Personality* 54 (1986): 262–93.

6. More details on the beeper study can be found in C. A. Constantian, *Solitude: Attitudes, Beliefs, and Behavior in Regard to Spending Time Alone* (Ph.D. diss., Harvard University, 1981); and in D. P. McAdams and C. A. Constantian, "Intimacy and Affiliation Motives in Daily Living: An Experience Sampling Analysis," *Journal of Personality and Social Psychology* 45 (1983): 851–61.

7. The seminal source in this regard is S. S. Tomkins, *Affect, Imagery, and Consciousness*, vols. 1 and 2 (New York: Springer, 1963).

8. P. Ekman, W. V. Friesen, and P. Ellsworth, *Emotion in the Human Face: Guidelines for Research and an Integration of Findings* (New York: Pergamon, 1972); C. E. Izard, *Human Emotions* (New York: Plenum, 1977).

9. K. S. Robson, "The Role of Eye-to-Eye Contact in Maternal–Infant Attachment," *Journal of Child Psychology and Psychiatry* 8 (1967): 13–25; R. A. Spitz, *The First Year of Life* (New York: International Universities Press, 1965).

10. M. Argyle and M. Cook, *Gaze and Mutual Gaze* (Cambridge: Cambridge University Press, 1976); A. Mehrabian, *Nonverbal Communication* (Chicago: Al-

dine, 1972); M. L. Patterson, "An Arousal Model of Interpersonal Intimacy," *Psychological Review* 83 (1976): 235–45.

11. J.-P. Sartre, *Being and Nothingness*, trans. Hazel Barnes (New York: Philosophical Library, 1956; orig. 1942).

12. D. P. McAdams, R. J. Jackson, and C. Kirshnit, "Looking, Laughing, and Smiling in Dyads as a Function of Intimacy Motivation and Reciprocity," *Journal of Personality* 52 (1984): 261–73.

13. Ignatow, "Two Friends" (n. 1 above), p. 26. Reprinted by permission.

14. The case of Marty N. appears in my *Power, Intimacy, and the Life Story* (Chicago: Dorsey Press, 1985), p. 30.

15. D. P. McAdams, "Motivation and Friendship," in *Understanding Personal Relationships: An Interdisciplinary Approach*, ed. S. Duck and D. Perlman (Beverly Hills, Calif.: Sage, 1985), pp. 85–105.

16. The study of high points and low points in friendship histories is reported in D. P. McAdams, "Human Motives and Personal Relationships," in *Communication, Intimacy, and Close Relationships*, ed. V. J. Derlega (New York: Academic Press, 1984), pp. 41–70.

17. D. P. McAdams, S. Healy, and S. Krause, "Social Motives and Patterns of Friendship," *Journal of Personality and Social Psychology* 47 (1984): 828–38.

18. The distinction between an agentic and a communal style to friendship and other personal relationships is discussed further in D. P. McAdams, "Personal Needs and Personal Relationships," in *Handbook of Personal Relationships*, ed. S. Duck (New York: Wiley, 1988), pp. 7–22.

19. Parts of this section are derived from D. P. McAdams, "Modern Peacemakers: A Personological Perspective," *Illinois Psychologist* 26.1 (1987): 27–33. In this very speculative paper, I discuss three different models for peacemaking, derived from three deities in ancient Greek mythology: Athene, Apollo, and Prometheus, the first one to be discussed in this section. In Athene, we see the linkage between peacemaking on the one hand and prudent counseling and arbitration, teaching, and androgyny on the other.

Apollo, by contrast, highlights a peacemaker's passion for order, organization, and balance. A great peacemaker in his own right, Albert Einstein firmly believed that "God did not throw dice" in creating the universe. For Einstein, the world was ordered and rational *by faith:* there simply could be no other reality, in his view. Einstein spoke out against war and actively worked for international cooperation and arbitration for most of his adult life. At least one biographer argues that Einstein's commitment to peace was intimately tied up with his vision of the universe as an intricately ordered totality (O. Nathan and H. Norden, eds., *Einstein on Peace* [New York: Schocken, 1968], p. ix):

When, in the summer of 1914, he rebelled against the war as "something unbelievable," when he lamented his belonging to the "rotten species of man," I believe he must have felt that man's actions in war violated the sublime laws of the universe, that the willful killing of millions interfered with nature's course for which he, the scientist, had the deepest reverence. It appears that *this* was the real source of his antipathy to brutality, the motive power behind his passionate, devoted efforts to help abolish the very institution of war.

A third model of the peacemaker is Prometheus, the revolutionary. In Greek mythology, Prometheus was the champion of mortals, the defender of the underdog who paid a handsome price for his sympathies. The image of Prometheus underscores sympathy for the oppressed, radical action against authority, suffering, and separation from the mainstream. All three models of peacemaking—conciliatory Athene, rational Apollo, and revolutionary Prometheus—provide patterns of living that are highly agentic and communal, powerful and intimate.

20. In the nationwide survey described in Chapter 4, intimacy and power motivation are not significantly correlated with each other among 505 men $(r = .03)$ and slightly positively and significantly associated with each other among 696 women $(r = .12, p \{ .01)$. Most other studies show that the two motives are generally uncorrelated: in other words, knowing the score of a person on one of the two motives tells you little about his or her score on the other. It is best, therefore, to think of intimacy and power motivation as separate dimensions that do not relate directly to each other. Therefore, many people score high on both motives, many score low on both, and many score high on one and low on the other.

21. E. H. Erikson, *Gandhi's Truth: On the Origins of Militant Nonviolence* (New York: Norton, 1969), p. 44.

22. M. K. Gandhi, "On Nonviolence" (1957), in *Peace and War*, ed. C. R. Beitz and T. Herman (San Francisco, Calif.: Freeman, 1973), pp. 345–48 at p. 346.

23. C. Downing, *The Goddess: Mythological Images of the Feminine* (New York: Crossroad, 1981), p. 126.

24. J. Hillman, *Facing the Gods* (Irving, Tex.: Spring Publications, 1980), p. 31.

25. P. Brock, *Twentieth-Century Pacifism* (New York: Van Nostrand Reinhold, 1970), p. 70.

26. Many thanks to Abigail Stewart for acquainting me with Vera Brittain, both through Brittain's works and through Abigail's own writings on her. See especially V. Brittain, *Testament of Youth* (New York: Wideview Books, 1980;

orig. 1933); A. J. Stewart, C. Franz, and L. Layton, "The Changing Self: Using Personal Documents to Study Lives," *Journal of Personality* 56 (1988): 41–72; and A. J. Stewart and J. M. Healy, Jr., "The Role of Personality Development and Experience in Shaping Political Commitment: An Illustrative Case," *Journal of Social Issues* 42 (1986): 11–32.

27. Brittain, *Testament* (n. 26 above), p. 11.

28. Ibid., p. 44.

29. Ibid., p. 21.

30. Ibid., p. 655.

Chapter 4: Health and Happiness

1. J. Keats, "Ode on a Grecian Urn" (1819), 3.1–5, in *Keats: Selected Poetry, with an Introduction by Howard Moss,* ed. R. Wilbur (New York: Dell, 1959), p. 99.

2. The case of Sandy appears in my *Power, Intimacy, and the Life Story* (Chicago: Dorsey Press, 1985), pp. 94–96.

3. My discussion of comedy, tragedy, and romance draws on the work of the literary critic Northrop Frye (*Anatomy of Criticism* [Princeton, N.J.: Princeton University Press, 1957]). Taking his lead from Aristotle's *Poetics*, Frye identifies four basic forms for narrative, or what he calls *mythic archetypes:* comedy, romance, tragedy, and irony. In *Power, Intimacy, and the Life Story* (n. 1 above), I suggest that each of these story forms corresponds to a general form of a person's *life* story (pp. 54–56, 91–98). If identity is a life story, then, Frye's archetypes may be seen as four different kinds of identities in human lives.

Comedy is the archetype of dawn, spring, and birth. Stories of the hero's birth, of revival and resurrection, of creation, and of the defeat of the powers of darkness, winter, and death come under this heading. In the classic comedy (which may or may not be "funny" or "comic"), a young man wants a young woman, or vice versa, but his (or her) desire is thwarted by some opposition, often a parent or some figure of authority. At the end of the story, some twist in the plot enables the hero to have his (her) will. Thus, the movement in comedy is always toward union, and comedies often end with a wedding. With respect to identity, a life story in the form of comedy sees as its central narrative problem finding happiness and stability in life and coming together with others with minimal constraints from the environment. The tone of the story is generally optimistic, and the emotions emphasized are positive, such as joy and contentment. The hero of the story is viewed as a common, ordinary person who comes together with other ordinary persons to find the simple and pure pleasures. One "moral" of the story is that the person is given the opportunity to achieve happiness that is free from guilt and anxiety and to provide a happy ending to his or her own life story on earth.

By contrast, romance is the archetype of the sun's zenith, summer, and the triumph of the hero. Stories of the hero's great exploits, of apotheosis, and of entering into paradise are manifestations of this mythic archetype. The essential ingredient in romance is adventure. The action consists of a series of heroic exploits as the protagonist oftentimes proceeds on a perilous journey, encounters fierce rivals, and emerges triumphant and exalted in the end. Subordinate characters in the story are divided between those for and those against the hero's quest. A prototypical romance is Homer's *Odyssey*. In life stories, the central problem of romance is moving onward and continuing to grow through life's journey, with the ultimate goal of emerging victorious. Like comedy, the tone of the story is generally optimistic. The emotions are also positive, but they tend to emphasize excitement and interest over joy and contentment. The hero of the story is elevated, not common, and he or she is viewed as a great adventurer embarking on a quest. One moral of the story is that the person must embark on a long and difficult journey through life in which circumstances constantly change and new challenges arise.

The mythic archetype of sunset, autumn, and death is tragedy. Included in tragedy are stories of "the fall," dying gods and heroes, violent death, sacrifice, and isolation. In the classic tragedy, the hero finds himself separated in some fundamental way from the natural order of things. This separation makes for an imbalance of nature, and the righting of the imbalance requires the tragic hero's downfall. Like Oedipus, the tragic hero may be supremely proud, passionate, and of soaring mind; yet, these extraordinary attributes are exactly what separate him or her from common people and bring about his or her eventual ruin. The central problem of tragedy in life stories is to avoid or minimize the dangers and absurdities of life, which threaten to overwhelm even the greatest human beings. The tone of the story is pessimistic, and the emotions emphasized are both negative and positive, such as sadness and fear as well as excitement. The hero is elevated, the extraordinary victim pursued by life's nemesis. One moral of the story is that the person confronts inescapable dangers and absurdities in which he or she finds that pain and pleasure, happiness and sadness are always mixed.

The archetype of darkness, winter, and dissolution is irony. Included in this category are stories of floods and the return of chaos: of the triumph of forces that bring mystery and confusion. Frye writes that irony attempts "to give form to the shifting ambiguities and complexities of existence" *(Anatomy,* p. 223). The hero of irony may assume many forms. One favorite is the successful rogue of the picaresque novel who employs satire (what Frye calls "militant irony") to expose the absurdities of modern convention. Another is the antihero of some modern novels, whose world appears to be devoid of opportunities for comedy, romance, or tragic heroism but instead manifests itself as a swirl of double meanings, ambiguities, and ambivalence, a puzzle or mystery that will never be understood. In life stories, irony poses the problem of solving the mysteries of life and trying to gain some perspective on the chaos, ambiguities, and contradictions of human existence. The tone of the story is generally pessimistic, and the emotions are negative, such as sadness and fear. Like comedy and unlike romance and tragedy, the hero is rather common, not exalted. One moral of the story is that the person encounters ambiguities and contradictions in life that are larger than him or her and that are, for the most part, beyond comprehension.

In *Power, Intimacy, and the Life Story,* I report the results of a study of fifty men and women between the ages of thirty-five and fifty years whose life stories were coded for Frye's four mythic archetypes. Adults high in intimacy motivation tended to score higher than adults low in intimacy motivation on the archetype of comedy. Adults high in power motivation tended to construct life stories that resemble romance to a greater extent than those low in power motivation. Tragedy and irony were unrelated to motives.

4. There are many variations on Harlow's studies. In addition to the isolation studies described briefly in Chapter 4, Harlow and his colleagues are also well known for studies of (1) surrogate mothers, (2) together-together monkeys, and (3) therapist monkeys.

In the studies of surrogate mothers, Harlow raised newborn rhesus monkeys in isolation but provided them with different kinds of inanimate mother figures, such as a soft terrycloth doll in the shape of a monkey and a corresponding doll made of wire mesh that dispensed milk from a nipple. A major finding in the surrogate studies was that baby monkeys are more likely to form an attachment bond to the soft cloth doll than to the wire mesh doll, even though the mesh doll provides nourishment. The studies suggest that attachment is not a derivative of nutritional intake and sucking, a theoretically critical departure from Freud and certain behaviorist theories that were prominent in the 1940s.

In the together-together monkey studies, two newborn monkeys were raised together in isolation. Over time, their development was not as impaired as that of the ones raised in total isolation, but they nonetheless exhibited many bizarre behaviors. When they emerged from isolation and were placed with their peers, together-together monkeys refused to interact with other monkeys and instead clung desperately to each other.

In the relatively recent studies of "therapist" monkeys, researchers have tried to rehabilitate monkeys who were isolated from birth. Previously, researchers had believed that after six months of isolation, rhesus monkeys suffered irreversible psychological damage. Recent research suggests, however, that six-month isolates benefit greatly from the introduction of a normal three-month-old monkey into their lives. Perhaps because the three-month-old monkey is still rather young and immature, the grossly deprived isolate is able to build a kind of therapeutic relationship with its younger peer. Exposure to younger therapist monkeys does not undo all of the damage of early isolation, but it seems to be a stronger palliative than any other procedure yet devised.

These studies are discussed in the following sources: H. F. Harlow, R. O. Dodsworth, and M. K. Harlow, "Total Social Isolation in Monkeys," (1965), in *Readings in Developmental Psychology,* ed. J. K. Gardner (Boston: Little, Brown, 1982), pp. 41–48; M. A. Novak, "Social Recovery of Monkeys Isolated for the First Year of Life: II. Long-Term Assessment," *Developmental Psychology* 15 (1979): 50–61; and M. A. Novak and H. F. Harlow, "Social Recovery of Monkeys Isolated for the First Year of Life," *Developmental Psychology* 11 (1975): 453–65.

5. The nature and effects of early deprivation in human development is an extremely controversial topic. While some psychologists point to early deprivation as the source of virtually all pathology in human living, others argue that babies are extremely resilient and can bounce back from some of the most daunting early experiences. Reviewing scientific literature from the 1970s on maternal deprivation, Michael Rutter concludes that separation from mother in the first year of life is indeed a stressor but that it may *not* be *the* crucial factor in most varieties of deprivation. Other features of deprivation appear more important. For instance, intellectual retardation has been related to lack of adequate meaningful experiences in the first year of life. Conduct disorders may be a function of family discord and disordered interpersonal relationships in the early years. Affectionless psychopathy may be a function of grossly abnormal patterns of bonding between mother and infant. See M. Rutter, "Maternal Deprivation, 1972–1978: New Findings, New Concepts, New Approaches," *Child Development* 50 (1979): 283–305; and A. M. Clarke and A. D. B. Clarke, eds., *Early Experience: Myth and Evidence* (New York: Free Press, 1979).

6. J. Bowlby, *Attachment and Loss,* vol. 3: *Loss* (New York: Basic Books, 1980).

7. F. M. Berardo, "Survivorship and Social Isolation: The Case of the Aged Widower," *Family Coordinator* 19 (1970): 11–25.

8. D. Maddison and A. Viola, "The Health of Widows in the Year After Bereavement," *Journal of Psychosomatic Research* 12 (1968): 297–306.

9. B. Bloom, S. J. Asher, and S. W. White, "Marital Disruption as a Stressor: A Review and Analysis," *Psychological Bulletin* 85 (1978): 867–94.

10. A. J. Stewart and P. Salt, "Life Stress, Life Styles, Depression, and Illness," *Journal of Personality and Social Psychology* 40 (1981): 1063–69; and E. M. Waring, "Psychosomatic Symptoms and Marital Adjustment," *Psychiatric Forum* 8 (1979): 9–13; R. L. Weiss and B. M. Aved, "Marital Satisfaction and Depression as Predictors of Physical Health Status," *Journal of Consulting and Clinical Psychology* 46 (1978): 1379–84.

11. G. J. Chelune and E. M. Waring, "Nature and Assessment of Intimacy," in *Advances in Psychological Assessment*, vol. 6, ed. P. McReynolds and G. J. Chelune (San Francisco: Jossey-Bass, 1984), pp. 277–311.

12. J. J. Lynch, *The Broken Heart: Medical Consequences of Loneliness* (New York: Basic Books, 1977).

13. C. B. Thomas and K. R. Duszynski, "Closeness to Parents and the Family Constellation in a Prospective Study of 5 Disease States," *Johns Hopkins Medical Journal* 134 (1974): 251–70.

14. S. Duck, *Human Relationships: An Introduction to Social Psychology* (London: Sage, 1986), p. 210.

15. K. S. Rook, "Research on Social Support, Loneliness, and Social Isolation," *Review of Personality and Social Psychology* 5 (1984): *Emotions, Relationships, and Health*, ed. P. Shaver, pp. 239–64.

16. R. S. Weiss, "The Provisions of Social Relationships," in *Doing unto Others*, ed. Z. Rubin (Englewood Cliffs, N.J.: Prentice-Hall, 1974), pp. 17–26.

17. J. S. House delineates four different kinds of social support: emotional, informational, appraisal, and instrumental *(Work Stress and Social Support* [Reading, Mass.: Addison-Wesley, 1981]).

18. F. W. Brown and T. Harris, *The Social Origins of Depression* (London: Tavistock, 1978).

19. E. S. Paykel, E. M. Emms, J. Fletcher, and E. S. Rassaby, "Life Events and Social Support in Puerperal Depression," *British Journal of Psychiatry* 136 (1980): 339–46.

20. J. M. LaRocco, J. S. House, and J. R. P. French, Jr., "Social Support, Occupational Stress and Health," *Journal of Health and Social Behavior* 21 (1980): 202–18.

21. N. Lin, R. L. Simeone, W. M. Ensel, and W. Kuo, "Social Support, Stressful Life Events and Illness: A Model and an Empirical Test," *Journal of Health and Social Behavior* 20 (1979): 108–19.

22. L. F. Berkman and S. L. Syme, "Social Networks, Host Resistance and Mortality: A Nine-Year Followup Study of Alameda County Residents," *American Journal of Epidemiology* 109 (1979): 186–204.

23. J. G. Bruhn and S. Wolf, *The Roseto Story* (Norman, Okla.: University of Oklahoma Press, 1979).

24. Researcher Everett Bovard points out that a number of studies have shown the critical effect of the presence or absence of social relationships on disease outcome and on the individual's growth and development. But what are the physiological mechanisms that account for these results? In a recent

article, Bovard suggests that certain brain mechanisms may be responsible for the positive effects of social support on viability.

Bovard's discussion centers on the hypothalamus, a small structure at the base of the brain that plays a vital role in the control of the autonomic nervous system, of the endocrine system, and of the major biological drives. The hypothalamus regulates various aspects of metabolism by releasing hormones directly into the blood and by activating the autonomic nervous system. The posterior zone of the hypothalamus is associated with the response to stress and expenditure of energy. Under stress, it uses a chemical signal to release adrenocorticotropic hormone (ACTH) from the anterior pituitary into the bloodstream. In turn, ACTH triggers the release of cortisol from the adrenal cortex. Cortisol elevates blood pressure and blood glucose, protecting the organism under shock. But it also inhibits cell growth. Under stress, the posterior zone of the hypothalamus also activates the sympathetic section of the autonomic nervous system, which results in elevation of the heart rate, digestive inhibition, and stimulated release of adrenalin. All in all, therefore, stimulation of the posterior hypothalamus leads to energy release and protein catabolism.

An antithetical pattern of responses follows the activation of the anterior region of the hypothalamus, resulting in the conservation of energy and protein anabolism. The anterior zone is associated with the release of human growth hormone (HGH) from the anterior pituitary. In turn, HGH promotes cell multiplication and growth throughout the body and is therefore associated with healing of wounds and fractures. Further, the anterior zone is associated with the activity of the parasympathetic division of the autonomic nervous system, which slows heart rate and promotes digestion, assimilation of food, and the elimination of waste products. In simple terms, then, while the posterior zone of the hypothalamus is involved in mobilizing the body's resources to do battle with the world, the anterior zone of the hypothalamus is involved in conserving the body's resources and maintaining equilibrium under minimal stress.

Bovard reviews evidence from stimulation and lesion studies to suggest that these two zones of the hypothalamus are reciprocally inhibitory. The activation of one zone inhibits the functioning of the other. He goes on to suggest that a socially supportive environment activates the anterior zone, thereby inhibiting the posterior zone and thus conserving the metabolic resources of the individual who has been subjected to disease, injury, or emotional stress. Social ties are hypothesized to "alter the the balance of internal metabolism from the protein catabolic to the protein anabolic side, from energy expenditure to energy conservation" (E. W. Bovard, "Brain Mechanisms in Effects of Social Support on Viability," in *Perspectives on Behavioral Medicine*, vol. 2: *Neuroendocrine Control and Behavior* [New York: Academic Press, 1985], pp. 103–29 at 115–16). "Social relationships, at first physical and then more symbolic, can alter internal metabolism of the individual and increase his or her viability" (ibid., p. 117).

25. S. E. Hobfoll and P. London, "The Relationship of Self-Concept and Social Support to Emotional Distress Among Women During War," *Journal of Social and Clinical Psychology* 3 (1985): 231–48.

26. S. O. C. Kobasa and M. C. Puccetti, "Personality and Social Resources in Stress Resistance," *Journal of Personality and Social Psychology* 45 (1983): 839–50.

27. K. S. Rook, "Social Support vs. Companionship: Effects on Life Stress, Loneliness, and Evaluation by Others," *Journal of Personality and Social Psychology* 52 (1987): 1132–47 at p. 1133.

28. N. O. Brown, *Love's Body* (New York: Random House, 1966), p. 80.

29. J. B. Jemmott III, "Social Motives and Susceptibility to Disease: Stalking Individual Differences in Health Risks," *Journal of Personality* 55 (1987): 267–98.

30. J. R. McKay, *Trust vs. Cynicism: The Relationship of Affiliative Orientation to Immunocompetence and Illness Frequency* (Ph.D. diss., Harvard University, 1987).

31. D. P. McAdams and G. E. Vaillant, "Intimacy Motivation and Psychosocial Adjustment: A Longitudinal Study," *Journal of Personality Assessment* 46 (1982): 586–93.

32. G. E. Vaillant, *Adaptation to Life: How the Best and the Brightest Came of Age* (Boston: Little, Brown, 1977).

33. G. E. Vaillant and C. C. McArthur, "Natural History of Male Psychologic Health: I. The Adult Life Cycle from 18–50," *Seminars in Psychiatry* 4 (1972): 415–27, at p. 417.

34. The sample consisted of fifty-seven men from the original study of more than two hundred. About half of the original sample had been given the TAT in 1950–52. The fifty-seven were all of the subjects who in the late 1960s consented to be interviewed on the issue of psychological health and for whom (1) sets of TAT stories written in 1950–52 and (2) total adult adjustment data were both available and intact in the late 1970s. Of the original sample, 80 percent of the men were Protestant in college, 10 percent Catholic, and 10 percent Jewish. Many were from middle- and upper-middle-class backgrounds, though there was marked variability. At the time of the initial contact in college (early 1940s), one-third of the subjects had fathers who earned more than $15,000 per year, but almost one-third had fathers who earned less than $5,000 annually. Although not all relevant data have survived, the fifty-seven subjects in this study do not appear to differ in any important respect

from the original two hundred. Class and ethnic breakdowns are essentially the same, and the various outcome variables that were available (e.g., physical health and mortality, college performance, adult adjustment, personal habits) show virtually no significant differences between the groups.

The correlation between intimacy motivation from 1950 to 1952 and total adult adjustment in 1967 was $+.39$, $p \{ .01$. Correlations between intimacy motivation and 1967 income, vacations, enjoyment of job, and marital enjoyment were .26 *(p $\{$ .05)*, .26 *(p $\{$ .05)*, .39 *(p $\{$ .01)*, and .38 *(p $\{$ .01)*, respectively.

35. P. B. Zeldow, S. R. Daugherty, and D. P. McAdams, "Intimacy, Power, and Psychological Well-Being in Medical Students," *Journal of Mental and Nervous Disease*, 176 (1988): 182–87.

36. C. G. Jung, *Memories, Dreams, Reflections* (New York: Vintage Books, 1961; orig.).

37. D. J. Levinson, *The Seasons of a Man's Life* (New York: Alfred Knopf, 1978).

38. D. P. McAdams and F. B. Bryant, "Intimacy Motivation and Subjective Mental Health in a Nationwide Sample," *Journal of Personality* 55 (1987): 395–413.

39. F. B. Bryant and J. Veroff, "Dimensions of Subjective Mental Health in American Men and Women," *Journal of Health and Social Behavior* 25 (1984): 116–35.

Chapter 5: Intimacy and Human Development

1. H. S. Sullivan, *The Interpersonal Theory of Psychiatry* (New York: Norton, 1953).

2. I owe this interpretation of the writings of Harry Stack Sullivan to George W. Goethals, whose lectures and writings on Sullivan have been extremely illuminating: "The Evolution of Sexual and Genital Intimacy: A Comparison of the Views of Erik H. Erikson and Harry Stack Sullivan," *Journal of the American Academy of Psychoanalysis* 4 (1976): 529–44.

3. Sullivan, *Interpersonal Theory* (n. 1 above), p. 32.

4. A. S. Thomas, S. Chess, and H. G. Birch, "The Origins of Personality," *Scientific American* 223 (August 1970): 102–9.

5. A. H. Buss and R. Plomin, *Temperament: Early Developing Personality Traits* (Hillsdale, N.J.: Erlbaum, 1984).

6. J. Kagan, *The Nature of the Child* (New York: Basic Books, 1984).

7. H. J. Eysenck, *Eysenck on Extraversion* (New York: Wiley, 1973).

8. Research on temperament has burgeoned over the past twenty years in developmental psychology. Currently, there exist a number of different formulations of temperament and different measuring devices for determining individual differences in temperament traits. One very interesting line of research has investigated ethnic differences in temperament. Psychologist Daniel G. Freedman has examined newborns of Caucasian (generally northern European), Chinese (Cantonese), and Native American (Navaho) descent for differences in behavioral style. Conducting a number of simple tests of newborn responsiveness, Freedman has observed that Chinese and Navaho babies are consistently calmer and more malleable than their Caucasian counterparts. For instance, Caucasian babies cry more easily and are harder to console, he claims. Chinese and Navaho babies adapt to most any position in which they are placed: "when placed face-down in their cribs, they tended to keep their faces buried in the sheets rather than immediately turning to one side, as did the Caucasians" ("Ethnic Differences in Babies," in *Readings in Developmental Psychology*, ed. J. K. Gardner, 2d ed. [Boston: Little, Brown, 1982], pp. 110–18 at p. 111). When Freedman pressed the newborn's nose with a cloth, most Caucasian babies fought back by taking a swipe at the cloth with their hands. By contrast, the typical Chinese or Navaho newborn "simply lay on his back and breathed through his mouth, 'accepting' the cloth without a fight" (p. 111).

Similar results have been obtained by W. B. Carey and S. C. McDevitt, who found that Chinese babies were less difficult and slower to warm up than their Caucasian counterparts ("Revision of the Infant Temperament Questionnaire," *Pediatrics* 61 [1978]: 735–39). Adopting a provocative interpretation emphasizing biological determinism, Freedman observes that Chinese and Caucasian newborns behave "like two different breeds" (p. 111), suggesting general temperament differences between ethnic groups that have been biologically separated for hundreds of years. He entertains the possibility that cultural differences between East and West may be partially a product of slightly different biological endowments. The traditional emphasis in Eastern cultures on serenity and spiritual harmony complements well the calm temperament of the Chinese infant; the West's emphasis on action and change, by contrast, is consistent with the rather irritable temperament of the Caucasian newborn.

9. S. Freud, *Introductory Lectures on Psychoanalysis* (New York: Norton, 1961; orig. 1916), p. 314.

10. J. Bowlby, *Attachment and Loss*, vol. 1: *Attachment* (New York: Basic Books, 1969).

11. According to Bowlby, the biological function of attachment can only be understood in the context of the "environment of evolutionary adaptedness." What he means here is that if attachment has evolved to be part and

parcel of human nature, then it must have proved adaptive for thousands and thousands of years of human evolution. In view of the fact that during most (more than 95 percent) of human evolution, human beings have lived in small groupings as nomadic hunters and gatherers, attachment must have proved adaptive in the context of a nomadic lifestyle and its attendant environment: generally wide-open savannahs offering little physical protection from predators. Group living proved efficient for food gathering and distribution and effective for defending members of the group from myriad dangers. Thus, attachment served to protect the relatively defenseless infant from predators and other dangers by assuring close physical proximity between caregiver and infant.

12. The evidence that "bonding" during the first few hours or days of life has a meaningful influence on later development is virtually nonexistent. Popular writing on bonding "carries the implication that parents who lack early contact do not love their babies or somehow are compromised." But "there is little or no research support for this position, especially for middle-class or advantaged populations" (M. J. Svejda, B. J. Pannabecker, and R. N. Emde, "Parent-to-infant Attachment: A Critique of the Early "Bonding" Model," in *The Development of Attachment and Affiliative Systems,* ed. R. N. Emde and R. J. Harmon [New York: Plenum, 1982], p. 91).

13. M. S. Mahler, F. Pine, and A. Bergman, *The Psychological Birth of the Human Infant: Symbiosis and Individuation* (New York: Basic Books, 1975).

14. J. Kagan, R. B. Kearsley, and P. R. Zelazo, *Infancy: Its Place in Human Development* (Cambridge, Mass.: Harvard University Press, 1978).

15. R. A. Spitz, *The First Year of Life* (New York: International Universities Press, 1965).

16. D. N. Stern, *The Interpersonal World of the Infant: A View from Psychoanalysis and Developmental Psychology* (New York: Basic Books, 1985).

17. E. H. Erikson, *Childhood and Society,* 2d ed. (New York: Norton, 1963).

18. M. D. S. Ainsworth, M. C. Blehar, E. Waters, and S. Wall, *Patterns of Attachment* (Hillsdale, N.J.: Erlbaum, 1978).

19. L. A. Sroufe, "The Coherence of Individual Development: Early Care, Attachment, and Subsequent Developmental Issues," *American Psychologist* 34 (1979): 834–41.

20. B. Egeland and L. A. Sroufe, "Attachment and Early Maltreatment," *Child Development* 52 (1981): 44–52.

21. Ainsworth et al., *Patterns of Attachment* (n. 18 above), p. 142.

22. Students often confuse the concepts of attachment and temperament. Attachment refers to the quality of the bond between the caregiver and the

infant as it develops during the first few years of life. Temperament, rather, refers to inborn individual differences in behavior. While attachment refers to a particular type of relationship, temperament refers to an individual's general relational style. To date, research does not support a direct relation between attachment and temperament. While many might expect that "easy babies" (temperament) should show "secure attachment" patterns with parents (attachment), very little evidence for such a correlation exists. Attachment seems instead to develop rather independently of temperament, according to researchers such as Sroufe and Ainsworth.

23. N. L. Hazen and M. E. Durrett, "Relationship of Security of Attachment to Exploration and Cognitive Mapping Abilities of 2-Year-Olds," *Developmental Psychology* 18 (1982): 751–59; L. Matas, R. Arend, and L. A. Sroufe, "Continuity of Adaptation in the Second Year: The Relationship Between Quality of Attachment and Later Competence," *Child Development* 49 (1978): 547–56; A. Slade, "Quality of Attachment and Early Symbolic Play," *Developmental Psychology* 23 (1987): 78–85.

24. P. J. LaFraniere and L. A. Sroufe, "Profiles of Peer Competence in the Preschool: Interrelations Between Measures, Influences of Social Ecology, and Relation to Attachment History," *Developmental Psychology* 21 (1985): 56–69.

25. Romantic love bears certain resemblances to mother–infant attachment: see C. Hazen and P. Shaver, "Romantic Love Conceptualized as an Attachment Process," *Journal of Personality and Social Psychology* 52 (1987): 511–24.

26. R. L. Selman, *The Growth of Interpersonal Understanding* (New York: Academic Press, 1980).

27. E. S. Person, "Love Triangles: From Oedipus Complex to Adultery, an Ancient Obsession," *Atlantic Monthly* (February 1988): 41–52, at p. 42.

28. T. J. Berndt, "The Features and Effects of Friendship in Early Adolescence," *Child Development* 53 (1982): 1447–60, at p. 1447.

29. D. P. McAdams and M. Losoff, "Friendship Motivation in Fourth and Sixth Graders: A Thematic Analysis," *Journal of Social and Personal Relationships* 1 (1984): 11–27. A total of fifty-two children who made up the fourth- and sixth-grade classes at a private elementary school outside St. Paul, Minnesota participated in the study. The school is affiliated with the Evangelical Lutheran Church. All fifty-two children were white, and most came from lower-middle- to middle-class backgrounds. Of the fifty-two, eight were from single-parent families in which parents had been divorced, and one child's father was deceased. In the fourth grade, eleven were boys, and sixteen were girls. In the sixth grade, fifteen were boys, and ten were girls. In each of the two grades children spent most of their time in one classroom supervised by one primary teacher, who completed rating forms for each student. Intelligence test scores

obtained at the beginning of the fourth grade for students in the school were available for forty-seven of the fifty-two students. Scores ranged from 81 to 142, mean = 114, standard deviation = 12.9.

Each child was interviewed individually in October and the following May. In October, the interview began with a storytelling exercise, in which the child told an imaginative story in response to each of four pictures. These stories were later scored for intimacy motivation. The storytelling exercise was followed by a sequence of questions about friends and peer relations: (1) Who is your best friend? (2) Tell me a little bit about him or her. (3) Why is he or she your best friend? (4) What does it mean to say that the two of you are best friends? What does your friendship with him or her mean? (5) Who are some other people in class whom you consider pretty good friends? These should be people that you like pretty much. (6) Is there anybody in class whom you do not like too much? If yes, who is he or she? (7) Why do you not like him or her?

In the followup interview in May, questions 1, 2, 3, 5, 6, and 7 were repeated. Ten factual questions about the child's best friend were added: (1) names of best friend's siblings, (2) street best friend lives on, (3) best friend's favorite sports, games, or activities, (4) best friend's other friends, (5) best friend's enemies, (6) best friend's favorite toy or possession, (7) best friend's favorite subject in school, (8) best friend's pets, (9) best friend's favorite television show, and (10) best friend's favorite food.

30. Erikson, *Childhood and Society* (n. 17 above).

31. D. P. McAdams, *Power, Intimacy, and the Life Story* (Chicago: Dorsey Press, 1985).

32. B. Inhelder and J. Piaget, *The Growth of Logical Thinking from Childhood to Adolescence,* trans. A. Parsons and S. Milgram (New York: Basic Books, 1958; orig. 1955).

33. E. H. Erikson, "Identity and the Life Cycle: Selected Papers," *Psychological Issues* 1 (1959): 5–165, at p. 111.

34. In a number of recent studies, psychologists have administered structured interviews to assess (1) maturity of identity formation and (2) depth and breadth of intimate relationships. The findings show that people who have explored various identity possibilities and made commitments to particular identity positions in life (especially in the realms of ideology and occupation) tend to show deeper friendships and greater levels of commitment and stability in love relations. See in particular S. Kahn, G. Zimmerman, M. Csikszentmihalyi, and J. W. Getzels, "Relations Between Identity in Young Adulthood and Intimacy at Midlife," *Journal of Personality and Social Psychology* 49 (1985): 1316–22; and S. A. Tesch and S. K. Whitbourne, "Intimacy and Identity Status in Young Adults," *Journal of Personality and Social Psychology* 43 (1982): 1041–51.

35. John Kotre distinguishes among four different kinds of generativity. *Biological* generativity involves the begetting, bearing, and nursing of offspring. *Parental* generativity involves raising offspring, providing care and guidance. *Technical* generativity concerns teaching the skills of a culture to successors. *Cultural* generativity involves creating, renovating, and conserving the culture's symbol systems. In biological generativity the object of one's generative efforts is the infant; for parental generativity the object is the child; for technical generativity the object is the apprentice and the skills that the apprentice learns; in cultural generativity the object is the culture itself and the disciples or followers who are initiated into that culture. See his *Outliving the Self: Generativity and the Interpretation of Lives* (Baltimore, Md.: Johns Hopkins University Press, 1984).

36. D. P. McAdams, J. M. Foley, and K. Ruetzel, "Complexity and Generativity at Mid-Life: Relations Among Social Motives, Ego Development, and Adults' Plans for the Future," *Journal of Personality and Social Psychology* 50 (1986): 800–7. In this study, sections of the life-story interview in which the individual described his or her hopes, dreams, and plans for the future were summarized and reduced to single paragraphs presenting the essence of the response. Each paragraph was then rated on a three-point scale, receiving a score of 1 for low generativity, 2 for medium generativity, or 3 for high generativity. The following paragraph received a score of 1:

> Subject (S) plans to get married in the near future to the individual with whom S now lives. S plans to travel extensively. S plans to buy a larger condominium. S plans to obtain a Master's degree. S states that the purpose of plan for the future is "satisfaction." S sees the future as being a time in which S is able to settle down and to be secure. S sees no way in which plan for the future provides opportunities for creativity or for making contributions to others.

The next paragraph received a score of 2, indicating that there was some mention of generativity but that the emphasis was not strong:

> S reports that S has "no big plans." However, lists a number of smaller ones: To continue to enjoy personal life. To provide children with incentive and ambition. To solve the problems S is having with spouse. To obtain a Master's in Business Administration so as to make more money, which S argues will facilitate all goals in the future. S reports that plan for the future offers little opportunity to be creative and little opportunity to contribute to others. S feels that it is now time to make self happy because in the past S has devoted self to happiness of others.

The last paragraph received a score of 3, indicating a strong emphasis on generativity:

S plans to leave present job in order to work in the nonprofit sector. S hopes to serve as a mentor for others in work and in personal relationships. S plans to make more friends and to become closer to the friends S already has. S wants to "make things happen" in the future. Overall, S clearly wants to contribute to others and believes that this can be done in a creative way by simplifying things that appear complicated to other people. This is S's general approach to present job as teacher and to many situations and problems outside the classroom. Further, S believes that S will be able to continue finding simplicity amidst complexity in new career.

(Each person or subject is designated as "S" so as to conceal the sex of the subject for the generativity raters.)

Chapter 6: Intimate Women, Intimate Men

1. D. Bakan *The Duality of Human Existence: Isolation and Communion in Western Man* (Boston: Beacon Press, 1966), p. 15.

2. S. Hite, *Women and Love* (New York: Alfred Knopf, 1987).

3. M. E. McGill, *The McGill Report on Male Intimacy* (New York: Holt, Rinehart and Winston, 1985).

4. Ibid., p. 14.

5. Ibid., pp. 162–63.

6. E. E. Maccoby and C. N. Jacklin, *The Psychology of Sex Differences*, vol. 1: *Text* (Stanford, Calif.: Stanford University Press, 1974), p. 349.

7. D. Eder and M. T. Hallinan, "Sex Differences in Children's Friendships," *American Sociological Review* 43 (1978): 237–50.

8. D. Perlman and B. Fehr, "The Development of Intimate Relationships," in *Intimate Relationships: Development, Dynamics, and Deterioration*, ed. D. Perlman and S. Duck (Newbury Park, Calif.: Sage, 1987), 13–42.

9. R. E. Sexton and V. S. Sexton, "Intimacy: A Historical Perspective," in *Intimacy*, ed. M. Fisher and G. Stricker (New York: Plenum, 1982), pp. 1–20.

10. D. Strassberg, K. Anchor, H. Gabel, and B. Cohen, "Client Self-Disclosure in Short-Term Psychotherapy," *Psychotherapy: Theory, Research, and Practice* 15 (1978): 153–57.

11. Perlman and Fehr, "Development of Intimate Relationships" (n. 8 above).

12. J. L. Fischer, "Transitions in Relationship Style from Adolescence to Young Adulthood," *Journal of Youth and Adolescence* 10 (1981): 11–23.

13. Perlman and Fehr, "Development of Intimate Relationships" (n. 8 above).

14. R. A. Lewis, "Emotional Intimacy Among Men," *Journal of Social Issues* 34.1 (1978): 108–21.

15. S. Duck, *Human Relationships: An Introduction to Social Psychology* (London: Sage, 1986).

16. E. Walster and G. W. Walster, *A New Look at Love* (Reading, Mass.: Addison-Wesley, 1978).

17. T. Wolfe, *The Bonfire of the Vanities* (New York: Farrar, Straus & Giroux, 1987).

18. D. P. McAdams, R. M. Lester, P. A. Brand, W. J. McNamara, and D. B. Lensky, "Sex and the TAT: Are Women More Intimate Than Men? Do Men Fear Intimacy?" *Journal of Personality Assessment*, 52 (1988): 397–409.

19. A highly significant sex difference in intimacy motivation, again in favor of women, is also reported in R. J. Smith, "The Concept and Measurement of Social Psychopathy," *Journal of Research in Personality* 19 (1985): 219–31.

20. R. May, *Sex and Fantasy: Patterns of Male and Female Development* (New York: Norton, 1980).

21. D. L. Gutmann, "The Post-Parental Years: Clinical Problems and Developmental Possibilities," in *Mid-Life: Developmental and Clinical Issues,* ed. W. H. Norman and T. J. Scaramella (New York: Bruner/Mazel, 1980), pp. 38–52.

22. P. Cramer and T. Carter, "The Relationship Between Sexual Identification and the Use of Defense Mechanisms," *Journal of Personality Assessment* 42 (1978): 63–73; P. Cramer and K. Hogan, "Sex Differences in Verbal and Play Fantasy," *Developmental Psychology* 11 (1975): 145–54.

23. E. F. Bernat, *The Relationship of Gender and Personality to Fantasy Patterns* (Master's thesis, Loyola University of Chicago, 1985); C. Fried, "Icarianism, Masochism, and Sex Differences in Fantasy," *Journal of Personality Assessment* 35 (1971): 38–55; and D. C. McClelland and N. Watt, "Sex Role Alienation in Schizophrenia," *Journal of Abnormal Psychology* 73 (1968): 226–39.

24. S. Pollack and C. Gilligan, "Images of Violence in Thematic Apperception Test Stories," *Journal of Personality and Social Psychology* 42 (1982): 159–67.

25. C. J. Benton, A. C. R. Hernandez, A. Schmidt, M. D. Schmitz, A. J. Stone, and B. Weiner, "Is Hostility Linked with Affiliation Among Males and with Achievement Among Females? A Critique of Pollack and Gilligan," *Jour-*

nal of Personality and Social Psychology 45 (1983): 1167–71; A. Colby and W. Damon, "Listening to a Different Voice: A Review of Gilligan's *In a Different Voice,*" *Merrill-Palmer Quarterly* 29 (1983): 473–81; B. Weiner, A. J. Stone, M. D. Schmitz, A. C. R. Hernandez, and C. J. Benton, "Compounding the Errors: A Reply to Pollack and Gilligan," *Journal of Personality and Social Psychology* 45 (1983): 1176–78.

26. H. B. Lewis, "Depression vs. Paranoia: Why Are There Sex Differences in Mental Illness?" *Journal of Personality* 53 (1985): 150–78.

27. A. Sagi and M. L. Hoffman, "Empathic Distress in Newborns," *Developmental Psychology* 12 (1976): 175–76.

28. J. Haviland and C. Malatesta, "The Development of Sex Differences in Nonverbal Signals," in *Gender and Nonverbal Behavior,* ed. C. Mayo and N. Henley (New York: Springer, 1981), pp. 183–206; J. H. Hittelman and R. Dickes, "Sex Differences in Neonatal Eye Contact Time," *Merrill-Palmer Quarterly* 25 (1979): 171–84.

29. H. Moss, "Early Sex Differences in the Mother–Infant Interaction," in *Sex Differences in Behavior,* ed. R. Friedman, R. Reichert, and R. Vande Weile (New York: Wiley, 1974), pp. 149–63.

30. M. Lewis, "Infants' Responses to Facial Stimuli During the First Year of Life," *Developmental Psychology* 1 (1969): 75–86.

31. Moss, "Early Sex Differences" (n. 29 above).

32. P. D. Blanck, R. Rosenthal, S. E. Snodgrass, B. M. DePaulo, and M. Zuckerman, "Sex Differences in Eavesdropping on Nonverbal Cues: Developmental Changes," *Journal of Personality and Social Psychology* 41 (1981): 391–96.

33. J. Hall, "Gender Effects in Decoding Nonverbal Cues," *Psychological Bulletin* 85 (1978): 845–57.

34. D. Dinnerstein, *The Mermaid and the Minotaur* (New York: Harper & Row, 1977).

35. N. Chodorow, *The Reproduction of Mothering* (Berkeley: University of California Press, 1978).

36. L. Wheeler, H. Reis, and J. Nezlek, "Loneliness, Social Interaction, and Sex Roles," *Journal of Personality and Social Psychology* 45 (1983): 943–53.

37. Chodorow, *Reproduction of Mothering* (n. 35 above), p. 167.

38. C. Gilligan, *In a Different Voice: Psychological Theory and Women's Development* (Cambridge, Mass.: Harvard University Press, 1982).

39. Gilligan's thesis, however, is a controversial one. Some researchers have recently questioned the pervasiveness of the sex difference she identifies

in moral reasoning. See M. Brabeck, "Moral Judgment: Theory and Research on Differences Between Males and Females," *Developmental Review* 3 (1983): 274–91; C. F. Ford and C. R. Lowery, "Gender Differences in Moral Reasoning: A Comparison of the Use of Justice and Care Orientations," *Journal of Personality and Social Psychology* 50 (1986): 777–83.

40. H. Witkin, D. Goodenough, and P. Oltman, "Psychological Differentiation: Current Status," *Journal of Personality and Social Psychology* 37 (1979): 1127–45.

41. D. J. Levinson, *The Seasons of a Man's Life* (New York: Ballantine, 1978).

42. M. Norman, "The Road to Self-Reliance," *New York Times Magazine* (December 13, 1987): 82.

43. F. M. Ford, *The Good Soldier* (New York: Vintage, 1983; orig. 1927), p. 115.

44. B. Bloom, S. J. Asher, and S. W. White, "Marital Disruption as a Stressor: A Review and Analysis," *Psychological Bulletin* 85 (1978): 867–94.

Index

241